THE LOW CARB VEGAN COOKBOOK BUNDLE

30-Day Ketogenic Meal Plan
(Including Breads, Fat Bombs & Cheeses)

By Eva Hammond
Version 3.1
Published by HMPL Publishing

Find us at **happyhealthygreen.life**

INTRODUCTION

Welcome to our ultimate guide to discovering the best recipes and nutritional information that caters to not only one, but two dietary lifestyles! Here, you will be able to effortlessly browse through our directory of endless recipes accommodating both a ketogenic and vegan diet, better known as the ketogenic vegan diet, also referred to as a low carb, high-fat vegan diet (LCHF vegan diet).

At first glance, the ketogenic vegan diet may seem to be a bit contradictory. We are taking the ketogenic diet, a more scientific approach towards our health and optimum energy by consuming minimal carbohydrates and focusing on fat-rich foods, and combining it with the vegan diet, a health-based diet that originally stems from the moral of consuming no animal products. For people who are unaware of the vegan diet, let us give you a brief introduction. A vegan diet is one that does not include meat. Not only that, it completely excludes any form of dairy products such as eggs or milk products.

Despite allegations that veganism is not a healthy lifestyle, the vegan diet has proven to be a healthy one over the years. It includes almost every color in the rainbow including fruits, vegetables, legumes, beans, and grains. The list is as infinite as the number of dishes that can be made by combining the above foods.

Ironically, people usually associate the keto diet with a focus on animal fats and the vegan diet with just the opposite. That's what makes this combination so interesting: following a ketogenic vegan diet not only allows you the freedom and peace of mind that comes with a cruelty-free vegan diet, but also the high nutritional levels that come with the ketogenic diet.

This is where you might pause and ask yourself: "So I just got my hands on a book that is going to give me amazing nutritional information and delicious, mouth-watering recipes, and they are completely kind to my body and all sentient beings around me?" That's exactly what this is, and it is only once people begin educating themselves and look into adopting this lifestyle and dietary path that they will realize how excruciatingly simple it all really is. Yes, you can get the best of both worlds. Sacrifice life? Sacrifice health? Sacrifice taste? No. Why have we put it in our minds that it is just not possible to simultaneously satisfy all of these categories? At the end of the day, we all deserve, not to mention are *allowed*, to satisfy all of our food-related wants in a guilt-free manner, and now that you know it is 100% possible, why not?!

Ultimately, as mentioned above, the ketogenic vegan diet combines two diets that would originally seem to be at opposite ends of the spectrum. Many people's first thoughts on it may be along the lines of this metaphor: Imagine this combination diet as a Venn-diagram, with one circle representing the ketogenic diet, and the other representative of the vegan diet. The small section in the middle created by the overlapping of both circles would represent the combined, compromised views of the ketogenic vegan diet. My point being that people may assume that the options of the two "limited" diets get even more restricted to satisfy both diet's perspectives; however, this is merely a misconception.

The ketogenic vegan diet extols just the opposite by unlocking the gateways to endless possibilities of wholesome, fresh foods. You know all the unnecessary filler aisles in your local grocery store consisting of processed foods, "fresh" flesh, or animal-based dairy that were originally considered to be the endless "options" we were being restricted from when accepting the keto-vegan diet? Well, each of those categories should have never really been considered options at all. Thus, what is left in the middle of this Venn-diagram is what should have been there from the start: real food.

This book will serve as your handy, detailed guide to how to begin going about the combination of these two moral and dietary spheres. Are you ready for the best of each world without having to sacrifice a single thing? It is possible, and we are here to show you how!

So how can you combine those two worlds?

You are going to minimize the carbohydrates you eat by ensuring all of the veggies and fruits you consume are on the lower end of the sugar scale. And on the flip side, you will enjoy all sorts of delicious vegan fats like those found in avocados and buttery nuts. And no, you don't have to do any of the guesswork; we've calibrated all of the recipes for you, so you will watch the pounds slide off while your energy increases and you feel better than you have ever felt before.

We have included delicious recipes for vegan cheeses to low carb vegan deserts and everything in between. You're going to love the flavors, and these dishes will fill you up while keeping you in a ketogenic state so your body is constantly burning fat. The dishes are also quite simple to make, and you don't need a lot of fancy ingredients.

Again, a simple way to eat clean is to stay away from a good majority of the aisles at your grocery store, which are often filled with junk foods that give you a load of calories without any of the nutritional benefits that a calorie is supposed to bring. (But remember this excludes your go-to aisles that contain dried nuts and fruits!) When you're eating vegan, you're eating plant-based, and that means you are eating all natural, all green, and all good for your body and the environment.

In terms of health and nutrition, the vegan diet is completely free of cholesterol and saturated animal fat. Plant-based foods don't have high amounts of cholesterol. Cholesterol is primarily found in animal products like eggs, dairy, and meat. Studies have shown that vegan diets tend to have lower levels of cholesterol in general. Cholesterol is not a bad thing, nor is it particularly good either. On a low-carb, high-fat eating plan, you may actually increase your HDL (the good cholesterol for the body) by consuming more saturated fats. Because of this, vegans are less likely to develop heart disease, type 2 diabetes, high blood pressure, and some forms of cancer.

Meat has many more calories and fat than plant food options, which means it's more likely for you to be overweight if you are eating the higher fat food options like meat and meat products. Nutritionists cite numerous studies showing people that eat meat as a staple in their diet are ten times more likely to be overweight than vegans. Add to that the fact that meat eaters also show a lifelong trend of gaining more weight as the years tick by.

In other words, it's safe to say opting for healthy vegan eating will help you slim down for life. When you need to lose weight, it is very unwise for you to adopt a fad diet that contains less nutrients and is low in fat. It will make your body feel deprived. A vegan diet is a healthy option containing foods such as olive oil, seeds, nuts, and avocados.

Losing weight happens when your calorie expenditure exceeds your calorie intake. That means you either eat less or exercise more. In general, it's easier to reduce your intake.

When practicing a keto-vegan diet, another concern is achieving ketosis. This is a metabolic process in which, with insufficient carbs to burn for energy, your body will burn fat instead. It occurs when you eat a diet high in healthy fats and low in carbohydrates.

As a side effect of this process, ketones are created. Once you start your keto vegan diet, you can buy test strips to check the amount of ketones in your blood or urine, thereby finding out whether or not you are in ketosis. You can get into ketosis in as little as one to two days.

Please consult with your doctor before attempting to go into ketosis if you have any particular concerns, especially if you are diabetic, have high blood pressure, or are pregnant or breastfeeding.

If you ever want to increase your calories or fat ratio, add some coconut oil or olive oil to your meals. You can also try eating a few nuts or adding a spoonful of flax seed or hemp seed to a meal. Increasing the amount of healthy fats you consume will also keep you feeling fuller longer. You may actually feel less hungry even though you're eating less than before.

More energy and improved mental focus are other possible benefits. This diet is also excellent for building and maintaining muscle. Many weightlifters and bodybuilders swear by the keto diet, a growing number of which prefer a keto vegan diet.

TABLE OF CONTENTS

DISCLAIMER

The recipes provided in this report are for informational purposes only and are not intended to provide dietary advice. A medical practitioner should be consulted before making any changes in your diet. Additionally, recipe cooking times may require adjustment depending on age and quality of appliances. Readers are strongly urged to take all precautions to ensure ingredients are fully cooked in order to avoid the dangers of foodborne viruses. The recipes and suggestions provided in this book are solely the opinion of the author. The author and publisher do not take any responsibility for any consequences that may result due to following the instructions provided in this book.

ABOUT US

Welcome to the reader's circle of happyhealthygreen.life.

You can subscribe to our newsletter using this link:

http://happyhealthygreen.life/vegan-newsletter

By subscribing to our newsletter, you will receive the latest vegan recipes, tips about health & nutrition and plant-based cooking articles that make your mouth water, right in your inbox.

We also offer you a unique opportunity to read future vegan cookbooks for absolutely free...

Get your hands on free vegan recipes and instant access to 'The Vegan Cookbook'. Subscribe to the vegan newsletter and grab your free copy here at:

http://happyhealthygreen.life/vegan-newsletter

Enter your email address to get instant access. Support veganism and say NO to animal cruelty!

We don't like spam and understand you don't like spam either. We'll email you no more than 2 times per week.

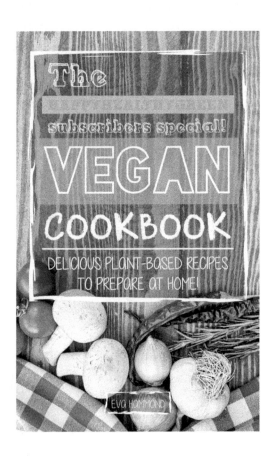

WHAT IS THE KETOGENIC DIET?

When you eat, your body breaks down all the carbohydrates present in the food into glucose. This glucose is what acts as fuel for your everyday functioning. The idea behind the ketogenic diet is to reduce the number of carbohydrates and force the body to enter ketosis. It is a state in which the body burns its fat instead of the carbs that you take in. The process starts when your liver releases ketones. The primary purpose of the ketogenic diet is to encourage your body to stop burning carbs as fuel and instead burn fat as fuel. This process is achieved by lowering the level of carb intake to 20 grams net carbs per day.

But what is ketosis? Ketosis is a metabolic process where the production of ketones by the liver is undertaken. Normally, when the intake of carbohydrates is lowered, the body adjusts and shifts into ketosis. A high percentage of cells in the human body utilizes ketones as a source of energy. The usage of ketones usually occurs at a time of a long fast or restricted consumption of carbohydrates. Ketones can provide energy for most organs in the body.

It is very important to know that glucose is the primary energy provider for most cells in the body. For the purpose of conserving energy for future use, the body stores excess glucose as glycogen. This glycogen is found in the liver and in the muscles. The glycogen stored in the liver is used to maintain normal levels of glucose in the blood, where glycogen that has been stored up in the muscles is for the purpose of fueling muscle activities.

When carbohydrate intake restriction is in high gear, protein—and fats—can be used as a source of energy. The majority of cells in the body can make use of fatty acids for energy. In a time of shortage or complete lack of carbohydrates, the liver breaks down fat. At such times, most cells can use ketone bodies. The production of ketones in excess of what the body requires makes the level of ketones increase, resulting in what is known as ketosis.

The key thing to remember is that if you are not following the ketogenic diet to perfection, it will lead to a number of medical situations. For instance, your body can produce too many ketones in uncontrolled diabetes making you ill. Therefore, whenever you follow a ketogenic diet, it is imperative that you follow it correctly.

Your body is responsible for thousands of operations at any given second. Right there, you blinked, breathed, your body is digesting your last meal, and it's doing all of these things without you having to think about it. So you can imagine that your body is quite busy, and it's going to try to do things with as little effort as possible.

The average person's diet consists of carbohydrates, protein, and fat. Carbohydrates are super easy for your body to break down and use for energy, but proteins and fats are more difficult. When you eat a meal, your body uses the carbohydrates right away. Proteins are usually used for other functions like muscle maintenance so the body doesn't use them for energy. Finally, fat is more difficult to break down than sugar, so the body uses it as a last resource.

So when you eat carbohydrates and fats together, the body uses the carbs and stores the fat. If you don't get enough carbs in your diet, the body will start to use the fat because it has to—and this is when your body goes into a ketogenic state. A ketogenic state simply means your body is using fat for energy, and that is great news for anyone trying to get lean.

In order for you to get your body to burn fat for fuel instead of carbohydrates, you need to feed your body a low amount of carbs and more fat. In addition, the carbs you eat should be complex carbs instead of simple carbs because complex carbs are also difficult for your body to break down. Complex carbs are found in veggies, whole grains, beans, and lentils. Carbs that are difficult for your body to break down require more energy, so when you eat them, the body will turn to fats to get more of that energy.

When you reduce your carbohydrate intake, your body has no choice but to start using fats for energy, and that is when you enter the ketogenic state. The ketogenic state is also known as the fat burning state because it is when your body doesn't have enough carbohydrates to use for energy so it uses fats.

Why eating more fat means burning more fat

When you eat a high amount of carbohydrates, you feel sluggish because your body uses the carbs quickly and you have no energy left. But when you consume fats, it takes longer for your body to break them down into energy, so you are fed a steady amount of fat energy as your body breaks down the fat molecules. This also means you feel fuller longer and have no need to reach for harmful snacks.

You must understand that your body has a lot of work to do, so it is going to try to make that as easy as possible. If you feed it a ton of carbohydrates, it will use these carbohydrates for energy and will always store your fat, but if you get rid of the carbs, then your body will burn your fat—it is as simple as that!

WHAT IS VEGANISM

Veganism goes beyond a diet. It is a lifestyle choice, one that people make with a fair amount of consideration to not just their own bodies but to the effect their choices are making in the world.

A vegan diet is focused on plant-based food, and all animal consumption is eliminated. The difference between vegetarianism and veganism is that although vegetarians will consume animal products like eggs and milk, vegans will not.

The choice to go vegan is a personal one, one that goes far beyond food consumption. One of the core reasons individuals decide to go vegan is because they no longer want to participate in a practice that harms animals. Another big reason for switching to a vegan lifestyle is that many people believe that the human body was not designed to consume animals, and since the body was not designed to consume animals, it doesn't have the tools to break down animal products in a good way—which is harmful to the body.

Once the decision has been made to follow a vegan diet, there are some very important things people must think about when it comes to the food they're eating. Since an animal-based diet provides most of the nutrients a person needs, most of us don't think about the individual nutrients we need. Going vegan means you must be conscious of the types of foods you eat to ensure you are getting everything your body needs.

One of the biggest concerns about turning to veganism is your amino acid consumption. You can get all the amino acids you need when you eat meat products, but when it comes to plant-based foods, you must get a mix of the right foods together to get all the amino acids your body must have.

What are amino acids?

Amino acids are the building blocks of your body, the ones that help form your muscle and tissue, so they are essential. Your body can form some amino acids on its own, but others must be obtained by outside sources. There are nine amino acids that are essential for optimal function that your body cannot create; they are: methionine, leucine, isoleucine, histidine, lysine, phenylalanine, tryptophan, valine, and threonine. It is easy to get the complete nine amino acids from animal products, but to get all nine from vegan products, you have to combine various foods.

Combining simple things like beans and quinoa is enough to make a complete protein. You have to remember that you don't need to get all the essential amino acids from one food; you can get them from combining foods throughout your day. Being vegan does not mean you lose any nutritional value; it only means that you have to make sure you are eating a variety of foods. Doing this will ensure you are getting all the amino acids your body requires.

Amino acids (AA) bond together to form peptides or polypeptides. From there, proteins are made. Your body requires twenty different kinds of amino acids to create proteins. Each type determines what the shape will be like when formed.

There are essential and non-essential amino acids that exist today. Some of them are present in your body, while others cannot be synthesized, and, as such, need to be obtained from food.

Essential amino acids perform critical functions in your body. For instance, in order to obtain normal sleep, you will need certain amino acids. They can also reduce anxiety and depression and make your immune system stronger.

Amino acids make up 75% of your body. Every bodily function depends on them. Every chemical reaction happening within your body relies on the proteins formed from their bond.

Their volume is considered to be the most common type in the human body. Hence, every human being, plant, or animal depends on them to survive.

These essential amino acids must be ingested every day. If you fail to supply your body with enough of them, it could lead to protein degradation because your system does not store them in your body like fats, starches, etc.

The good thing is that amino acids are found in nature. You can obtain them from diverse sources like microorganisms and plants, among others.

You can also take food and dietary supplements that contain amino acids. They are proven to offer health benefits such as decreasing your risk of developing life-threatening medical conditions and improving your energy levels each day.

Your body needs amino acids to develop and repair muscle and organ tissue. They are also essential in the production of hormones and enzymes. Your hair, skin, teeth, and nails need amino acids for proper growth. They can also generate antibodies to help in defending against infection. Essentially, they maintain the overall growth of your body and control its metabolic functions.

You may think that those categorized as non-essential amino acids are not important in your bodily functions. Although the term non-essential is misleading, the amino acids that fall into this category are still extremely important. They cannot be produced without the essential amino acids. So, in a way, they are still influenced by diet.

When you consume protein, your body digests and metabolizes the protein to produce amino acids. Then, the amino acids produced are utilized by the system to generate different cell types and chemical compounds.

In order to maintain proper levels of amino acids, you need to maintain a balanced diet, which is required for overall health and fitness.

The levels of amino acids in your body are constant. They do not depend on your diet. Then again, your body attacks itself by breaking down muscle and other tissues in order to keep the amino acids' concentration level.

How to ensure you have enough energy on a vegan diet

As you travel down the vegan roadway, make sure that you are getting enough calories in your diet since all calories are not made equal, and neither are the calories you get from animal products versus vegetable products. A cup of veggies is not going to give you the same energy or nutrients that a cup of meat would. A cup of almonds will give you a lot more fat.

Consult an expert

It is also important that you consult your doctor before you make such a drastic change in your diet. One of the major challenges for individuals is replacing what they are missing from not consuming animal products. Vitamins like B12 can only be found in meat products, and many people end up taking supplements to make up for a lack of B12. Determine with your health professional what the best choice is for you, but the most important thing is you getting everything you need to function at your best.

Understanding the value of the energy you get from your carbs and fats is critical, and we're here to help you do that. It isn't difficult to understand this, and once you do, you'll be armed with the knowledge of life.

What exactly is B12 and how do vegans get it.

When many people hear of a vegan or vegetarian based diet, or any diet largely absent of "flesh foods" one of the first questions you might hear may be along the lines of "Aren't you going to have iron or vitamin deficiency? That's not healthy". Actually, with a bit of proper education, the above statement can be completely false. Following a wholesome, animal free diet may have a few initial challenges in the vitamin department. Some new vegans, vegetarians, or keto vegans may, in fact, initially struggle with their B12 levels, since it can only be found naturally in foods such as red meat, fish, crab and dairy related products. But with appropriate knowledge multiple healthy alternatives can always be identified.

A common misconception is that a meat and dairy free diet means never taking vitamins such as B12, which would lead to fatigue, iron deficiency, and unhealthy nerve and blood cells. The reason the above statement is believed by many to be true is that the B12 vitamin is one that is only found naturally in a majority of meat-related products as mentioned above. However, while that is true, B12 intake for people with accommodated dietary needs is in fact possible! Essentially, while daily intake levels for the B12 vitamin only reach 2.4 micrograms to 2.8 micrograms, consumption is extremely vital for the nutrients it provides your body with.

You'll be glad to hear that B12 is now found in multiple "fortified foods" (meaning foods that have been injected with certain nutrients) such as soy based dairy. In addition, if that's not up your alley, the B12 vitamin is even offered as gelatin free supplements.

Being knowledgeable of this information will allow you to jump into your dietary changes with no problems at all. At the end of the day, you can still be receiving all the nutrients you need with no harm done to you or any living being around you.

YOUR MACROS

Macronutrients are to the body what gasoline is to the gas-powered car. The three main macronutrients are protein, carbohydrates, and fat; these three nutrients provide us with the energy we need to function. The three macronutrients are not created equal, so each one provides a different amount of energy per serving. Most researchers have found that fats provide the most energy per serving compared to proteins and carbohydrates.

Protein

We are essentially walking protein, which means our hair, nails, muscles, and organs are all made out of protein. Through complex biological processes, proteins are broken down into amino acids. These amino acids further break down into other compounds and become the basic tools our body needs to repair itself after the strain of daily life (or hard workouts). Amino acids facilitate connections between neurons in our body and brain. Protein itself is broken down into amino acids, and our body is capable of making some amino acids, but not all that we require. Our body needs twenty amino acids, and it can produce eleven of them, but the remaining nine we have to get from food. Ingest too much protein, and it becomes stored as glucose which, as we've seen already, is sugar that the body will then rely on for energy.

Protein is necessary for the body's and brain's development and function, and the body uses a lot of it. If there isn't enough protein in the body, the body then starts taking it from your muscles, so it is important to be steadily fueled with protein.

Good sources of keto-vegan protein include hemp-fu, nuts, and seeds like flax and chia.

Carbohydrates

Carbohydrates are molecules made up of a combination of hydrogen, carbon, and oxygen. Carbohydrates are a pre-ketogenic person's energy supply. They become glucose (sugar), which the body uses for a boost. Unfortunately, that sugar rush releases insulin, which stockpiles glucose in the forms of both glycogen (a different kind of sugar) and fat cells. The ketogenic diet is designed to minimize carb-consumption and maximize burning glucose, glycogen, and fat. On this diet, your body becomes far more efficient at processing.

The most common forms of carbohydrates are sugar, fiber, and starch. Our body certainly needs some carbohydrates in the diet, but most people consume carbohydrates in excess. Carb-rich foods are satisfying and usually inexpensive, which is one of the reasons they are consumed so readily. But carb-heavy foods are often void of the necessary nutrients. It is possible to get energy from carbs like white bread and soda pop, but these things don't have the nutrients you need. There is, however, a way to eat the right carbs that will give you what you need.

There are two types of carbohydrates: complex and simple. Simple carbohydrates, high-level Glycemic Index foods such as white bread or potatoes, are generally sugars and are easily broken down by the body and used right away, causing a spike in your insulin levels. This means your blood sugar instantly soars for a short period of time, soon dropping back down, and you get hungry quite quickly after since the carb is rapidly used up. Complex carbohydrates are take your body a longer period of time to break down, thus being on the lower end of the Glycemic Index (which is best for helping your body efficiently metabolize fat). For example, eating a bowl of lentils, a low-level GI food, would allow you to have steady blood glucose levels, which in turn would keep you satiated longer, as well as significantly aid in the metabolizing of their fat levels. In summary, complex carbs take longer to break down, your blood glucose levels do not spike out of control, and you feel fuller longer.

When you are eating carbohydrates, you should ensure that you're getting most of your carbs from the complex carb family. This would mean that most of the carbs you consume would not be considered net carbs or, in other words, carbs that you are trying to decrease as much as possible. This means eating things like vegetables and whole grain while staying away from simple things like white sugar and white flour. However, if you are following a gluten-free regimen, you would probably opt for other great gluten-free fiber sources, such as lentils, beans, green peas, and so on.

Fats

Over the past three decades, it has been drilled into our minds that fat is bad. Period. The truth of the matter, however, is that the body needs fat. For one, we need fat to absorb certain fat-soluble vitamins like A, D, E and K. Without fat, the body is not able to absorb those much-needed vitamins. Additionally, we need fat for healthy skin and hair as well as a protective insulator.

Your body is unable to produce essential fatty acids, so it is critical that you consume good fat sources. These essential fats help with numerous body processes like regulating blood pressure, protecting organs, and brain development functions.

Consuming unsaturated fats is the best bet. Unsaturated fats are in a liquid state and generally come from plant sources. Saturated fats are solid and generally come from animal sources. Trans fats are a third major fat. These fats are more often than not produced by companies trying to increase the shelf life of their products. Trans fats are unsaturated fats that are turned into saturated fats by hydrogenizing the unsaturated fat. Needless to say, trans fats are super bad and should, in fact, be avoided.

Plant-based oils are a great keto-vegan source of unsaturated fats. Butters like cocoa butter and coconut cream are also great sources of Keto Vegan fats. For added nutrition, there have been studies stating coconut oil is "overrated" as it only temporarily aids your body's nutritional levels. In fact, while coconut oil may claim to decrease LDL levels, your "bad" cholesterol levels, it eventually adds to your LDL levels in the long run. As a result, while many recipes lean towards the use of coconut oil, remember that any oil of your choice works just as well. These include sunflower oil, flax seed oil, and olive oil, to name a few, which gives your body a well-balanced array of fats.

KETO-FLU AND MINERAL DEFICIENCIES

When you enter the first phase of a ketogenic diet, you'll most likely experience a 'keto-flu'. This is a direct result of the limited amount of carbohydrates you're consuming. With this lower carb consumption, you want to pay extra attention to a sufficient consumption of Electrolytes. A diet insufficient in minerals like magnesium and potassium can result in you feeling tired and in worst case scenarios, even heart-related problems. Let's look at the minerals that you should pay extra attention to when enjoying a low carb vegan diet.

Potassium

This mineral is most commonly deficient in vegans that consume foods low in carbs. Even though the Estimated Daily Minimum for potassium is around 2,000 mg, it's recommended to top this up with another 1,000 mg. Note that too much potassium can be toxic to the body. But if you get your potassium from foods, there's no need to worry. Unless you supplement, you won't be consuming too much potassium.

You want to eat enough potassium-rich foods to avoid extreme problems like hypertension, cardiac arrhythmia, muscular weakness and muscle cramps, weakness, constipation, depression and irritability, heart palpitations, skin problems, and respiratory depression. It's very easy. Plant-based foods are rich in potassium. One avocado is good for 1,000 mg potassium. Also nuts are an excellent source of this mineral; 90 grams is good for 300-900 mg of potassium. Alternatively, dark leafy greens are a good source of potassium.

Magnesium

Modern diets, including a ketogenic vegan diet, are commonly deficient in magnesium. The RDA is 400 mg per day for an adult. Magnesium is responsible for proper muscle function and other bodily functions. A deficiency can result in muscle cramps, dizziness and fatigue.

Consume nuts, cacao, spinach and artichokes for enough magnesium in your body. You can supplement, but be careful not to consume more than necessary.

Sodium

If you're enjoying a ketogenic vegan diet, you're going to need some more sodium. Insulin, which has the effect of reducing the rate at which sodium is extracted through the kidneys, drops when you're consuming a diet low in carbohydrates. This can cause sodium levels to drop too.

Make sure to consume between 2300 and 3500 mg of sodium. Some foods high in sodium are beets, spinach, and artichokes.

Consult a doctor before adding supplements to your diet if have high blood pressure or are experiencing problems with your kidney or heart.

Calcium

Calcium is responsible for more than bone and teeth growth. It's also required for blood coagulation and nerve impulse conduction. Consume between 800 and 1200 mg per day to stay healthy. Great sources of calcium are tahini, tofu, almonds, and kale.

Zinc

Zinc is also very important for our bodies. If you're enjoying a vegan diet, you want to make sure your nutrition contains enough zinc to help your body function. This mineral plays an important role in protein and DNA synthesis. Also the production of testosterone depends on zinc. That's why males need a little bit more zinc than females; 9 mg per day for women and 11 mg per day for men.

There's a lot of plant-based nutrition that is rich in zinc. Legumes, soy, grains, nuts, and seeds make it easy to get enough zinc in your body. Since you'll find plenty of nuts and soy in low carb vegan recipes, consuming enough zinc should be a walk in the park.

Iron

Iron is one of the most abundant metals on earth. Unfortunately, this is not always the case for vegans. Plant-based sources of iron are often enhancing or inhibiting the absorption of this metal. This problem can be fixed with vitamin C. Consume vitamin C-rich ingredients low in carbohydrates. Some examples are bell peppers, broccoli, tomatoes, and dark leafy greens like kale and spinach. You'll have no problem using these ingredients in low carb recipes.

To ensure good absorption of iron by the body, it's best to avoid coffee, tea, cocoa, and spices that contain polyphenols and phytates that prevent this absorption. These spices include turmeric, coriander, chilies, and tamarind.

Iodine

The intake of iodine is usually not a problem, but you're still going to need 150 mg on a daily basis. This mineral supports thyroid function and can be found in nori, cranberries, and ionized salt.

Phosphorus

This mineral is essential for bone density, kidney function and energy storage by the body. Phosphorus also contributes to the use and balance of other vitamins and minerals in our bodies. A plant-based diet can cause difficulties due to the lower absorption rate of phosphorus. Sources loaded with this mineral are tofu, nuts, and garlic.

OMEGA 3-6-9

Fatty Acids are vital for your body's functions from your respiratory system to your circulatory system to your brain and other vital organs. Ultimately, while the body does produce fatty acids such as the Omega-9 fatty acid on its own for multiple different tasks, there are two essential fatty acids (EFAs) it does not produce: Omega-3 and Omega-6.

The Omega-3 fatty acid is responsible for aiding in brain function as well as preventing cardiovascular disease. This fatty acid prevents asthma, certain cancers, arthritis, high cholesterol, blood pressure, and so on. Many say that our dosage of Omega-3 can be satisfied by consuming fatty fish such as salmon; however, it's a great misconception that vegans lack this vital nutrient due to not consuming fatty-flesh foods. While Omega-3 is most popularly taken from fish, it has a plethora of different sources as well, including green vegetables, chia seed oil, flaxseed oils, raw walnuts, and hempseed oil to name a few!

On the other hand, the Omega-6 fatty acid is responsible for many of the benefits mentioned above when consumed with Omega-3. The trick is to consume the right levels of these nutrients; you should be consuming double the amount of Omega-6 fatty acid as the Omega-3, or the benefits of these EFAs may actually be cancelled. The world has become victim to fast food and frozen pre-made dishes, which have dangerously high amounts of Omega-6; however, following a whole foods based diet ensures your health, as you'll get balanced amounts of each and every nutrient. Ultimately, Omega-6 can be found in seeds, nuts, green veggies, and oils, such as olive oil.

Lastly, the Omega-9 fatty acid is a non-essential fatty acid that the body can, in fact, produce. The body will produce this fatty acid only once there are appropriate levels of both Omega-3 and Omega-6, thus making it dependent on the consumption of the two fatty acids the body cannot produce. If you do not have appropriate amounts of Omega-3 and Omega-6, then you can get additional Omega-9 from your diet (since your body wouldn't be producing it in this case). Omega-9 can be found naturally in plenty in avocados, nuts, chia seed oil, and olive oil.

THE TRUTH ABOUT COCONUT OIL

As mentioned above, plant-based oils are great ketogenic vegan options containing unsaturated fats; however, coconut oil has received a more glorified view compared to the others. While coconut oil has a great, complementary flavor and can be used periodically, it has become overrated in the nutritional sense. While it has benefits such as decreasing bad cholesterol levels (LDL), these are only short term. Surprisingly, recent studies have uncovered that, in the long term, coconut oil can in fact negate health benefits by increasing the originally lowered LDL levels. So you can use coconut oil periodically, as a majority of keto-vegan recipes these days call for it; however, you can substitute as you wish with other plant-based oils like hemp seed oil, flax seed oil, or olive oil to name a healthful few, as they not only lower LDL, but also increase HDL (good cholesterol).

Healthy Oils and Fats

Unsaturated fats decrease blood cholesterol when they replace saturated fats in the diet. You will find two types of unsaturated fat: monounsaturated fat and polyunsaturated fat. Monounsaturated fats have been shown to raise the level of HDL (the "good" cholesterol that protects against heart attacks) within the blood, so in moderation, they can be a component of a healthy diet. This is why they are referred to as the excellent fats. Olive, canola, and peanut oils are excellent sources of monounsaturated fats.

All fats, even the excellent ones, will still make you gain weight if too much is consumed. The key here is maintaining all fats in moderation and attempting to make the majority of your fat intake come from the good ones whenever possible. Note that a lot more than 20% of your daily calorie intake needs to be from fat of any kind, especially in the event you are attempting to lose weight.

THE KETOGENIC VEGAN DIET?

So now that we understand the concept of keto and veganism, let's dive into the brilliance of combining the two together. Both lifestyle choices are designed to help us help our bodies perform in the best way possible. Both are also about clean eating; however, applying the clean eating concepts of a ketogenic diet to the ethical eating view of veganism can torpedo your health and wellness substantially.

A vegan can also opt to take up a ketogenic vegan diet. A vegan is a person who prefers to eat plants such as potatoes, kale, plant products, and beans. Some vegans also do not eat or use honey. It is therefore evident that a vegan diet contains a high level of carbohydrates as a result of the sugar content and starch that is higher in plants than in animal products. As such, a ketogenic vegan diet may appear to be impossible. However, it can be done.

A ketogenic vegan diet has to be obtained from plant based foods that are particularly fatty, avoiding those that have high sugar or starch contents. It is, however, a challenge, as the access of fatty plant-based foods commercially is less than plants that are either sugary or starchy. This hinders the food selection. Therefore, the sole difference between a ketogenic diet and a vegan ketogenic diet is the strict consumption of plants in the latter. The end goal, however, is similar.

In the above chapters, we have explained both vegan and ketogenic diets. The focus of this chapter is going to be on a form of diet that came into existence by combining these two, called the Vegan Ketogenic Diet.

The ketogenic diet lately has become the ultimate diet in terms of fat loss and ethical consumption, but meeting in the middle is never without compromise. The traditional ketogenic diet is mainly based on consuming heavy animal fats. It would seem that the ketogenic diet and vegan diet are two opposite sides of a coin. This is because the ketogenic diet promotes the consumption of mainly fats and some protein, while maintaining very low levels of carbohydrates, whereas a vegan diet is an ideology based on the premise that all living creatures, including animals, should be respected, and that the killing and consumption of animals and animal-based ingredients breaches this premise.

Depending on the side you are on, we are sure that you would have ample reason to support your cause. But the question is: could these diets actually overlap? Is it possible to follow the principles of veganism while enjoying the fat burning benefits of ketosis? The answer is YES! You can enjoy the best of both diets while still adhering to the ethical principles.

According to the conventional keto rules, a person is only allowed to consume 20g of net carbs every day. However, for a vegan following the ketogenic vegan diet, consuming 30g of net carbs is easier to achieve, compared to the original 20g especially when no animal products are involved, since all plant foods tend to have higher carbohydrates as opposed to animal foods that are low in carbohydrates. So, consuming plant foods can potentially increase the number of carbohydrates.

If you want to maintain the 20g carbs routine, it requires a strict diet plan or routine, especially on a higher daily caloric intake. To maintain ketosis, it is recommended to not go over 30g depending on your caloric needs, although there are many vegan-keto people who consume up to 50g of carbohydrates and still lose weight, while maintaining a healthy, cruelty-free lifestyle. It is very dependent on the individual.

Below is the correct macronutrients ratio required for the keto diet
- *5-10 percent of calories should come from carbs.*
- *15-30 percent of calories should come from protein.*
- *60-75 percent of calories should come from fatty foods.*

On a vegan diet, you focus on consuming plant-based foods, however, not all plant-based foods are equal in nutritional value for your body, nor are they equal in energy value for your body.

When applying the ketogenic philosophy to your vegan diet, you can ensure that you are getting a stable level of green energy. The ketogenic lifestyle plan espouses the virtues of eating whole foods, which help keep you energized and full. Ketogenic-vegan foods ensure you are getting your nutrients without inundating your body with sugar.

We know that when you flood your body with sugar, you will get a short sugar high, but then your energy levels will plummet. When your energy levels drop, you get hungry again quickly, and this could easily lead you to snack on quick snack foods that are high in fat and low on the nutrient scale. However, when you apply the ketogenic philosophy to the vegan diet, you will ensure that you are only eating foods that are high in nutrients and energy without the influence of bad sugars.

GETTING ENOUGH LYSINE FROM A KETOGENIC VEGAN DIET

What is Lysine?

Lysine is one of the nine amino acids our body cannot produce, as mentioned above. However, lysine is a necessary building block for our body as it plays extremely important roles in the development and creation of our proteins. More importantly, lysine is mandatory for our growth, as well as converting the fatty acids that our body consumes into energy, which in turn keeps cholesterol levels at bay. Since lysine cannot be produced by our body, we must find it through the foods we eat on a daily basis.

The importance of Lysine and how it works

There are many uses of lysine. One of its interesting uses is in caramelization, which is applied to some desserts, like pastries. When it is heated, it links with fructose, glucose, or any type of sugar to create a caramelized substance. Even though it offers many uses in the culinary field, the caramelized substance from lysine cannot be absorbed by the body. For that reason, all caramelized foods contain a low amount of lysine.

When inside the body, lysine is converted to acetyl CoA, an essential component in the metabolism of carbohydrates and in energy production.

It is the precursor to another amino acid known as carnitine, an amino acid required for transporting fatty acids into the mitochondria to produce energy and perform metabolic functions.

Lysine competes with arginine, another amino acid involved in the replication of the human simplex virus. In in vitro studies, it was shown that arginine's growth-promoting action was inhibited by the presence of lysine. This is one of the reasons lysine is being given to treat and manage the HSV outbreak.

Just like other essential amino acids, a deficiency of lysine may cause negative effects, including:

- Fatigue
- Nausea
- Dizziness
- Anorexia
- Slow growth
- Anemia

Why vegans sometimes don't get enough Lysine

Lysine is an essential amino acid. This means that it cannot be synthesized by the body on its own. Therefore, it needs to come from dietary intake. Rich sources of this amino acid include animal proteins like meats and poultry. Milk is rich in this type of AA, but proteins from grains are low in lysine, and wheat germ has high amounts of it. It is a generally known fact that foods containing the protein building block lysine are found in flesh foods as well as dairy.

How much Lysine do you need and how can you get it?

Many sources say that adults should be consuming about 38-40mg per 1 kg of body weight of lysine daily. Vegans can easily consume lysine in foods such as beans, nuts, lentils, and soy products. While it is essential to consume lysine in order for your body to have the appropriate nutrients it needs, there is a limit. Even though it can be pretty rare for keto-vegans, too much Lysine can in fact be a bad thing. A spike in lysine amino acids can cause an increase in cholesterol as well as stomach uneasiness and cramps.

Lysine rich protein vegan foods

Remember that lysine is one of the nine vital amino acids that our body cannot produce. Moreover, it is commonly and mainly found in non-vegan foods including dairy, meat, and poultry; however, there are a few vegan options. Foods that contain high amounts of lysine include tempeh, lentils, black beans, quinoa, soy milk, pistachios, and seitan.

Tempeh:	30g protein/cup	754mg lysine
Lentils:	16g protein/cup	1248mg lysine
Black beans:	14g protein/cup	1046mg lysine
Quinoa:	8g protein/cup	442mg lysine
Soy milk:	9g protein/cup	439mg lysine
Pistachios:	12g protein/cup	734 mg lysine
Seitan:	6.7g protein/oz	219mg lysine

NUTRIENT RICH VEGAN FOODS

Low carb vegan foods

If you decide to embark on a ketogenic-vegan diet, you want to understand the nutritional value of nuts. They contain both protein and fat. They're tasty, and they're some of nature's best nutrient sources. Essentially, they are foods with a lower carb amount than many other plant-based foods.

Carbs in nuts & seeds

Nuts and seeds are easy to consume and are very portable. They can be salty and oily, making you yearn for them. Limit their consumption and do not eat those that are high in carbs like chestnuts, pistachios, and cashews.

The serving size has been set to 1 ounce to make it easy to calculate a larger serving.

Food	Serving	Fats(g)	Carbs(g)	Fiber(g)	Protein(g)	Net Carbs(g)
Chai seed	1 oz.	9	12	11	4	1
Pecan	1 oz.	20	4	3	3	1
Flax seed	1 oz.	12	8	7	5	1
Brazil nut	1 oz.	19	4	2	4	2
Hazelnut	1 oz.	17	5	3	4	2
Walnut	1 oz.	18	4	2	4	2
Coconut, unsweetened	1 oz.	18	7	5	2	2
Macadamia nut	1 oz.	21	4	2	2	2
Almond	1 oz.	15	5	3	6	2

Food	Serving	Fats(g)	Carbs(g)	Fiber(g)	Protein(g)	Net Carbs(g)
Almond flour	1 oz.	14	6	3	6	3
Pumpkin seed	1 oz.	6	4	1	10	3
Sesame seed	1 oz.	14	7	3	5	4
Sunflower seed	1 oz.	14	7	3	6	4

Carbs in greens

As we know, vegetables play an important role in a healthy, low-carb diet. make sure that you choose the right kind of vegetables. Avoid those with high sugars; they do not make you lose weight. Choose the non-starchy options. Be careful when eating greens because some have a carb count that adds up at a rapid rate.

Food	Serving	Metric	Fats(g)	Carbs(g)	Fiber(g)	Protein(g)	Net Carbs(g)
Endive	2 oz.	56g	0	2	2	1	0
Butter head lettuce	2 oz.	56g	0	1	0.5	1	0.5
Chicory	2 oz.	56g	0	2.5	2	1	0.5
Beet greens	2 oz.	56g	0	2.5	2	1	0.5
Bok choy	2 oz.	56g	0	1	0.5	1	0.5
Alfalfa sprouts	2 oz.	56g	0	2	1	2	1
Spinach	2 oz.	56g	0	2	1	1.5	1
Swiss Chard	2 oz.	56g	0	2	1	1	1
Arugula	2 oz.	56g	0	2	1	1.5	1
Celery	2 oz.	56g	0	2	1	0.5	1
Chives	2 oz.	56g	0	2.5	1.5	2	1
Collard greens	2 oz.	56g	0	3	2	1.5	1
Romaine lettuce	2 oz.	56g	0	2	1	1	1
Asparagus	2 oz.	56g	0	2	1	1	1

Food	Serving	Metric	Fats(g)	Carbs(g)	Fiber(g)	Protein(g)	Net Carbs(g)
Eggplant	2 oz.	56g	0	3	2	0.5	1
Radishes	2 oz.	56g	0	2	1	0.5	1
Tomatoes	2 oz.	56g	0	2	1	0.5	1
White mushrooms	2 oz.	56g	0	2	0.5	2	1.5
Cauliflower	2 oz.	56g	0	3	1.5	1	1.5
Cucumber	2 oz.	56g	0	2	0.5	0.5	1.5
Dill pickles	2 oz.	56g	0	2	0.5	0.5	1.5
Bell green pepper	2 oz.	56g	0	2.5	1	0.5	1.5
Cabbage	2 oz.	56g	0	3	1	1	2
Fennel	2 oz.	56g	0	4	2	1	2
Broccoli	2 oz.	56g	0	3.5	1.5	1.5	2
Green beans	2 oz.	56g	0	4	2	1	2
Bamboo Shoots	2 oz.	56g	0	3	1	1.5	2

Carbs in fruits

Fruit is the part of the plant that houses the seeds. Some fruits are known to be so simply because they are sweet. Other fruits include okra, avocado, and green beans, among others. Avocado has a very low carb concentration compared to others.

Food	Serving	Metric	Fats(g)	Carbs(g)	Fiber(g)	Protein(g)	Net Carbs(g)
Rhubarb	2 oz.	56g	0	2.5	1	1	1.5
Lemon juice	1 oz.	28g	0	2	0	0	2
Lime juice	1 oz.	28g	0	2	0	0	2
Raspberries	2 oz.	56g	0	7	4	1	3
Blackberries	2 oz.	56g	0	6	3	1	3
Strawberries	2 oz.	56g	0	4	1	0	3

Protein rich vegan foods

Proteins are commonly referred to as the building blocks of a person's life. Proteins are broken down into amino acids that are responsible for promoting the growth and repair of cells. They take longer to be digested compared to carbs. They make you feel fuller longer and have fewer calories. Some of the good vegetarian and vegan sources like tofu and lentils are outlined below.

Food	Serving	Metric	Fats(g)	Carbs(g)	Fiber(g)	Protein(g)	Net Carbs(g)
Tofu	100g	100g	9	4	2	16	2
Pumpkin seed	1 oz.	28g	6	4	1	10	3
Almond	1 oz.	28g	15	5	3	6	2
Flax seed	1 oz.	28g	12	8	7	5	1
Chia seed	1 oz.	28g	9	12	11	4	1
Brazil nut	1 oz.	28g	19	4	2	4	2
Hazelnut	1 oz.	28g	17	5	3	4	2
Walnut	1 oz.	28g	18	4	2	4	2
Pecan	1 oz.	28g	20	4	3	3	1
Unsweetened coconut	1 oz.	28g	18	7	5	2	2
Macadamia nut	1 oz.	28g	21	4	2	2	2

Fat rich vegan foods

It should be noted that our bodies need healthy fats like monounsaturated and polyunsaturated fats. These fats have good levels of cholesterol and play a role in reducing diseases of the heart. Generally, fats from plant sources are very healthy. Avoid sources that have trans fats.

Food	Serving	Metric	Fats(g)	Carbs(g)	Fiber(g)	Protein(g)	Net Carbs(g)
Avocado oil	1 oz.	28g	28	0	0	0	0
Cocoa butter	1 oz.	28g	28	0	0	0	0
Coconut oil	1 oz.	28g	28	0	0	0	0
Flaxseed oil	1 oz.	28g	28	0	0	0	0
Macadamia oil	1 oz.	28g	28	0	0	0	0
MCT oil	1 oz.	28g	28	0	0	0	0
Olive oil	1 oz.	28g	28	0	0	0	0
Red palm oil	1 oz.	28g	28	0	0	0	0
Coconut cream	1 oz.	28g	10	2	1	1	1
Olives, green	1 oz.	28g	4	1	1	0	0
Avocado	1 oz.	28g	4	2	2	1	0

LOSING WEIGHT WITH A KETOGENIC VEGAN DIET

Casual low carb diets (the kind people use for getting in shape, looking better, and weight loss) are typically less than 20g-50g/day of carbs.

If you want to lose weight, a healthy weight-loss diet should not fall under 1700 calories daily for women and 2200 for men. Lower calorie counts would not be considered a responsible diet. With the recipes in this book, you'll be able to calculate your daily calorie intake with respect to your personal goals. If you would like to speed up the weight loss process, you can always add exercise or cardio routines to your daily and/or weekly schedules.

Obviously, you can also add your own nutrients and foods to the mix. In general, you should consume 20 to 50 grams of net carbs on a daily basis for your body to enter ketosis. Consuming a lesser amount of carbohydrates—and staying on the lower end of the scale at 20g per day—will ensure the body is in optimum ketosis and help you shed the weight right off.

According to various studies, the ketogenic diet for weight loss is characterized by the consumption of a maximum of 100g of carbs per day, representing approximately 5% of a diet having 3000 calories consumed in the day, whereas carbohydrates provide between 45 and 65% of our calories in a typical diet. The remainder is distributed between lipids and proteins. In the ketogenic diet, the calories ingested in the form of lipids can reach up to 75%, and proteins occupy the remaining 20%.

Usually, the body uses the consumed carbohydrates as the energy needed for proper functioning of the body. In this ketogenic diet with extremely limited carbohydrates, the body begins to tap into the carbohydrates that are stored in the muscles and liver called "glycogen" stores. As each gram of glycogen is bound to 3-4 g of water in the body, significant early weight loss in the ketogenic diet is actually a loss of water.

When glycogen stores are depleted, the body begins to use lipids or fats to produce energy. When the body uses fat in the absence of carbohydrates, it produces waste products called ketones. Next, the ketone bodies begin to accumulate in the blood, and their odor, similar to that of nail polish, becomes perceptible in that person's breath. This is the primary indicator that the body is in a ketosis state. It takes around 2 to 4 weeks before arriving at this condition. The state of ketosis can be checked by using ketone urine (acetoacetate) test strips, such as Ketostix. Not all ketones are used when produced by the body. They will spill over into the urine, as noted through the change of color in the urine strip.

This state of ketosis causes a marked decrease in appetite, which contributes to reducing the amount of food consumed. This condition can also lead to nausea and fatigue. Although the ketogenic-vegan plan does not focus on counting calories, those who follow the diet absorb fewer calories because they do not get hungry, therefore leading to weight loss.

Many people experience increased energy levels a few days after withdrawing from carbohydrates. Why? Because a gram of fat has dense nutritional energy. Once you feel more energetic, you can engage in different activities to burn fat. In addition, once you start feeling better, you are unlikely to succumb to emotional eating, which is the main culprit for many people who are overweight and/or obese.

The ketogenic diet also works because it is satiating. As mentioned earlier, a ketogenic diet is high in fat, adequate in protein, and low in carbs. Fats and proteins are satiating. As such, you will feel full longer and have no need to overeat.

The ketogenic diet also works because it helps activate fat metabolism due to the drastically reduced level of insulin in the body. Given that you reduce your intake of carbs, your blood has less glucose, meaning there won't be any need for the secretion of high amounts of insulin. Besides facilitating the cells to absorb glucose, insulin inhibits fat metabolism (lipolysis). Instead, it actually promotes fat storage and glycogen accumulation (glycolysis). As such, with reduced insulin levels, your body can effectively start metabolizing fats since there is nothing stopping it.

Other factors that contribute to weight loss

Besides counting carbs, it's important to pay attention to how much protein and fat are consumed. It's a huge mistake to think that you can consume any amount of calories and still burn fat. If you eat too much, you will gain weight, even on a low-carb diet. To avoid that mistake, here are some very important principles to keep in mind.

- Be sure to eat enough protein, not just fat, because protein is the most sating macronutrient and helps combat cravings.
- Proper low-carb diets are naturally sating and act as appetite suppressants, which helps in the process of losing weight. In fact, you won't need to count calories all the time to lose weight and/or stay in ketosis.
- A mistake most people make is consuming far too many nuts, seeds and other fat bombs when trying to lose weight. You can hit a weight plateau or even gain weight simply because these are very calorie-dense per serving and thus exceed your caloric goals in order to lose weight.
- If there is no progress on your weight loss for more than 2-3 weeks, you should consider monitoring your calorie intake closely. There are several reasons why this could be happening. You might not be eating enough or you may be eating too much. As you get close to your ideal weight, losing weight generally gets harder.
- It is no problem to eat non-starchy vegetables such as cauliflower, spinach, kale, broccoli, zucchini and bell peppers, as well as fruits like avocados or berries. These fruits and vegetables pack a lot of micronutrients and are low in carbs so they won't impair your weight loss efforts at all and will, in fact, have a positive effect on overall metabolic health.

THE RELATIONSHIP BETWEEN EPILEPSY AND A KETOGENIC DIET

E pilepsy is usually defined as a neurological condition and as a group of neurological disorders. It has been observed to have long term effects in the life of the affected individual. Episodes of seizures characterize this condition, and they are one of its main symptoms.

Symptoms of Epilepsy

Epilepsy is one of the more difficult neurologic conditions to diagnose because of the multiple ways in which it can be caused. It is also because epilepsy can take on a wide variety of forms, manifesting unique symptoms on a case-by-case basis. Epileptic symptoms depend on which region of the brain is affected. Understanding the different signs and symptoms of this disease would go a long way in getting the proper diagnosis, and ultimately proper treatment. The symptoms include:

- Seizures (generalized seizures and focal seizures)
- Stiffening of all muscles
- Loss of muscle control
- Presence of clonus, a condition with repeated, rhythmic, jerking muscle movements
- Temporary loss of awareness
- Sensory disturbances, emotional swings, and spontaneous sensory disturbances

Some cases of epilepsy are caused by birth defects, brain tumors, stroke, or brain injury, but most cases of epilepsy have unknown etiologies.

It is estimated that 1% of people around the world have epilepsy. That amounts to around 65 million individuals. It should be noted that almost 80 percent of the cases of epilepsy are found in developing countries.

There are several treatment options available for people with epilepsy. One of them is brain surgery, which is one of the more frightening prospects that the general public faces. Medical experts say that years ago, a surgeon would wait for years, even decades, before recommending surgery for epilepsy patients. However, surgical procedures have become better, safer, and more effective.

Specific diets have been developed to prevent seizures with mixed results. Specific diet plans aim to reduce the incidences of epileptic attacks by manipulating how the brain works. This makes us arrive at another option of treatment which is the adoption of a ketogenic diet. Medical experts have achieved success at treating epileptic seizures using this diet. Medical experts admit that it works even though they do not know exactly how or why.

Since a ketogenic diet is a diet that features high fat, low carbohydrates, and controlled consumption of protein, it causes the body to use fat as the main source of energy. In many epileptic cases, switching to a ketogenic diet has resulted in a less seizures. However, the use of the ketogenic diet, especially for children, must be strictly monitored by trained medical specialists.

This diet has shown that it can also reduce the episodes of epileptic seizures in adults when a less strict form of the diet is used. The results of current research studies suggest that the ketogenic diet protects neurons and modifies diseases for many adults who have neurodegenerative disorders. Some of the researches include *A ketogenic diet as a potential novel therapeutic intervention in amyotrophic lateral sclerosis'* by Zhao et al, *'Ketogenic diet protects dopaminergic neurons against 6-OHDA neurotoxicity via up-regulating glutathione in a rat model of Parkinson's disease'* by Cheng et al, and *'The ketogenic diet: metabolic influences on brain excitability and epilepsy'* by Lutas & Yellen. Still, the use of the diet to treat any form of epilepsy other than pediatric epilepsy is considered to be in the research stage.

A ketogenic diet allows patients to reduce the amount of anti-epileptic drugs they use as well as remain seizure-free. It is possible to stay seizure-free and completely stop depending on the drugs, which is highly beneficial to the patients since all medications administered as anti-seizure have side effects, including reduced IQ, reduced concentration, and drowsiness as well as personality changes.

ALCOHOL ON A KETOGENIC VEGAN DIET

As a vegan that consumes only low carb products, you want to be careful with alcohol. Carbs are found in many places and one of them is the bar. That's why sticking with limited amounts of hard liquor is your best choice. Don't be mistaken. Hard liquor is made from carb-rich ingredients like grains and potatoes but after the sugar present in these ingredients is converted into ethanol, there's next to zero carbs left in your glass.

Do take in mind that alcohol effects liver metabolism, meaning more ketones will be produced when you drink more alcohol. This can deepen the level of ketosis. People on a ketogenic diet can experience an increased buzz compared to people who don't stick to a low carb diet. Also, hangovers can be worse with the absence of carbs in your food. Finally, the temptation to consume carbs might increase after enjoying an alcoholic drink.

Stick to hard liquor like whiskey, rum, vodka, gin, and tequila. Choose the unsweetened versions and stay responsible. Drink 1 glass of water per 1 shot or glass of alcohol.

RECIPES

1. Flax Egg

Serves: 1
Prep Time:
~1 min

Nutrition
information
(per serving)

Calories: 37 kcal
Carbs: 2.1g
Fat: 2.7g
Protein: 1.1g
Fiber: 1.9g
Sugar: 0g

INGREDIENTS:

- 1 tbsp. ground flaxseed
- 2 tbsp. spring water

Total number of ingredients: 2

METHOD:

1. Mix flaxseed and spring water.
2. Allow to sit covered for 10 minutes.

Note: You can use this mixture to replace a single egg in any recipe.

TIP: Many ketogenic recipes contain eggs; however, to be vegan-friendly, flax or chia seeds pose as great, low-carb alternatives.

2. Almond Milk

INGREDIENTS:

- 1 cup raw almonds
- 5 cups filtered water
- 2 medjool dates, pitted
- 1 tsp. vanilla extract
- 1 pinch sea salt

Total number of ingredients: 5

METHOD:

1. Mix tap water with salt.
2. Place almonds in salt mixture.
3. Soak almonds overnight or for about 12 hours.
4. Remove almonds from salt mixture.
5. Rinse almonds in cold tap water.
6. Preheat oven to lowest setting.
7. Place rinsed almonds on a baking pan and put in oven to dry.
8. Once dry, remove almonds from oven and rinse under cold water.
9. Add rinsed almonds to spring water.
10. Place mixture in a blender. Blend until creamy and smooth.
11. Strain mixture.
12. Place mixture back in blender.
13. Add vanilla and dates to mixture.
14. Blend until preferred milk consistency is reached.

Serves: 5
Prep Time: ~60 min

Nutrition Information (per serving)

Calories: 191 kcal
Carbs: 12.8g
Fat: 13.2g
Protein: 5.4g
Fiber: 4.1g
Sugar: 7.6g

3. Coconut Whipped Cream

Serves: 5
Prep Time:
~60 min

_____

Nutrition
information
(per serving)

Calories: 166 kcal
Carbs: 4.2g
Fat: 16.0g
Protein: 1.4g
Fiber: 1.6g
Sugar: 2.5g

INGREDIENTS:

- 1 can (1 ½ cups) unsweetened coconut milk
- 1-2 tbsp. stevia sweetener (to taste)
- 1 tsp. vanilla extract

Total number of ingredients: 3

METHOD:

1. Refrigerate the can of coconut milk for 8 hours.
2. Refrigerate a metal mixing bowl and beaters for 1 hour.
3. Open the cooled can of coconut milk and scoop the coconut cream solids into the cold mixing bowl.
4. Use the cool beaters to beat the coconut cream with a mixer on medium speed for 7-8 minutes.
5. Add the stevia sweetener to taste. Beat the mixture for another minute.

4. Hummus

Serves: 8
Prep Time:
~15 min

___

Nutrition
information
(per serving)

Calories: 157 kcal
Carbs: 17.6g
Fat: 7.7g
Protein: 4.4g
Fiber: 4.0g
Sugar: 0.6g

INGREDIENTS:

- 2 cups of cooked or jarred chickpeas
- 2 garlic cloves
- ⅓ cup tahini
- 8 tbsp. lemon juice
- 2 tbsp. chickpeas liquid (cooking left over from jar filling)
- 1 tbsp. olive oil
- 1 tbsp. sweet paprika powder
- Salt (to taste)
- 5 drops of tabasco (more to taste)

Total number of ingredients: 9

METHOD:

1. Chop the garlic cloves.
2. Use a food processor to mix all the ingredients except the salt.
3. Add salt and extra tabasco to taste.

Note: Add more lemon juice, olive oil, and sweet paprika powder to taste as well. The preference varies a lot by person. Find your right combination. You can store this mixture for up to 5 days in the fridge.

5. Guacamole

INGREDIENTS:

- 3 medium avocados, pitted and halved
- 1 lime, juiced
- ⅓ cup red onion, minced
- 1 clove garlic, minced
- 1 handful chopped cilantro
- Pinch of salt
- Black pepper to taste

Total number of ingredients: 7

METHOD:

1. Combine all the ingredients in a food processor and blend.
2. Place the guacamole in tightly covered containers to prevent browning.
3. Add pepper to taste when served.

Serves: 8
Prep Time:
~15 min

Nutrition
information
(per serving)

Calories: 157 kcal
Carbs: 6.0g
Fat: 8.0g
Protein: 1.0g
Fiber: 4.0g
Sugar: 0.6g

6. Vegan Half & Half Cream

INGREDIENTS:

- ½ can full-fat coconut milk
- ½ cup coconut cream

Total number of ingredients: 2

METHOD:

1. Pour coconut milk in small pan on stove with low heat.
2. Cut up the coconut cream if necessary and add an equal part to the coconut milk.
3. Keep stirring until the cream is dissolved.
4. Use warm or cold. Refrigerate for up to two days.

Serves: 8
Prep Time:
~60 min

Nutrition
information
(per serving)

Calories: 106 kcal
Carbs: 2.4g
Fat: 10.3g
Protein: 1.0g
Fiber: 0.7g
Sugar: 0.8g

7. Mexican Salsa

Serves: 6
Prep Time:
~5 min

Nutrition
information
(per serving)

Calories: 30 kcal
Carbs: 6.1g
Fat: 0.3g
Protein: 0.8g
Fiber: 2.1g
Sugar: 4.2g

INGREDIENTS:

- 4 large, firm tomatoes
- 1 fresh jalapeno
- ½ medium red onion
- 2 tbsp. fresh cilantro
- 1 lime
- Salt & black pepper to taste

Total number of ingredients: 6

METHOD:

1. Skin and seed tomatoes, halve the jalapeno, and remove stem, seeds, and placenta.
2. Cut the tomatoes and jalapeno in fine pieces and add to bowl.
3. Chop cilantro and red onion into tiny bits and add to bowl.
4. Juice the lime into the bowl, mix the ingredients, and season to taste with salt and black pepper.
5. After all ingredients are combined, let it sit for one hour before serving!

8. Avocado Pesto

Serves: 8
Prep Time:
~35 min

Nutrition
information
(per serving)

Calories: 335 kcal
Carbs: 4.7g
Fat: 36.1g
Protein: 1.0g
Fiber: 3.7g
Sugar: 0.4g

INGREDIENTS:

- 2 ripe avocadoes
- 1 cup extra virgin olive oil
- 1 cup fresh spinach
- ¼ cup fresh basil
- 2 cloves garlic
- 1 tsp. black pepper
- 1 tbsp. fresh oregano
- 1 tbsp. fresh rosemary
- 1 tbsp. fresh parsley

Total number of ingredients: 9

METHOD:

1. Combine all ingredients in blender and process thoroughly until smooth.
2. Serve with shirataki noodles to create a low-carb vegan pesto lasagna.

KETOGENIC
BREAD RECIPES

1. Banana Bread

Serves: 13
Prep Time:
~5 min

Nutrition
information
(per serving)

Calories: 106 kcal
Carbs: 12.1g
Fat: 17.9g
Protein: 5.3g
Fiber: 2.3g
Sugar: 5.2g

INGREDIENTS:

- 4 bananas
- 4 flax eggs
- 2 ½ cups almond flour
- ⅓ cup olive oil
- ½ tbsp. baking soda

Total number of ingredients: 5

METHOD:

1. Preheat oven to 350 °F.
2. Slightly grease a loaf pan.
3. Chop bananas in quarter inch circular slices.
4. Place chopped bananas in a bowl.
5. Add flax eggs, almond flour, olive oil, and baking soda to bowl.
6. Mix with spoon until well blended.
7. Pour mixture into loaf pan.
8. Bake for one hour.
9. Remove from oven, and let cool at room temperature.

People on a ketogenic diet usually steer clear of eating bananas due to their high carb content (around 27g for an average sized banana). While this number seems scary, this recipe allows you to satisfy your banana sweet tooth while cutting the carb consumption per piece to about 12g.

2. Mini Italian Toast Crackers

Serves: 13
Prep Time:
~5 min

Nutrition information (per serving: about 4 crackers)

Calories: 225 kcal
Carbs: 5.4g
Fat: 20.9g
Protein: 6.2g
Fiber: 0.5g
Sugar: 1g

INGREDIENTS:

- 1 ¼ cups almond flour
- 1 flax egg
- 2 tbsp. olive oil
- ¾ tsp. salt
- 1 ½ tbsp. Italian seasoning (or ¼ tsp. each of: basil, garlic powder, thyme, oregano and onion powder).

Total number of ingredients: 5

METHOD:

1. Preheat oven to 300 °F.
2. Place all ingredients into a bowl.
3. Mix ingredients into a dough-like consistency.
4. Once dough is formed, place on a cutting board.
5. Shape dough into a thin, long, rectangular prism.
6. Using a knife, cut dough into thin pieces of your liking.
7. Lightly grease a baking tray.
8. Place cut dough on baking tray.
9. Bake for 10 minutes or until crisp.

These Italian crackers are sure to hit that savory spot with the Italian herbs adding a twist to your everyday cracker! Use these as crackers when you're craving a quick, crispy snack, or munch on them in the morning, spreading avocado on them to make a quick breakfast.

3. 2-Minute Microwave Burger Bun

Serves: 1
Prep Time:
~3 min

**Nutrition
information
(per serving:
1 bun)**

Calories: 280 kcal
Carbs: 10g
Fat: 23.9g
Protein: 9.5g
Fiber: 4.4g
Sugar: 1.4g

INGREDIENTS:

- ⅓ cup almond flour (or any other nut flour of your choice)
- 1 flax egg
- ½ tsp. baking powder
- ½ tsp. cocoa powder
- ¼ tsp. salt
- ¾ tsp. sesame seeds

Total number of ingredients: 6

METHOD:

1. In a bowl, add the almond flour, baking powder, cocoa powder, and salt. Mix thoroughly, or you will end up tasting weird bits of baking powder, salt, or cocoa in your burger bun!
2. Add the flax egg to mixture and stir until well blended.
3. Slightly grease a cup large enough to fit the batter.
4. Sprinkle some of the sesame seeds at the bottom of the cup.
5. Pour batter on top of the seeds.
6. Sprinkle the rest of the seeds on top of the batter.
7. Place cup in microwave.
8. Microwave for about 2 minutes or until firm.

Sounds too easy to be true, right? Not to mention it makes the perfect complement to the perfect ketogenic vegan burger. This bun would be great with a seasoned tofu patty, grilled mushrooms, and crisp, fresh veggies like tomato and lettuce.

4. Almond Pan Loaf

Serves: 15
Prep Time:
~10 min

Nutrition
information
(per serving)

Calories: 381 kcal
Carbs: 9.5g
Fat: 33g
Protein: 11.7g
Fiber: 5.2g
Sugar: 2.0g

INGREDIENTS:

- 6 cups almond flour (or any other nut flour that you prefer)
- 3 flax eggs
- ½ cup olive oil
- ¼ cup almond milk (or water, if you want to reduce the caloric content)
- 2 tsp. baking powder
- 1 tsp. baking soda
- ¼ tsp. salt

Total number of ingredients: 7

METHOD:

1. Preheat oven to 350 °F.
2. Lightly grease a large loaf pan with oil.
3. Combine all ingredients in a bowl, ensuring they are well mixed.
4. Pour mixture into loaf pan and bake for about 1 hour.
5. Remove pan from oven and let cool.
6. Once cooled, remove loaf by flipping pan upside down.
7. Slice evenly.

Note: Though this bread does not rise as much as a "normal" loaf would, per se, its plain taste is the perfect complement to a sandwich on the go! Also, if you decide to use this to make a quick, easy lunch, two slices yield only 3 grams of carbs for your daily count compared to a whopping 22 grams of regular bread!

5. Italian Herb Rolls

Serves: 6
Prep Time:
~10 min

Nutrition
information
(per serving)

Calories: 257 kcal
Carbs: 16.6g
Fat: 18.6g
Protein: 5.8g
Fiber: 11.7g
Sugar: 1.5g

INGREDIENTS:

- 1 ¼ cups coconut flour
- ¾ tsp. baking soda
- 6 tbsp. melted coconut oil
- 3 tbsp. Italian seasoning (If you don't have this, you can just use 2/3 tsp. each of: basil, garlic powder, thyme, oregano and onion powder)
- 2 flax eggs
- ¾ tsp. salt

Total number of ingredients: 6

METHOD:

1. Preheat oven to 300 °F.
2. Add coconut flour, oil, baking soda, and flax eggs to a bowl.
3. Mix well.
4. Add Italian seasoning (or herbs if you don't have this seasoning) and salt to the mix.
5. Using your hands, mold the dough, small handfuls at a time, to make mini rolls. You should have about 6 rolls when done.
6. Place on a greased baking sheet.
7. Bake at 300 °F for about 45 minutes.
8. Remove from oven and cool at room temperature.

TIP: The bread is naturally a bit crumbly, but if you don't let it cool for an extended period of time, it will completely fall apart.

These lovely rolls are sure to satisfy cravings for carbs and make a delectable side roll to any balanced meal, whether it be a salad, soup, or even as a snack with a drizzle of olive oil.

6. Tortilla Wraps

Serves: 6
Prep Time:
~10 min

Nutrition
information
(per serving)

Calories: 157 kcal
Carbs: 4.2g
Fat: 13.8g
Protein: 5.0g
Fiber: 1.9g
Sugar: 1.5g

INGREDIENTS:

- ¼ cup ground flaxseed
- ¼ cup hot water
- 1 cup almond flour
- ¼ tsp. baking powder
- ½ tsp. salt

Total number of ingredients: 5

METHOD:

1. Mix ground flaxseed with hot water until you get a gel-like substance.
2. In a separate bowl, mix almond flour, salt and baking powder.
3. Add ground flaxseed mixture to almond flour mixture.
4. Mix thoroughly.
5. Add hot water as needed in order to achieve a perfect dough-like consistency.
6. Knead dough, then separate dough into about 6 balls.
7. Flatten each ball as thinly as possible.
8. Grease a pan.
9. Place each tortilla on greased pan and bake each tortilla until brown on both sides.
10. Remove pan from oven.
11. Let cool completely before using as they are easier to mold and fold once cool.

This bread-based recipe comes in handy if you're craving a good old tofu wrap or even a vegan-styled quesadilla!

TIP: Psyllium husk and flaxseed mixed with hot water allows for a gel-like substance to form, which is extremely convenient for achieving a dough-type consistency.

7. Keto-Vegan Pizza Crust

INGREDIENTS:

- 1 tsp. salt
- 1 tbsp. olive oil
- 1 cup warm water
- 2 ½ tsp. active yeast
- 3 cups almond flour
- 1 pinch dried oregano, ground
- 1 pinch dried basil leaf

Total number of ingredients: 7

METHOD:

1. Preheat oven to 300 °F.
2. Place warm water in a cup (Note: It must be the right temperature or it will not work).
3. Add yeast to cup.
4. Stir for one minute until you see a light brown mixture.
5. Let sit for 5 minutes until a thin layer of foam forms on top.
6. In a separate bowl, add almond flour and salt.
7. Mix almond flour and salt. Once done mixing, form a well in the middle of the almond flour-salt mixture.
8. Pour yeast mixture and olive oil into well center and begin mixing ingredients.
9. Mix until a dough is achieved. Add more or less flour depending on consistency of dough.
10. Separate into 2 balls.
11. Using a rolling pin, flatten balls into circles of dough.
12. Place dough in oven and allow to cook halfway for about 6 minutes.
13. Take out dough.
14. Place pizza toppings on dough.
15. Place pizza dough back in oven to finish baking for 3-6 minutes.
16. Once baked, remove from oven.
17. Let cool for 2 minutes, then use a pizza slicer to slice into 8 pieces per pizza.

This adapted ketogenic vegan pizza crust is the perfect substitute if you're looking for a quick pizza without the excess carbs. This crust works best as thin to regular crust, but not deep dish. Pair with some fresh tomato sauce, vegan cashew-parmesan cheese, mushrooms, spinach, or even tofu if you like!

Serves: 2
Prep Time:
~10 min

Nutrition
information
(per serving:
1 Crust Slice)

Calories: 134 kcal
Carbs: 3.4g
Fat: 11.8g
Protein: 4.9g
Fiber: 6.3g
Sugar: 1.6g

8. Panini Flat Bread

Serves: 10
Prep Time:
~10 min

___

Nutrition
information
(per serving: 2 half
slices/one sandwich)

Calories: 280 kcal
Carbs: 8.1g
Fat: 24.4g
Protein: 8.5g
Fiber: 3.7g
Sugar: 3.1g

INGREDIENTS:

- 3 cups almond flour
- 4 flax eggs
- ⅓ cup coconut flour
- 1 tsp. baking soda
- ½ tsp. garlic powder
- ¼ cup water
- ¼ cup olive oil

Total number of ingredients: 7

METHOD:

1. Preheat oven to 350 °F.
2. Mix dry ingredients (coconut flour, almond flour, garlic powder and baking soda) together in a bowl.
3. To this bowl, add in flax eggs, olive oil, and water, and mix completely until a dough forms (add extra flour or water accordingly; it should be a bit sticky!).
4. Place dough onto a parchment paper-covered tray and mold into a rough rectangular loaf shape.
5. Place 1 piece of parchment paper on top of loaf.
6. Place loaf in oven and bake for 15-20 minutes until firm.
7. Remove loaf from oven.
8. Remove top piece of parchment paper and let loaf cool completely.
9. Once cool, cut into about 10 square pieces, then cut each piece in half.

9. Herb Cracker Crisps

Serves: 20
Prep Time:
~5 min

Nutrition
information
(per serving:
about 4 crackers)

Calories: 201 kcal
Carbs: 4.7g
Fat: 18.4g
Protein: 5.5g
Fiber: 0.4g
Sugar: 1.8g

INGREDIENTS:

- 1 cup almond flour
- 2 flax eggs
- 1 tbsp. rosemary (can be fresh or dried, but freshly chopped rosemary is preferable as it will give a beautiful, strong taste!)
- 2 tbsp. canola oil
- 2 tbsp. water
- ½ tsp. garlic powder
- ¼ tsp. dried oregano, ground
- ¼ tsp. dried basil leaf
- ¼ tsp. salt
- 1 pinch black pepper

Total number of ingredients: 10

METHOD:

1. Preheat oven to 350 °F.
2. Place all ingredients in a bowl and mix well.
3. Line a pan with non-stick parchment paper.
4. Taking the dough formed in step 2, scoop ½ tbsp. of dough and place on pan. Flatten with your finger to make it as thin as a cracker.
5. Bake for about 5-10 minutes until the outsides are crisp and the insides are just the slightest bit soft (they'll harden even more when cooling).
6. Remove from oven, and let cool.

Eat these lovely crisps alone or with a spread to please any cracker-snack cravings you may be having. The infusion of herbs is sure to hit your taste buds and leave you satisfied, with only 4.7g of carbs and 1.8g of sugar per serving!

10. Dried Fruits and Nuts Breakfast Bread

Serves: 15
Prep Time:
~15 min

Nutrition information (per serving)

Calories: 315 kcal
Carbs: 21.1g
Fat: 19.4g
Protein: 6.1g
Fiber: 3.6g
Sugar: 15.1g

INGREDIENTS:

- 2 cups almond flour
- 1 medium banana
- 2 flax eggs
- ¼ cup coconut oil
- 2 tbsp. whole flax seeds
- ¼ tsp. salt
- ½ tsp. baking soda
- 1 ½ cups roughly chopped dried mixed fruit (e.g., cranberries, strawberries, pineapple, cherries)
- 1 ½ cups roughly chopped dried nuts (e.g., pecans, almonds, walnuts)

Total number of ingredients: 10

METHOD:

1. Preheat oven to 300 °F.
2. Lightly grease a loaf pan with olive oil.
3. Place bananas in a bowl, and mash extremely well.
4. To the mashed bananas, add coconut oil and flax eggs.
5. Mix well.
6. Add in flour, baking powder, and salt to the mixture, and mix thoroughly.
7. Top with fruits, nuts, and seeds, and mix until everything is evenly mixed.
8. Pour batter in greased loaf pan, and let bake for about 45 minutes or until knife comes out of the center clean.
9. Remove pan from oven, and let cool completely before slicing.

This bread does not rise, so no worries if you don't see that happening!

You will realize how many nutrients you are getting when you eat a slice, as well as how satisfied and strengthened you feel! Due to the amount of dried fruits and nuts in the recipe, as well as the density of the loaf, one to two slices is more than enough to get you energized and full until lunch time. You can even grab a slice if you're looking for a boost in between your meals.

The great thing about this recipe is that it is very adaptable. You can choose whatever assortments of dried fruits or nuts you want to add to the recipe.

11. Seed and Nut Topped Loaf

INGREDIENTS:

- 2 cups almond flour
- 2 tbsp. coconut flour
- ⅓ cup coconut oil
- ½ cup whole almonds
- 3 tbsp. sesame seeds
- ½ cup pumpkin seeds
- ¼ cup whole flax seeds
- ½ tsp. salt
- 3 flax eggs
- 1 ½ tsp. baking soda
- ¾ cup almond milk
- 3 drops stevia sweetener
- 1 tbsp. apple cider vinegar

Total number of ingredients: 13

Serves: 15
Prep Time:
~15 min

Nutrition
information
(per serving)

Calories: 172 kcal
Carbs: 8.1g
Fat: 13.2g
Protein: 6.1g
Fiber: 3.5g
Sugar: 2.4

METHOD:

1. Preheat oven to 350 °F.
2. Blend almonds in a blender until fine.
3. Add flax seeds, sesame seeds, and pumpkin seeds and blend.
4. Add almond flour, coconut flour, salt, and baking soda and blend.
5. In a separate bowl, add flax eggs, coconut oil, almond milk, vinegar, and sweetener. Stir well.
6. Add almond mixture to flax egg mixture and let sit for a few minutes.
7. Grease a loaf pan.
8. Pour batter in pan.
9. Sprinkle left over seeds atop batter (pumpkin, flax, and sesame seeds).
10. Bake for about 45 minutes, or until a knife comes clean out of the middle.
11. Remove from oven, and let cool completely before slicing.

This loaf recipe is a dry, nutty spin on a regular bread loaf. What makes it even better is its low-carb, high-fat content, allowing you to consume a few pieces guilt free.

12. Low Carb Corn Bread

Serves: 18
Prep Time:
~10 min

Nutrition
information
(per serving)

Calories: 138 kcal
Carbs: 7.2g
Fat: 10.7g
Protein: 3.5g
Fiber: 1.2g
Sugar: 2.6g

INGREDIENTS:

- 2 cups almond flour
- 6 drops stevia sweetener
- 1 tsp. salt
- 2 flax eggs
- 3 ½ tsp. baking powder
- ½ cup vanilla flavored almond milk
- ⅓ cup coconut oil
- 15 oz. can baby corn, finely chopped

Total number of ingredients: 8

METHOD:

1. Preheat oven to 350 °F.
2. In a bowl, mix almond flour, salt, and baking powder.
3. Add stevia, chopped corn, flax eggs, almond milk, and coconut oil.
4. Mix well, ensuring no clumps.
5. Lightly grease a pan.
6. Pour batter in pan.
7. Place pan in oven and let bake 50-60 minutes or until knife comes cleanly out of the middle.

You would think that people on a ketogenic diet would need to steer clear of corn, but here's a recipe that has been tweaked to prove otherwise! The stevia acts as a natural sweetener with almond meal acting as a substitute for high carb flour options. You can eat a slice for breakfast or in between meals to satisfy cravings.

13. Low Carb Sub Bread

Serves: 4 mini subs
Prep Time:
~5 min

Nutrition
information
(per serving)

Calories: 292 kcal
Carbs: 13.3g
Fat: 23.2g
Protein: 9.9g
Fiber: 2,5g
Sugar: 3.2g

INGREDIENTS:

- 1 ½ cups almond flour
- 5 tbsp. psyllium husk powder, finely ground
- 2 tsp. baking powder
- 1 tsp. salt
- 2 ½ tbsp. apple cider vinegar
- 2 flax eggs
- 1 cup boiling water

Total number of ingredients: 7

METHOD:

1. Preheat oven to 350 °F.
2. In a bowl, mix together almond flour, psyllium husk powder, baking powder, and salt.
3. Add flax eggs and apple cider vinegar and mix well until a dough forms.
4. Add boiling water and continue mixing.
5. Mold dough into 4 mini subs or one large sub (remember the dough should and will rise).
6. Place dough on a slightly greased baking pan. Bake for 45 minutes or until firm.

Yes, while 13.3g carbs may seem like a lot, it must be taken in comparison to a traditional sub sandwich's carb levels: a whole 40g. Enjoy this recipe when you find yourself reminiscing on those tasty sub sandwiches, and simply indulge the guilt-free way!

14. Plain Loaf

Serves: 15
Prep Time:
~5 min

Nutrition
information
(per serving)

Calories: 142 kcal
Carbs: 13.4g
Fat: 43.1g
Protein: 3.9g
Fiber: 3,5g
Sugar: 1.5g

INGREDIENTS:

- 1 cup coconut flour
- 6 cups almond flour
- ¼ cup flax seed
- 5 flax eggs
- ½ cup water
- ½ cup MCT oil
- 3 tsp. baking powder
- 1 tsp. salt
- 1 tbsp. apple cider vinegar

Total number of ingredients: 8

METHOD:

1. Preheat oven to 350 °F.
2. In a bowl, mix together dry ingredients: almond flour, coconut flour, baking powder, salt, and flax seeds.
3. In a separate bowl, mix together coconut oil, water and apple cider vinegar.
4. Combine dry and liquid ingredients from Steps 2 and 3. Mix well.
5. Pour batter in a slightly greased large loaf pan.
6. Bake for 30-45 minutes or until firm.

NOTE: Make sure the loaf is completely cooled before slicing it.

Here is another spin on a plain bread type loaf that you could use a spread on, or for on-the-go sandwiches!

15. Seed-Based Crackers

Serves: 25 crackers
Prep Time:
~5 min

___

Nutrition
information
(per serving)

Calories: 53 kcal
Carbs: 3.5g
Fat: 3.6g
Protein: 1.6g
Fiber: 1.6g
Sugar: 0.1g

INGREDIENTS:

- 1 cup flaxseed, ground
- 1 cup pumpkin seeds
- ½ cup sesame seeds
- ½ tsp. salt
- 1 cup hot water

Total number of ingredients: 5

METHOD:

1. Preheat oven to 300 °F.
2. Place all ingredients in a bowl and mix.
3. Let sit for five minutes (the flaxseed will form a gel with the water).
4. Spread mixture on a parchment paper-lined pan.
5. Using a knife, cut dough evenly into about 25 crackers.
6. Place in oven and bake until firm.
7. Turn oven off, leaving crackers in oven for about 1 hour so that crackers dry out.

Simple and quick homemade crackers are sure to satisfy your need of a quick snack, or even to use as a base for a low-carb spread.

16. 2-Minute Microwave Fruit Bread in a Mug!

INGREDIENTS:

- ⅓ cup almond flour (or any other nut flour of your preference)
- 1 flax egg
- ¼ tsp. baking soda
- ¼ tsp. salt
- 2 tbsp. of your desired dried fruit (For this recipe, raspberries and strawberries were chosen)

Total number of ingredients: 5

METHOD:

1. To a bowl, add almond flour, baking soda, dried fruits, and salt. Mix thoroughly.
2. Add flax egg and stir until evenly distributed. Also make sure dried fruits are evenly distributed in the batter.
3. Lightly grease a mug that is big enough to hold batter.
4. Pour batter into mug and microwave for about 2 minutes.
5. Remove mug from oven, and slice mini loaf into about 4 pieces.

This recipe is an adaptation of the new craze of "microwave bread" which allows you to exhaust minimal effort yet indulge to the maximum.

Raspberries and strawberries are great for those on a ketogenic diet as fresh raspberries contain 3.3g of carbs per ounce and strawberries 2.2g. Ultimately, this recipe is such an efficient, tasty, and filling way to put a spin on your normal loaf of bread.

Serves: 4 slices
Prep Time: ~3 min

Nutrition information (per serving: 1 circled slice)

Calories: 165 kcal
Carbs: 25.5g
Fat: 6.2g
Protein: 4.1g
Fiber: 0.8g
Sugar: 13.3g

17. Seed-Based Herb Crackers

Serves: 16
Prep Time:
~50 min

Nutrition information (per serving)

Calories: 190 kcal
Carbs: 5.5g
Fat: 14.7g
Protein: 9.0g
Fiber: 5.3g
Sugar: 0.3g

INGREDIENTS:

- 2 cups ground flaxseed
- 2 cups ground hemp seed
- 2 cups warm water
- 1 tsp. salt
- 1 tsp. black pepper
- Italian herbs or other herbs to taste

Total number of ingredients: 6

METHOD:

1. Preheat oven to 350°F.
2. Line your baking plate with parchment paper.
3. Combine flax seeds, hemp seeds, salt, and herbs in mixing bowl and stir thoroughly.
4. Pour in water and stir.
5. Let mixture sit for 5 minutes until water is absorbed.
6. Spread out mixture evenly on the baking plate, about 1/8 inch thick.
7. Divide into 16 pieces without damaging parchment paper.
8. Bake for 50 minutes.
9. Remove from oven and cool down.
10. Break into 16 pieces for serving.
11. Can be stored up to a week or frozen.

Check out this delicious keto friendly cracker recipe that is suitable for ketogenic vegans and is extremely simple to make!

KETOGENIC VEGAN CHEESES

Vegan Cheeses are an amazing alternative for dairy-based cheeses. There is a plethora of plant-based cheese alternatives that ketogenic vegans can lean on.

However, combining both dietary needs, you will have to watch out as many plant-based cheeses have different nutrition profiles than their dairy-based alternatives. Vegan cheeses are often rich in beans, nuts, and oils.

Please be aware that some of the cheeses are made with soybeans and nuts. If you have any allergies, make sure to read the ingredients carefully before you prepare a recipe.

Below, you'll find some of the best vegan cheeses with a lower carb profile that you can prepare in your own kitchen. This way, you're safe to satisfy your taste buds and indulge in your cruelty-free and carb-free cheese cravings!

Dig into these mouth-watering recipes for keto-vegan cheeses, such as feta and garlic-herb cream cheese. Beyond enjoying your cheese, you will enjoy the process of making it as well!

1. Feta Cheese

Serves: 6
Prep Time:
~10 min

———————

Nutrition
information
(per serving)

Calories: 103 kcal
Carbs: 5.8g
Fat: 5.0g
Protein: 8.6g
Fiber: 1.9
Sugar: 0.7g

INGREDIENTS:

- 1 block tofu (cut into ½ inch cubes, firm of extra firm)
- 1 ½ cups water
- ¼ cup light miso
- 3 tbsp. white wine vinegar
- 2 tsp. salt

Total number of ingredients: 5

METHOD:

1. In a saucepan, let the tofu simmer with water for about 5 minutes.
2. While the tofu is simmering, separately mix the miso, vinegar, salt, and water in a bowl.
3. Once the tofu is done, transfer it into a Tupperware container big enough to contain the mix and the tofu.
4. Pour the mixture over the tofu, and let this sit uncovered in the fridge for a few hours.
5. Then cover the container for 2-7 days until ready to serve.

Check out this great "fake feta" that is suitable for ketogenic vegans and is extremely simple to make!

2. Cashew Cheese

**Serves: 1 block /
15 wedge slices
Prep Time:
~25 min**

**Nutrition
information
(per slice)**

**Calories: 100 kcal
Carbs: 3.8g
Fat: 8.5g
Protein: 2.1g
Fiber: 0.5g
Sugar: 0.7g**

INGREDIENTS:

- 1 ¼ cup cashews
- 1 tsp. salt and pepper
- ½ tsp. oregano
- ½ tsp. basil
- ¼ tsp. garlic powder
- 1 tbsp. coconut vinegar
- 1 ½ cup almond milk
- ¼ cup olive oil
- 1 tsp. nutritional yeast

Total number of ingredients: 9

METHOD:

1. Boil the cashews for up to 15 minutes; then strain and dump the cashews in a blender.
2. Add oregano, basil, yeast, salt, pepper, and garlic powder; then blend.
3. Bring the almond milk, olive oil, and vinegar to a simmer; then dump in a mixing bowl. Slowly add the previous mixture and mix until it's a smooth puree.
4. Mold into a block of cheese and keep refrigerated.

If you're looking for a good spread for crackers or breads, try this cashew moldable cheese that's sure to satisfy those cravings!

3. Cheddar Cheese

**Serves: 1 block /
15 wedge slices
Prep Time:
~10 min**

**Nutrition
information
(per slice)**

**Calories: 47 kcal
Carbs: 3.7g
Fat: 3.0g
Protein: 1.3g
Fiber: 1.0
Sugar: 0.7g**

INGREDIENTS:

- 1 ½ cups water
- 2 tbsp. agar-agar
- ½ cups raw cashews
- 1 tsp. nutritional yeast
- 3 tbsp. fresh lemon juice
- 2 tbsp. sesame tahini
- 3 tbsp. paprika
- 3 tsp. onion powder
- 1 ½ tsp. sea salt
- ½ tsp. garlic powder
- ¼ tsp. cayenne
- ¼ tsp. dry mustard

Total number of ingredients: 12

METHOD:

1. Combine the agar-agar with water and bring to a boil for one minute; then set aside.
2. Pour this and all other ingredients into a blender and blend until smooth.
3. Using coconut oil, grease a ceramic bowl, and pour the mixture into it. Refrigerate this, uncovered, for up to three hours.
4. Cover and allow to chill overnight. This cheese can stay good for up to 10 days!

For all you cheddar cheese lovers, try out this vegan and keto option that's sure to make you feel like you are eating very normal cheese without the cruelty or carbs!

4. Cream Cheese

**Serves: 1 block /
15 wedge slices
Prep Time:
~2 min**

**Nutrition
information
(per slice)**

**Calories: 74 kcal
Carbs: 2.3g
Fat: 6.8g
Protein: 1.0g
Fiber: 0.4g
Sugar: 0g**

INGREDIENTS:

- 2 cups organic coconut cream
- 1 tsp. non-dairy probiotic powder
- 1 tsp. nutritional yeast
- 1 tsp. garlic powder
- ½ tsp. sea salt
- Fresh herbs (to taste)

Total number of ingredients: 5-6

METHOD:

1. Whisk the salt, probiotic powder, yeast, and chilled coconut cream until smooth.
2. For about 24 hours, leave the mixture wrapped in a cheese cloth or coffee filter in a cup to cope with leaking. Make sure that the area you store the mixture in is dimmed or dark.
3. Unwrap the cheese, and add salt and garlic powder; then cool the cheese in the fridge for up to 6 hours.

With only 2.3 grams of carbs, this cheese works perfectly when cubed as a spread for dried keto-friendly crackers with a pinch of herbs on top for added flavor. Also, as a perfect cream cheese substitute, try pairing this with keto-vegan friendly bagels.

5. Zucchini-Based Nacho Cheese

Serves: 10 slices
Prep Time:
~5 min

Nutrition
information
(per slice)

Calories: 62kcal
Carbs: 8.0g
Fat: 1.5g
Protein: 1.0g
Fiber: 1.7g
Sugar: 2.1g

INGREDIENTS:

- 5 cups zucchini (peeled and cubed)
- ½ cup water
- 1 cup red pepper (diced)
- 1 tbsp. coconut oil
- 1 tbsp. lemon juice
- ½ cup agar-agar
- 1 tsp. salt
- ¼ cup jalapenos (finely chopped)
- 1 tsp. nutritional yeast
- ½ tsp. cumin

Total number of ingredients: 10

METHOD:

1. Steam the zucchini, red pepper, and the water until they are softened (about 5 minutes).
2. Transfer the strained veggies into a blender with the salt, lemon juice, yeast, and coconut oil and blend until smooth. Add the agar-agar and blend again. Lastly, add the jalapeños, and blend one last time.
3. Pour the mix into a rectangular dish and refrigerate for up to 6 hours. Gently place the hardened cheese on a tray and slice the cheese.
4. Melt a chunk of it in a microwaveable dish for a nacho cheese dipping sauce!

A party favorite, this nacho cheese is versatile, as it can be added in sandwiches, on crackers, and even melted as a dipping sauce. The agar-agar is a popular vegan substitute for gelatin and necessary for many cheese recipes as it allows for the unique texture of the cheese.

6. Nut-Free Cheese Sauce

INGREDIENTS:

- ¼ cup sesame seeds
- ¾ cup water
- 2 tsp. lemon juice
- 1 tbsp. coconut oil
- 1 tsp. nutritional yeast
- 1 tsp. yellow mustard
- ¼ tsp. onion powder
- ¼ tsp. garlic powder
- ¼ tsp. salt

Total number of ingredients: 10

METHOD:

1. In a blender, add the sesame seeds, lemon juice, and water and blend for 2 minutes.
2. In an oiled saucepan, add the nutritional yeast and stir until all yeast is covered in oil.
3. Pour in the blended mixture and stir until all is boiling.
4. Add the mustard, garlic powder, onion powder, and salt. Mix well. Take off stove top and leave for about 2 minutes until thickened.

This 15-minute cheese sauce can be served with pasta for a keto-vegan friendly mac n' cheese or even the healthier option tossed with carrots, broccoli, and whatever steamed veggies you prefer!

Serves: 4
Prep Time:
~5 min

Nutrition
information
(per serving)

Calories: 84 kcal
Carbs: 2.7g
Fat: 7.4g
Protein: 1.8g
Fiber: 1.2g
Sugar: 0.2g

7. Cashew Cheese Spread

Serves: 1 cup of
cheese / 5 servings
Prep Time:
~5 min

___

Nutrition
information
(per serving)

Calories: 151.7 kcal
Carbs: 8.8g
Fat: 10.9g
Protein: 4.6g
Fiber: 1.0g
Sugar: 1.7g

INGREDIENTS:

- 1 tsp. nutritional yeast
- ½ tsp. salt
- 1 cup water
- 1 cup raw cashews
- 1 tsp. garlic powder

Total number of ingredients: 5

METHOD:

1. Soak cashews for 6 hours in the water.
2. Drain and transfer to a food processor along with all the other ingredients and blend.
3. For the best flavor, chill the mix before serving.

Try this heart-healthy alternative for all those cruelty-based cheeses nowadays! Made from cashews and spices, the spread works best as a cracker spread.

8. Peanut Cheese Spread

Serves: 14
Prep Time:
~10 min

Nutrition
information
(per serving)

Calories: 207.7 kcal
Carbs: 5.0g
Fat: 17,3g
Protein: 8.0g
Fiber: 2.6g
Sugar: 1.2g

INGREDIENTS:

- 3 cups unsalted shelled peanuts
- ½ tsp. salt
- 2 tbsp. peanut oil

Total number of ingredients: 3

METHOD:

1. Heat oven to 350°F.
2. Add the nuts to a round or square baking pan (or rimmed baking sheet).
3. Roast nuts for 3 minutes, shake, and then roast again for 3 to 5 minutes until the peanuts smell nutty and lightly browned, but be careful—they can burn quickly.
4. Allow to cool for handling.
5. Add all ingredients to a blender
6. Blend until achieving the desired consistency.
7. The peanut butter will be ready in 1 or 2 minutes.

These yellow cheese slices ensure minimal carb intake so you can enjoy it as a dipping sauce (when melted) or even for a classic grilled cheese sandwich.

9. Sharp Cheddar Shredded Cheese

Serves: 10
Prep Time:
~10 min

Nutrition
information
(per serving)

Calories: 261.4 kcal
Carbs: 11.8g
Fat: 19.4g
Protein: 9.9g
Fiber: 6.5g
Sugar: 2.1g

INGREDIENTS:

- 1 cup water
- ¾ cup flax seed
- 2 cups unsalted shelled peanuts
- 1 red pepper (marinated in vinegar and roasted)
- 1 tsp. nutritional yeast
- 1 tbsp. paprika
- 2 ½ tsp. salt and pepper
- 1 tsp. onion powder
- 1 tsp. garlic powder
- 2 tbsp. lemon juice
- 1 cup water (for blending)
- 2 ½ tbsp. agar-agar powder
- 1 ¼ cup water (for the agar-agar powder)

Total number of ingredients: 13

METHOD:

1. Heat oven to 350°F.
2. Add the nuts to a round or square baking pan (or rimmed baking sheet).
3. Roast nuts for 3 minutes, shake, and then roast again for 3 to 5 minutes until the peanuts smell nutty and lightly browned, but be careful—they can burn quickly.
4. Blend all the ingredients except the last amount of water and agar-agar powder. Place half of the water in the blender, followed by all the ingredients, then the remainder of the water. Blend.
5. In a medium saucepan, stir the agar-agar powder on low heat until it has a thick consistency; then add to the blender and mix for about 30 seconds.
6. Once the mix has uniform consistency, pour it into loaf pans and place in the fridge for 30 minutes or until firm.

While the carb intake on this specific cheese recipe is a bit higher than most, you don't need much sprinkled on any dish for added flavor.

10. Sesame Seed Cheese

Serves: 1 wheel of cheese / 12 wedges
Prep Time:
~10 min

Nutrition information (per wedge)

Calories: 57 kcal
Carbs: 2.0g
Fat: 4.9g
Protein: 1.0g
Fiber: 0.8g
Sugar: 0g

INGREDIENTS:

- 1 cup water
- 1 tbsp. agar-agar
- 1 tsp. nutritional yeast
- ½ cup sesame seeds
- ¼ tsp. salt
- ¼ tsp. garlic powder
- 2 tbsp. olive oil

Total number of ingredients: 7

METHOD:

1. Grind the nutritional yeast, sesame seeds, olive oil, and salt until a butter consistency is formed.
2. On low heat, simmer the water and agar-agar, mixing well until it is smooth. Turn off heat, and let cool for 5 minutes.
3. Blend the agar-agar mixture and the garlic powder in the sesame seed mixture.
4. Pour the cheese mix into a bowl and cover it with plastic wrap. Refrigerate it until firm.

Nut-free, dairy-free, and sugar-free, this sesame seed-based wedge cheese is sure to meet all of a ketogenic-vegan's dietary needs!

11. Seed-Based Cheese Spread

Serves: 12
Prep Time:
~10 min

___

Nutrition
information
(per serving)

Calories: 155.7 kcal
Carbs: 3.9g
Fat: 12.5g
Protein: 6.9g
Fiber: 1.7g
Sugar: 0.7g

INGREDIENTS:

- 1 cup hemp seeds
- 1 cup sunflower seeds (soak in hot water for 10 minutes)
- 1 tsp. nutritional yeast
- ¼ cup sun-dried tomatoes
- 1 tbsp. basil

Total number of ingredients: 5

METHOD:

1. In a blender, combine the hemp, sunflower seeds, and water until the mix is uniform.
2. Add the rest of the ingredients and water as needed and blend once more.

While the seeds in this recipe give for the texture, the sun-dried tomatoes add the flavor needed to make this cheese-spread a favorite.

12. Spicy Peanut Garlic Cream

Serves: 12
Prep Time:
~5 min

Nutrition
information
(per serving)

Calories: 40 kcal
Carbs: 4.3g
Fat: 14.2g
Protein: 6.3g
Fiber: 2.0g
Sugar: 0.9g

INGREDIENTS:

- 2 cups unsalted shelled peanuts
- 2 tbsp. peanut oil
- 1 garlic clove
- 1 jalapeno
- Salt and pepper to taste

Total number of ingredients: 5

METHOD:

1. Heat oven to 350°F.
2. Add the nuts to a round or square baking pan (or rimmed baking sheet).
3. Roast nuts for 3 minutes, shake, and then roast again for 3 to 5 minutes until the peanuts smell nutty and lightly browned, but be careful—they can burn quickly.
4. Combine all the ingredients in a food processor until they are thoroughly mixed. Don't over blend, however, as the mix might become too soft.

This cheesy, corn-based texture works best for keto-friendly quesadillas or burritos! The garlic, salt, and pepper ensure this cheese's flavorful addition to any meal.

13. Almond Cream Cheese

Serves: 6
Prep Time:
~15 min

___

Nutrition
information
(per serving)

Calories: 311 kcal
Carbs: 11.1g
Fat: 25.0g
Protein: 10.4g
Fiber: 5.9g
Sugar: 1.95g

INGREDIENTS:

- 2 cups raw almonds
- 2 tsp. olive oil
- 3 cloves garlic
- 1 ¼ cups water
- 1 tsp black pepper to taste
- 1 tsp. salt
- 1 tbsp. lemon juice
- ¼ cup nutritional yeast

Total number of ingredients: 8

METHOD:

1. Toss the olive oil, almonds, and garlic in a frying pan, and roast them for a few minutes until brown and smelling nutty.
2. Transfer these to a blender and add all other ingredients, adjusting any ingredient to your taste.
3. Blend until smooth and serve.

14. Gouda Nut Cheese

Serves:
8 oz. of cheese /
8 servings
Prep Time:
~15 min

**Nutrition
information
(per serving)**

Calories: 481 kcal
Carbs: 15.7g
Fat: 38.9g
Protein: 17.2g
Fiber: 4.4g
Sugar: 1.4g

INGREDIENTS:

- 2 cups unsalted, shelled peanuts
- 2 cups raw almonds
- 2 tbsp. vegan butter (any store brand you prefer or find)
- ¼ cup almond milk
- 1 tbsp. agar-agar
- 1 tsp. paprika
- 1 tbsp. mustard
- Salt and pepper (to taste)

Total number of ingredients: 8

METHOD:

1. Blend the peanuts and almonds together, adding the paprika, mustard, salt, and pepper.
2. In a saucepan, heat the milk and butter over medium heat. Once the butter has melted add the agar-agar and stir constantly for about 5 minutes.
3. Add the heated, stirred mixture to the blender, and blend again until all ingredients are mixed evenly.
4. Pour the mix into molds of your choice, letting it rest for 10 minutes. Refrigerate for about 30 minutes.

15. Cheese Wheel

Serves: 12 slices
Prep Time:
~15 min

Nutrition
information
(per slice)

Calories: 281 kcal
Carbs: 11g
Fat: 26.2g
Protein: 9.4g
Fiber: 3.7g
Sugar: 2.5g

INGREDIENTS:

- ½ cup aquafaba (liquid from a can of chickpeas)
- 3 tsp. agar-agar powder
- ½ cup almond milk
- 2 cups raw almonds
- 2 cups cashews
- 1 tsp. nutritional yeast
- 2 tsp. tapioca starch
- 1 tsp. salt
- ½ tsp garlic powder
- 2 tsp. dark miso (not mellow white miso)
- 1 tsp. Worcestershire sauce (vegan)

Total number of ingredients: 11

METHOD:

1. In a saucepan, mix together the agar-agar and the chickpea liquid WITHOUT HEAT until combined. Set this aside.
2. Combine the milk, yeast, almonds, cashews, salt, garlic, miso, and Worcestershire sauce in a blender and mix well; then set aside.
3. On low heat let the aquafaba mixture boil for 1 minute; then slowly add the blender mixture and allow it to boil again. With a spatula, mix this for about 5 minutes while heating.
4. Transfer the mixture into a mold of your choice and let cool. Once cool, refrigerate the mold to chill and harden. Remove from the mold, slice, and serve.

Looking for a dairy-free alternative with added flavor? Not to mention 26 grams of fat per wedge, this cheese recipe works great alone or on crackers for a flavorful snack!

16. Raw Spiced Cashew Cheese

Serves: 8 Wedges
Prep Time:
~5 min

Nutrition
information
(per wedge)

Calories: 221 kcal
Carbs: 8.0g
Fat: 17.6g
Protein: 7.7g
Fiber: 5.3g
Sugar: 1.4g

INGREDIENTS:

- 2 cups raw cashews (soaked for at least 4 hours)
- ½ lemon's juice
- 2 tsp. apple pectin
- Salt to taste
- 1 tsp. nutritional yeast
- Spices of your choice (garlic powder, herbs, etc.)
- Coconut oil or olive oil to grease

Total number of ingredients: 7

METHOD:

1. Add the apple pectin, yeast, lemon juice, and salt to the drained cashews, and blend all contents in a blender.
2. Remove from the blender and place in a well-greased bowl. Smooth the surface. Set aside for about an hour.
3. After an hour, carefully remove the cheese and incorporate (roll in) the spices of your choice; then refrigerate until fully firm.

The spices added to this cheese really give it a unique flavor you won't find in ordinary spreads. Tweak this recipe to your taste-bud preferences for the best results.

17. Garlic Herb Cream Cheese

Serves: 8
Prep Time:
~15 min

─────────

**Nutrition
information
(per serving)**

Calories: 181 kcal
Carbs: 11.4g
Fat: 28.1g
Protein: 12.3g
Fiber: 4.5g
Sugar: 2.4g

INGREDIENTS:

- 1 cup cashews (soaked 2-12 hours)
- 2 cups unsalted shelled peanuts
- ¼ cup fresh basil
- A small sprig of thyme
- ½ tsp. salt
- 2 garlic cloves
- 1 ½ tsp. apple cider vinegar
- 1 tsp. nutritional yeast
- 2 tbsp. olive oil
- Water (if needed)

Total number of ingredients: 10

METHOD:

1. Drain the nuts and transfer to a blender with all the other ingredients except the olive oil and blend well. If the mixture doesn't have the desired consistency, add water accordingly.
2. When the cheese looks creamy enough, add the oil and blend again.
3. Let the mix set so the flavors fully develop; then, pour into a strainer lined with cheesecloth. Place this strainer with the mix in another bowl so any leakage can fall into the larger bowl.
4. Refrigerate until firm.

18. Baked Cashew-Herb Cheese

INGREDIENTS:

- ¾ cup raw cashews (soaked overnight)
- ¾ cup raw blanched almonds (soaked overnight)
- ¼ cup lemon juice
- 1 tsp. nutritional yeast
- 3 tbsp. olive oil
- 1 large garlic clove (minced)
- Sprinkle of fresh thyme, basil, and rosemary (dried is okay)
- Salt and pepper to taste

Total number of ingredients: 8

METHOD:

1. With the olive oil, yeast, lemon juice, and spices, blend the nuts until very smooth.
2. In a large bowl, place a strainer lined with a cheese cloth, and carefully scoop the mixture into this. Bring together the corners of the cloth to form a ball, and close it with a rubber band. Squeeze the ball to let excess water drain.
3. Chill overnight so excess fluids will continue to drain.
4. Preheat the oven to 390°F, and line a tray with parchment paper.
5. Scoop the cheese onto this and form it into a smooth log shape.
6. Sprinkle the salt, pepper, and spices on top, and bake for about 45 minutes until firm.
7. Allow to cool completely before slicing and serving.

While this recipe does contain nuts, each serving only comes out to around 7 grams of carbs and 13 grams of fat, suitable for a ketogenic-vegan's dietary needs. The herbs allow you to eat this spiced cheese alone or spread on your favorite crackers.

Serves: 10 slices of cheese
Prep Time: ~10 min

Nutrition information (per slice)

Calories: 169kcal
Carbs: 5.8g
Fat: 13.2g
Protein: 3.8g
Fiber: 2.0g
Sugar: 0.6g

19. Queso Peanut Dip

Serves: 8
Prep Time:
~15 min

Nutrition
information
(per serving)

Calories: 93 kcal
Carbs: 10.6g
Fat: 18.1g
Protein: 7.0g
Fiber: 3.7g
Sugar: 2.1g

INGREDIENTS:

- 1 cup peanut cheese spread
- 1 ripe avocado
- 1 small onion
- ¼ cup vegetable broth
- ½ cup rice milk
- ½ cup cashews (soaked in water for 4-6 hours)
- 1 ½ tsp. paprika
- ½ tsp. cumin
- ¼ tsp. ground turmeric
- ½ tsp. garlic powder
- 1 garlic clove
- ½ tsp. sriracha (optional)

Total number of ingredients: 12

METHOD:

1. Combine all ingredients in a blender for about 2-3 minutes until soft.

The beauty of this recipe is the way you can play with it, serving it with anything such as tomatoes, avocadoes, beans, parsley, and more. Perfect for a party dip!

20. Spreadable Feta Cheese

Serves:
20 spreadable
blocks
Prep Time:
~10 min

Nutrition
information
(per serving)

Calories: 50 kcal
Carbs: 1.3g
Fat: 4.8g
Protein: 0.6g
Fiber: 0.7g
Sugar: 0.4g

INGREDIENTS:

- 1 cup macadamia nuts (soaked, rinsed, drained)
- ½ cup water
- 2 tbsp. lemon juice
- 1 clove garlic
- 1 tsp. nutrition yeast
- 1 tsp. white miso paste
- ¼ tsp. citric acid
- ½ tsp. dried oregano
- ½ tsp. dried thyme
- ½ tsp. salt and pepper

Total number of ingredients: 10

METHOD:

1. Mix the nuts and sea salt in a blender for a few minutes, stirring occasionally, until the mixture is smooth and thick.
2. Spoon out about half of the mixture and pour into a glass container lined with cheesecloth. Place all of the spices on top evenly. Then, spoon out the remaining cheese and press it on top.
3. Fold over the cheesecloth and put something heavy over it before placing it in the fridge.
4. Refrigerate for 24 hours to set.

21. Cashew Dill Cheese

Serves: 6 cheese circles
Prep Time: ~15 min

Nutrition information (per circle)

Calories: 127 kcal
Carbs: 7.7g
Fat: 9.1g
Protein: 3.8g
Fiber: 2.2g
Sugar: 1.3g

INGREDIENTS:

- 1 cup water
- 1 tsp. agar-agar powder
- 1 cup raw cashews
- 1 tsp. nutritional yeast
- 1 tsp. onion powder
- 1 tsp. salt
- ¼ cup fresh dill (chopped)

Total number of ingredients: 7

METHOD:

1. Mix together the salt, onion powder, cashews, and yeast in a blender until the cashew mixture is smooth.
2. In a saucepan, bring the water to a boil; then mix in the agar-agar powder mix for 5 minutes while simmering.
3. Add the cashew mix to the saucepan and stir a few times; then add the dill and mix again.
4. Pour the mix into a lightly-greased muffin tray, and let cool in the fridge for up to an hour before serving.

For those of you whose taste buds do miss a fine dill cheese, check out this cashew-based version with less than 10 grams of carbohydrates per indulgence sure to act as a great substitute to dairy-based cheeses.

22. Mozzarella Cheese

Serves: 8
Prep Time:
~10 min

Nutrition
information
(per serving)

Calories: 469 kcal
Carbs: 16g
Fat: 39.0g
Protein: 13.5g
Fiber: 5.4g
Sugar: 6.8g

INGREDIENTS:

- 2 cups raw cashews (soaked for several hours and drained)
- 2 cups almonds
- 1 cup hot water
- 2 tbsp. tapioca starch
- 1 garlic clove (small and minced)
- ¾ tsp. salt
- 1 tsp. fresh lemon juice

Total number of ingredients: 7

METHOD:

1. Combine all ingredients in a blender for 1 minute; then transfer to a skillet, constantly stirring over medium heat.
2. Keep stirring, so it doesn't burn. Stop stirring when the mixture thickens, which will take a few minutes.
3. Remove from the heat, and let cool.

23. Peanut Pepper Jack Cheese

Serves: 5
Prep Time:
~15 min

Nutrition
information
(per serving)

Calories: 372 kcal
Carbs: 12.7g
Fat: 28.8g
Protein: 15.5g
Fiber: 8.3g
Sugar: 2.6g

INGREDIENTS:

- ½ package Pomona's pectin (must use this brand)
- 1 cup water
- 2 cups unsalted shelled peanuts
- 2 tsp. lemon juice
- 1 tsp. nutritional yeast
- 1 tsp. sea salt
- ½ tsp. onion powder
- 1 tsp. garlic powder
- 2 tsp. red pepper flakes
- Canned green chilies (to taste, optional)

Total number of ingredients: 10

METHOD:

1. Mix half the pectin along with lemon juice and water in a blender, then transfer to a saucepan simmering over low heat.
2. In the blender grind the cashews, onion powder, garlic powder, salt, and nutritional yeast until very smooth.
3. On the side, mix ½ cup of water with the calcium packet that comes with the Pomona's pectin and mix.
4. Transfer the skillet mix into the blender and mix. It will start to thicken quickly, so pour in half the calcium mix as well as the pepper flakes and chilies.
5. Once everything is smooth and creamy, transfer to a lightly-greased six-cupcake tin and refrigerate uncovered for an hour until firm.

24. Sriracha and Lime Cheeseball

Serves: 8
**Prep Time:
~10 min**

**Nutrition
information
(per serving)**

Calories: 190 kcal
Carbs: 9.2g
Fat: 14.7g
Protein: 5.1g
Fiber: 1.5g
Sugar: 0.3g

INGREDIENTS:

- 1 ½ cup cashews (soaked for 4-6 hours)
- 3 tbsp. sriracha
- Lime zest and juice from ½ a lime
- 1 tsp. nutritional yeast
- 3 tbsp. almond milk
- ½ lemon's juice
- 1 tsp. salt
- Pinch of garlic and onion powder to taste
- ½ cup walnuts (toasted)

Total number of ingredients: 9

METHOD:

1. Combine all ingredients in a blender and keep adding water for fluidity; mix until smooth.
2. When the desired consistency is reached, transfer to a cheesecloth and squeeze until firm.
3. Roll the cheese ball in the toasted walnuts, and refrigerate until firm.

25. Herb-Encrusted Cheese Log

INGREDIENTS:

- 2 cups raw cashews (soaked for several hours and drained)
- 2 cups unsalted shelled peanuts
- ½ tbsp. agar-agar powder
- 2 tbsp. tahini
- 2 tbsp. water
- ¾ tbsp. nutritional yeast
- ¼ tsp. salt
- 2 tbsp. light miso
- 4 tsp. lemon juice

Coating:

- 1 large garlic clove (minced)
- 3 large sundried tomatoes (chopped and rinsed)
- 2 tbsp. green onions (chopped)
- 4 tbsp. toasted nuts (optional, pecans, walnuts, pine nuts, almonds)
- 3 tbsp. fresh herbs (chopped)

Total number of ingredients: 14

METHOD:

1. Blend the agar-agar powder, water, tahini, nuts, and salt in a food processor until very smooth. Place this in a saucepan on medium heat until it bubbles and becomes thick.
2. Add the lemon juice, garlic, and miso to the mix. Transfer to the blender and pulse briefly.
3. Have a long container prepared to pour the mixture into, and let refrigerate for 30 minutes.
4. While the cheese is in the fridge, mix coating ingredients together in a blender or by hand, and spread out along a sheet of plastic wrap.
5. Quickly transfer the cheese and roll on the herb-encrusted plastic wrap, then let this refrigerate for the next few hours until firm and the plastic wrap can be removed.

Serves: 6
Prep Time:
~15 min

Nutrition
information
(per serving)

Calories: 173kcal
Carbs: 21.1g
Fat: 59.2g
Protein: 23.1g
Fiber: 7.4g
Sugar: 6.0g

26. Hazelnut Spread

Serves: 16
Prep Time:
~60 min

Nutrition
information
(per serving)

Calories: 138 kcal
Carbs: 3.2g
Fat: 12.9g
Protein: 2.2g
Fiber: 1.7g
Sugar: 0.7g

INGREDIENTS:

- 2 cups raw hazelnuts
- ¼ cup hemp oil
- ½ tsp. salt
- ½ tsp. ground black pepper

Total number of ingredients: 4

METHOD:

1. Roast hazelnuts on baking sheet lined with parchment paper on 300°F for 12 minutes.
1. Take out and let the nuts cool.
2. Put all ingredients in blender or food processor.
3. Blend until smooth, stop and scrape down edges container when necessary.
4. Serve at room temperature, store in a cool place, or freeze up to 12 months.

27. Spicy Cheese Sauce

Serves: 8
Prep Time:
~5 min

**Nutrition
information
(per serving)**

Calories: 162 kcal
Carbs: 6.9g
Fat: 12.2g
Protein: 6.1g
Fiber: 1.8g
Sugar: 1.1g

INGREDIENTS:

- ½ cup hemp seeds
- 1 cup cashews
- 1 tbsp. nutritional yeast
- 1 jalapeno
- 1 clove minced garlic
- 1 tbsp. flaxseed oil
- ½ tsp. onion powder
- 1 tsp. black pepper
- ½ cup of water
- 1 tsp. salt

Total number of ingredients: 10

METHOD:

1. Halve the jalapeno, and remove seeds, stem, and placenta
2. Add all ingredients to blender and blend until smooth.
3. Store cooled for 2-3 days, or freeze up to two months.

28. No-Salt Cream Cheese

Serves: 1 block/15 wedge slices
Prep Time: ~25 min

Nutrition information (per serving)

Calories: 133 kcal
Carbs: 5.6g
Fat: 10.9g
Protein: 3g
Fiber: 0.6g
Sugar: 1.1g

INGREDIENTS:

- 2 cups cashews
- ½ tbsp. coconut vinegar
- ½ cup almond milk
- ¼ cup olive oil
- 1 tsp. nutritional yeast

Total number of ingredients: 5

METHOD:

1. Boil the cashews for up to 15 minutes; then strain and dump the cashews in a blender.
2. Blend until smooth.
3. Bring the almond milk, olive oil, and vinegar to a simmer, then dump in a mixing bowl. Slowly add the previous cashew mixture and mix until a smooth puree.
4. Mold into a block of cheese and keep refrigerated.

29. Vegan Nutella

INGREDIENTS:

- 2 cups raw hazelnuts
- ¼ cup MCT oil
- ½ tbsp. cocoa powder
- 1 tsp. stevia
- ½ tsp. vanilla extract
- ½ tsp. coffee beans, ground (optional)

Total number of ingredients: 6

METHOD:

1. Roast hazelnuts on baking sheet lined with parchment paper in a preheated oven at 300°F for 12 minutes.
2. Take out and let the nuts cool.
3. Put all ingredients in blender or food processor.
4. Blend until smooth. Stop and scrape down edges container when necessary.
5. Serve at room temperature, store in a cool place, or freeze up to 12 months.

Serves: 8
Prep Time:
~60 min

Nutrition
information
(per serving)

Calories: 281kcal
Carbs: 5.8g
Fat: 26.4g
Protein: 4.4g
Fiber: 3.4g
Sugar: 1.5g

30. Sweet Cashew Cheese Spread

Serves: 1 cup of
cheese/5 servings
Prep Time:
~5 min

Nutrition
information
(per serving)

Calories: 151 kcal
Carbs: 8.8g
Fat: 10.9g
Protein: 4.6g
Fiber: 1.0g
Sugar: 1.7g

INGREDIENTS:

- 1 tsp. nutritional yeast
- 1 cup water
- 1 drop stevia
- 1 cup raw cashews

Total number of ingredients: 5

METHOD:

1. Soak cashews for 6 hours in the water.
2. Drain and transfer to a food processor along with all the other ingredients and blend.
3. For the best flavor, make sure to chill the mix before serving.

Try this heart-healthy alternative for all those cruelty-based cheeses nowadays! Made from cashews and spices, the spread works best as a cracker spread.

LOW CARB VEGAN BREAKFASTS

Breakfast is the most important meal of the day and kick starts our metabolism. The morning is the ideal time to consume complex carbohydrates like fruit and oatmeal because these are heavier on the stomach.

Below, you'll find delicious recipes that are limited to 20-minute preparation time or less. From ketogenic pudding, pancakes, and smoothies to imitation spinach-fueled smoothies and casseroles, there are enough recipes below to satisfy your taste buds.

Even more so, they don't include crazy ingredients that are unpractical, but everyday items you can find in your fridge and pantry.

1. Overnight Bowl

Serves: 2
Prep Time:
~5 min

___

Nutrition
information
(per serving)

Calories: 424 kcal
Carbs: 11.5g
Fat: 35.8g
Protein: 13.6g
Fiber: 7.3g
Sugar: 3.4g

INGREDIENTS:

- ¾ cup coconut milk
- ½ cup hemp seeds
- 1 tbsp. chia seeds
- 4 drops stevia sweetener
- ½ tsp. vanilla
- Pinch of salt to taste
- 6 raspberries (or fruit of choice)

Total number of ingredients: 7

METHOD:

1. Combine all ingredients except fruits in a lidded plastic container and mix well.
2. Leave overnight in the fridge.
3. The next day, add more coconut milk until desired consistency and taste is reached.
4. Add fruit and enjoy.

This simplistic go-to keto-vegan breakfast option requires no prep time. Make it at your convenience at night and grab it in the morning for a quick boost of energy.

2. Berry Smoothie

Serves: 1
Prep Time:
~5 min

Nutrition
information
(per serving
- using optional
ingredients)

Calories: 549 kcal
Carbs: 15g
Fat: 46.1g
Protein: 18.6g
Fiber: 9g
Sugar: 2.7g

INGREDIENTS:

- 1 cup almond milk
- 2 tbsp. peanut oil
- ½ avocado
- 3-inch piece of cucumber
- 6 berries of choice (optional)
- 2 tbsp. vegan protein powder of choice (optional)

Total number of ingredients: 6

METHOD:

1. Combine all ingredients in a blender and add more or fewer berries of choice until desired flavor is reached.

3. Chocolate & Protein Smoothie

Serves: 2
Prep Time:
~5 min

___

Nutrition
information
(per serving)

Calories: 506 kcal
Carbs: 23.2g
Fat: 40.4g
Protein: 12.4g
Fiber: 8.9g
Sugar: 10.1g

INGREDIENTS:

- 1 cup full fat coconut milk
- 20 grams of vegan protein powder (neutral taste)
- 50 grams of dairy-free dark chocolate
- 2 tbsp. chia seeds
- ¼ cup water
- ½ cup ice
- ½ tsp. vanilla extract

Optional:

- ½ tsp. stevia sweetener

Total number of ingredients: 8

METHOD:

1. Combine all ingredients in a blender.
2. Drink the smoothie from a glass and enjoy.

Delicious protein-packed smoothie. Use more vegan protein powder for even more building blocks in your smoothie.

4. Chia Seed Pudding

Serves: 1
Prep Time:
~5 min

Nutrition information (per serving)

Calories: 331 kcal
Carbs: 20.8g
Fat: 24.6g
Protein: 6.6g
Fiber: 17.2g
Sugar: 2.1g

INGREDIENTS:

- ¼ cup chia seeds
- ¼ cup coconut milk
- ½ cup water
- 1 tbsp. cocoa powder
- 5 drops stevia sweetener
- ½ tsp. cinnamon

Total number of ingredients: 6

METHOD:

1. Combine all ingredients in a blender, adding more or less of what you prefer.
2. Let sit overnight in the fridge to thicken.
3. Top with cocoa nibs and enjoy.

Here is another overnight option for those of you in a rush in the morning. While satisfying a sweet tooth, this recipe provides high fat content to give you a boost for a couple of hours.

5. Veggie Quiche

Serves: 5
Prep Time:
~10 min

Nutrition
information
(per serving)

Calories: 461 kcal
Carbs: 18.6g
Fat: 36g
Protein: 14.4g
Fiber: 9.9g
Sugar: 4.3g

INGREDIENTS:

- 1 low carb crust (you can find the recipe in 'The Low Carb Vegan Cookbook')
- ½ tsp. salt
- 4 tbsp. water
- 1 leek (chopped)
- 1 ½ cups zucchini (chopped)
- Black pepper to taste
- 2 tbsp. olive oil
- 14 oz. firm tofu
- ¼ tsp. turmeric powder
- 1 cup spinach

Total number of ingredients: 10

METHOD:

1. Preheat oven to 350°F.
2. Fry leek and zucchini in a lightly-greased skillet until soft.
3. Blend the tofu with the salt, pepper, turmeric, and water until you achieve a thick batter. Add the veggies and mix.
4. Spoon the mixture over low carb crust and cook for about 30 minutes.

This recipe can satisfy multiple preferences, as you can be versatile with your ingredients. Add more or less of the veggies you prefer for the all-in-one breakfast.

6. Original Pancakes

Serves: 1
Prep Time:
~10 min

———

Nutrition
information
(per serving -
including protein
powder)

Calories: 657 kcal
Carbs: 17.2g
Fat: 33.7g
Protein: 77.7g
Fiber: 7.7g
Sugar: 0.3g

INGREDIENTS:

- 1 flax egg
- 1 tbsp. flax seeds
- 1 ½ tbsp. coconut oil
- 3 scoops of protein powder (vegan-friendly, optional)
- Salt (to taste)
- ¼ tsp. baking powder

Total number of ingredients: 6

METHOD:

1. In one bowl, mix the protein powder, baking powder, salt, and flax seeds.
2. In another bowl, mix the flax egg and coconut oil.
3. Pour the wet ingredients into the dry and mix well.
4. In a lightly-greased pan, measure out and pour batter for three individual pancakes. Be sure to flatten the poured batter so that the pancakes are ½ cm thick.
5. Keep cooking until browned on both sides. Top with syrup or berries of choice and enjoy.

The protein powder in this recipe works perfectly for those of you looking to get a boost in your protein levels while keeping the carbohydrates at bay in order to get lean. With three pancakes as a serving size, you are sure to feel energized and satisfied.

7. Avocado Breakfast Bowl

Serves: 2
Prep Time:
~10 min

Nutrition
information
(per serving)

Calories: 503 kcal
Carbs: 14.1g
Fat: 47.8g
Protein: 4.1g
Fiber: 8.7g
Sugar: 2.1g

INGREDIENTS:

Dressing:
- ¼ cup olive oil
- ¼ cup lemon juice
- ¼ tsp. ginger
- ¼ tsp. salt

Breakfast Bowl:
- 1 avocado (medium)
- ¼ cup carrot (shredded)
- 2 tbsp. tahini

Total number of ingredients: 7

METHOD:

1. Pour all the dressing ingredients, and shake until mixed well in an airtight Tupperware container. This will make dressing for up to 4 servings of this breakfast bowl.
2. Pour 2 tbsp. of the dressing onto the shredded carrots, and let sit for 5 minutes.
3. Transfer into the center of a pitted and halved avocado, and drizzle the tahini on top of it, adding more dressing if you prefer.

Avocados are a heart-healthy, keto- and vegan-friendly start to any morning. With barely any prep time, this recipe serves those in a rush in the morning, yet not willing to sacrifice their taste buds or health!

8. Nuts & Seeds Bagels

Serves: 8
Prep Time:
~10 min

**Nutrition
information
(per serving)**

Calories: 139kcal
Carbs: 14.0g
Fat: 13.8g
Protein: 4.1g
Fiber: 9.4g
Sugar: 0.5g

INGREDIENTS:

- 3 tbsp. ground flax seed
- ½ cup mixed nuts
- ½ cup tahini
- ½ cup psyllium husk powder
- 1 tsp. baking powder
- 1 cup water
- Salt to taste

Total number of ingredients: 7

METHOD:

1. Preheat oven to 375°F.
2. Grind mixed nuts into small, but not too small, pieces with a mortar and pestle.
3. Mix all the dry ingredients together; then add the water and mix until it has been absorbed.
4. Mix in the tahini well while kneading the dough to ensure it is a uniform mixture.
5. Make patties four inches in diameter and cut small circles out in the middle.
6. Lay on a baking tray and put in the oven for about 40 minutes.

Here is a simple recipe for keto vegan-friendly bagels that act as a base for eating plain or with whatever toppings you desire.

9. Matcha Pudding

Serves: 2
Prep Time:
~5 min

Nutrition
information
(per serving)

Calories: 244 kcal
Carbs: 9g
Fat: 21.8g
Protein: 3.1g
Fiber: 4.7g
Sugar: 3.6g

INGREDIENTS:

- ½ tsp. matcha powder
- ¾ cup coconut milk
- 1 ½ tbsp. chia seeds
- 2 strawberries
- 3 drops stevia sweetener (more or less to taste)

Total number of ingredients: 5

METHOD:

1. Combine all ingredients other than the strawberries into a lidded cup and shake well for about 10 seconds so everything mixes.
2. Place in the fridge for about 4 hours.
3. Take out, add the sliced strawberries on top, and enjoy.

With only five ingredients, this breakfast recipe is a great start to your day by giving you the added nutrients you need plus the flavor.

10. Peanut Butter Kale Blend

Serves: 2
Prep Time:
~10 min

Nutrition
information
(per serving)

Calories: 759 kcal
Carbs: 28.2g
Fat: 59.8g
Protein: 26.4g
Fiber: 16.0g
Sugar: 10.1g

INGREDIENTS:

- 2 cups kale
- 1 cup peanut butter
- 2 cups unsweetened almond milk
- ½ cup blackberries
- ½ cup crushed oats
- 3 tbsp. almond butter

Total number of ingredients: 6

METHOD:

1. Blend all ingredients together in a blender.
2. Add more or less of what you prefer.

Freeze the blackberries before blending. The frozen fruits will make your smoothie cold and delicious to drink on warmer days. Kale can be switched with spinach for a different flavor profile.

11. Avocado Chocolate Bread

Serves: 6
Prep Time:
~20 min

Nutrition
information
(per serving)

Calories: 728 kcal
Carbs: 27.4g
Fat: 61.7g
Protein: 16.0g
Fiber: 12.5g
Sugar: 13.4g

INGREDIENTS:

- 1 ½ cup avocado (pitted and peeled)
- 1 cup of almonds
- 3 tbsp. coconut oil
- 1 cup coconut milk
- 1 tsp. vanilla extract
- 1 tsp. baking soda
- 2 tbsp. stevia sweetener
- 2 flax eggs
- ½ cup pecans
- 2 cups almond flour
- ¼ cup raw cacao powder
- ½ cup pure chocolate chips
- Pinch of salt

Total number of ingredients: 13

METHOD:

1. Leave a cup of coconut milk in the fridge for 8 hours (overnight) and scrape the top of the cup for 2 tablespoons coconut cream.
2. Put the coconut cream and the sliced avocado in a food processor.
3. Add the coconut oil, vanilla, stevia sweetener, and flax eggs to the mix.
4. In a separate bowl, crush the pecans, and mix them with the almond flour, baking soda, chocolate chips, and raw cacao powder.
5. Mix all the ingredients together.
6. Put the batter into a pan, and sprinkle it with chocolate chips.
7. Preheat oven to 350°F.
8. Bake mixture for 40 minutes.
9. Allow the avocado chocolate bread to cool down before serving.

You can keep this bread longer than just a day. By storing it in airtight containers, you can keep it in the fridge for up to 2 days, and up to 2 months in the freezer.

12. Dried Fruit and Nut Granola

Serves: 8
Prep Time:
~25 min

Nutrition
information
(per serving)

Calories: 231 kcal
Carbs: 7g
Fat: 19.8g
Protein: 6.3g
Fiber: 3.3g
Sugar: 1.3g

INGREDIENTS:

- ½ cup chopped walnuts
- ½ cup chopped pecans
- ½ cup sliced almonds
- ⅓ cup roasted sunflower seeds
- ⅓ cup roasted pumpkin seeds
- 1 flax egg
- ¼ cup dried cranberries (unsweetened)
- 3 tbsp. stevia extract
- 1 tbsp. coconut oil
- Pinch of salt
- ½ tsp. cinnamon

Total number of ingredients: 11

METHOD:

1. Preheat the oven to 350°F.
2. Add the nuts, seeds, and dried fruit to a medium bowl.
3. Mix everything with the stevia extract, flax egg, and coconut oil.
4. Add a pinch of salt and the optional cinnamon.
5. Distribute the mixture in a large pan.
6. Bake for 20 minutes, until slightly gold in color.
7. Remove from oven and enjoy.

You will realize how many balanced nutrients you are getting when you eat this granola mixture.

13. Peanut Cream Scramble

Serves: 2
Prep Time:
~10 min

Nutrition
information
(per serving)

Calories: 1129 kcal
Carbs: 17.4g
Fat: 105.6g
Protein: 27.3g
Fiber: 7.9g
Sugar: 5.0g

INGREDIENTS:

- 1 cup tofu, extra firm
- 1 cup peanut cheese spread
- ½ cup spinach (chopped)
- ½ cup cherry tomatoes
- ¼ cup peppers (dices, optional)
- Onion powder, garlic powder, salt and pepper (to taste)

Total number of ingredients: 8

METHOD:

1. Sautee everything together in a lightly-greased pan until soft and combined.
2. Add more or less of whichever ingredient as you prefer.

14. Herb Crackers with Avocado Spread

Serves: 5
Prep Time:
~10 min

Nutrition
information
(per serving -
four crackers)

Calories: 266 kcal
Carbs: 8.3g
Fat: 23.7g
Protein: 6.3g
Fiber: 5.7g
Sugar: 2.4g

INGREDIENTS:

- 1 cup almond flour
- 2 flax eggs
- 2 tbsp. olive oil
- 2 tbsp. water
- 1 tbsp. rosemary (either fresh or dried, but freshly chopped rosemary will give that beautiful, strong taste!)
- ½ tsp. garlic powder
- ¼ tsp. oregano
- ¼ tsp. basil
- ¼ tsp. salt
- Pinch of black pepper
- 1 avocado
- ½ cup cherry tomatoes (halved)

Total number of ingredients: 12

METHOD:

1. Preheat oven to 350°F.
2. Pour all ingredients in a bowl and mix well.
3. Have a non-greased pan ready lined with non-stick parchment paper.
4. Make each cracker about ½ tbsp. in volume and press down gently with your finger to make the appropriate width.
5. Bake for about 5-10 minutes until the outsides are crisp and the insides are just the slightest bit soft (they will harden even more when cooling).
6. Spread mashed avocado and a few cherry tomatoes on the crackers.
7. Sprinkle salt and pepper on top and enjoy.

Eat these crisps with the avocado spread to satiate you early in the day. The infusion of herbs is sure to kick your taste buds and leave you satisfied with only 8g of carbs and 2g of sugar per serving!

15. Nut Free Granola

Serves: 8
Prep Time:
~15 min

Nutrition
information
(per serving)

Calories: 533 kcal
Carbs: 16.1g
Fat: 46.9g
Protein: 12.3g
Fiber: 10.1g
Sugar: 2.6g

INGREDIENTS:

- ¼ cup coconut oil (melted)
- 1 tsp. vanilla extract
- 6 drops stevia sweetener
- 1 tsp. cinnamon
- Salt to taste
- 1 cup sesame seeds (raw)
- 1 cup hemp hearts
- 2 cups coconut (shredded, unsweetened)
- ¼ cup chia seeds

Total number of ingredients: 9

METHOD:

1. Preheat oven to 350°F.
2. Whisk the wet ingredients until a thin paste is formed; then add the dry ingredients and mix well.
3. Transfer the mix to a lightly-greased baking sheet and bake for 15 minutes.
4. Transfer to another baking tray to let cool for 10 minutes before putting in an airtight plastic container.

16. Waffles

Serves: 4
Prep Time:
~15 min

Nutrition information (per serving)

Calories: 573 kcal
Carbs: 21.8g
Fat: 44.7g
Protein: 11.2g
Fiber: 19.9g
Sugar: 1.1g

INGREDIENTS:

- 2 cups ground flax seed
- 1 tbsp. baking powder
- 1 tsp. salt
- 5 flax eggs
- ½ cup water
- ⅓ cup olive oil
- 2 tsp. ground cinnamon
- Berries of choice (optional)

Total number of ingredients: 8

METHOD:

1. Heat waffle maker to medium heat.
2. Mix flax seed, baking powder, and salt. Set aside.
3. Add flax eggs, water, and oil to a blender and blend for approximately 30 seconds until it looks foamy.
4. Pour the blender mix into the dry ingredients bowl and mix well. Set aside for about 5 minutes.
5. Add the cinnamon and mix well.
6. Separate the mixture into 4 servings and pour each into the waffle maker.
7. Serve directly with fruits of choice, or freeze waffles in a container.

If you have a waffle maker at home, check out this simple recipe! Topping the waffles with fruits of your choice, you can expect a sweet and savory start to your energized day!

17. Tofu-Pepper Bake

Serves: 2
Prep Time:
~10 min

—————

Nutrition
information
(per serving)

Calories: 209 kcal
Carbs: 11.1 g
Fat: 12.4 g
Protein: 13.3 g
Fiber: 3.7g
Sugar: 6.1 g

INGREDIENTS:

- 1 large, green bell pepper, chopped
- 1 large, red bell pepper, chopped
- 2 tsp. olive oil
- Salt and pepper to taste
- 10 oz. extra firm tofu, chopped)

Total number of ingredients: 6

METHOD:

1. Preheat oven to 350°F.
2. Grease a baking tray with olive oil and lay out the chopped peppers and sprinkle with salt, pepper, and olive oil and bake for 20 minutes.
3. While the peppers are cooking, sauté tofu in a greased skillet with salt, pepper, and olive oil.
4. Take peppers out of the oven and let cool. Transfer to a baking dish and mix with the cooked tofu, adding vegan cheese if you like.
5. Put back in the oven for 10 minutes and mix well, adding any additional seasoning to taste.

18. Coconut Berry Bomb Bars

INGREDIENTS:

- ⅓ cup coconut butter
- ⅓ cup coconut oil
- ½ tbsp. 100% cocoa powder
- 2 drops stevia sweetener
- ⅓ cup fresh strawberries
- 1 tbsp. shredded coconut

Total number of ingredients: 6

METHOD:

1. In a saucepan, add coconut butter, coconut oil, syrup, and cocoa powder over low heat until melted. Stir well.
2. In a heated frying pan, add strawberries with a bit of water and mash them until a half solid-liquid mix is formed. Mix constantly.
3. Put the strawberries in the blender with one tablespoon of coconut oil mixture and blend.
4. Fill molds of your choice with the coconut oil mixture and one tablespoon of the strawberry mixture.
5. Sprinkle shredded coconut atop each.
6. Refrigerate overnight.

Check out this vegan-friendly fat bomb that can fill you up at the start of your day as well as give you a needed boost. If you aren't a fan of strawberries, you can switch them out for berries of your choice. With only 0.8 grams of carbs per bar, you can pair it with a filling smoothie or eat a few more!

Serves: 15 bars
Prep Time:
~15 min

Nutrition
information
(per serving)

Calories: 65 kcal
Carbs: 0.8g
Fat: 6.7g
Protein: 0.2g
Fiber: 0.3g
Sugar: 0.2g

19. Green Berry Smoothie

INGREDIENTS:

- ¼ cup coconut milk
- ½ avocado (pitted and peeled)
- ½ cup water
- 1 tbsp. fresh mint
- 2 tbsp. pistachios
- 1 tbsp. vanilla extract
- 2 drops of stevia sweetener
- ¼ cup spinach
- ¾ cup fresh raspberries

Total number of ingredients: 9

METHOD:

1. Blend all ingredients together. Add more or less of what you prefer.

For those of you that enjoy a quick, mess-free breakfast with loads of nutrients and energy, smoothies are your way to go. Check out this smoothie recipe for a serving of fruits and veggies in less than 5 minutes, perfect for busy mornings.

Serves: 2
Prep Time:
~5 min

Nutrition
information
(per serving)

Calories: 348 kcal
Carbs: 14g
Fat: 30.9g
Protein: 3.6g
Fiber: 8.2g
Sugar: 4.8g

20. PB&J Chia Pudding

Serves: 2
Prep Time:
~15 min

***

Nutrition
information
(per serving)

Calories: 160 kcal
Carbs: 20g
Fat: 45.9g
Protein: 21.5g
Fiber: 10.7g
Sugar: 4g

INGREDIENTS:

- 2 tbsp. chia seeds
- 2 tbsp. peanut butter
- ½ cup frozen raspberries (or berry of choice)
- ¾ cup water

Total number of ingredients: 4

METHOD:

1. Combine all ingredients well in a mason jar.
2. Add 6 ounces of boiling water.
3. By the time the water cools down, the pudding should have set.

21. Fuel-Full Iced Coffee

Serves: 1
Prep Time:
~5 min

Nutrition information (per serving)

Calories: 247 kcal
Carbs: 5.9g
Fat: 23.6g
Protein: 2.9g
Fiber: 2.5g
Sugar: 0.5g

INGREDIENTS:

- 1 ¾ cup brewed coffee (slightly more or less, depending on your preference)
- 1 tbsp. almond butter
- 1 tsp. cocoa powder
- 1 tbsp. coconut oil
- 4 drops stevia sweetener
- ¼ tsp. vanilla powder
- ¼ tsp. cinnamon
- 4 ice cubes

Toppings:
- 1 tbsp. coconut whipped cream
- 1 tsp. dairy-free cocoa-nibs

Total number of ingredients: 8

METHOD:

1. Blend all ingredients except for the toppings and ice cubes.
2. Place mix in a mason jar and set in fridge overnight so it chills.
3. Place back in blender and add the ice cubes. Blend until smooth.
4. Pour coffee into mug or jar of choice, add toppings, and enjoy!

22. Fat-Packed Iced Coffee

Serves: 4
Prep Time:
~5 min

Nutrition
information
(per serving)

Calories: 288 kcal
Carbs: 7.7g
Fat: 26.4g
Protein: 5.0g
Fiber: 2.6g
Sugar: 3.4g

INGREDIENTS:

- 1 (14 oz). can of coconut milk
- 8 ice cubes
- 1 tbsp. vanilla-flavored protein powder (make sure it's vegan-friendly)
- 1 ½ cup brewed coffee (of choice)
- 2 tbsp. almond butter

Total number of ingredients: 5

METHOD:

1. Blend all ingredients except the ice cubes until smooth.
2. Divide the mixture into four cups, add 2 ice cubes in each, and enjoy!

Here's a twist on a normal cup of caffeine to start off your morning. Using a protein powder you like, this coffee recipe has you covered for a more healthful twist to your day.

23. Coconut-Almond Loaf

Serves: 10
Prep Time:
~30 min

———

Nutrition
information
(per serving)

Calories: 250 kcal
Carbs: 7.5g
Fat: 20.4g
Protein: 6.5g
Fiber: 5.4g
Sugar: 1.9g

INGREDIENTS:

- 1 ½ cups almond flour
- 2 tbsp. coconut flour
- ¼ cup ground flax seed
- ¼ tsp. salt
- 5 flax eggs
- 1 ½ tsp. baking soda
- 3 drops stevia sweetener
- ¼ cup coconut oil
- 1 tbsp. apple cider vinegar
- ½ cup almonds (sliced)

Total number of ingredients: 10

METHOD:

1. Preheat the oven to 350°F.
2. Mix all dry ingredients: almond flour, coconut flour, salt, flax seed, and baking soda in a blender.
3. Add the stevia, flax eggs, apple cider vinegar, and coconut oil.
4. Mix extremely well, making sure there are no clumps.
5. Add chopped almonds, and mix manually.
6. Pour batter in a lightly-greased loaf pan.
7. Bake for 30-35 minutes.
8. Let it cool before serving.

Looking for a more filling, yet sweet and flavorful breakfast option? Make this simple recipe at night and grab a loaf on the go with either a smoothie or on its own. It's sure to fill you up and keep you going until lunch!

24. Hemp Porridge

Serves: 1
Prep Time:
~30 min

Nutrition
information
(per serving)

Calories: 815 kcal
Carbs: 28.6g
Fat: 61.8g
Protein: 36.1g
Fiber: 20.2g
Sugar: 2.4g

INGREDIENTS:

- 1 cup almond milk
- ½ cup hemp hearts
- 2 tbsp. ground flax seeds
- 1 tbsp. chia seeds
- 5 drops stevia sweetener
- ¾ tsp. vanilla extract
- ½ tsp. cinnamon
- ½ cup almonds (crushed)

Total number of ingredients: 8

METHOD:

1. Add all ingredients except the almond flour to a small saucepan on low heat, and stir constantly until it begins to boil. Turn off heat.
2. Leave covered in hot saucepan for about 2 minutes.
3. Remove from heat, stirring in the crushed almonds.
4. Pour in a bowl and serve.

Want a filling, warm breakfast before you start your day? Go for this quick and easy 10-minute porridge. With only 8.4 net grams of carbs, it is sure to be a keto favorite.

25. Peach Protein Bars

Serves: 6
Prep Time:
~60 min

————

Nutrition
information
(per serving)

Calories: 270 kcal
Carbs: 15.0g
Fat: 19.3g
Protein: 9.1g
Fiber: 11.1g
Sugar: 2.0g

INGREDIENTS:

- 1 cup flax seeds
- ½ cup peanuts
- ¼ cup hemp seeds
- 15g dehydrated peaches
- 2 tbsp. psyllium husk
- ¼ tsp. stevia
- ½ tsp. salt
- 1¼ cup water

Total number of ingredients: 8

METHOD:

1. Preheat oven at 350°F.
2. Grind up nuts and seeds with ½ cup water in a blender, but make sure the mixture is not finely ground.
3. Transfer and combine mixture with psyllium husk and cinnamon in a mixing bowl.
4. Crush the dehydrated peaches into small bits and add to mixing bowl.
5. Stir in the remaining water and salt until all ingredients are combined.
6. Let the mixture sit for a few minutes.
7. Spread the mixture out on a baking sheet lined with parchment paper, and make sure the dough is about ¼ inch thick.
8. Bake for 45 minutes, remove around 30 minutes to cut the dough carefully in six pieces, and bake for another 15 minutes.
9. Remove from oven and cool for 30 minutes.
10. Can be stored for a week or frozen up to two months.

26. Protein Pancakes

Serves: 4
Prep Time:
~35 min

**Nutrition
information
(per serving)**

Calories: 113 kcal
Carbs: 5.3g
Fat: 7.6g
Protein: 7.8g
Fiber: 3.8g
Sugar: 0.7g

INGREDIENTS:

- 1 scoop vegan protein powder
- ¼ cup almond flour
- 1 tbsp. glucomannan powder
- 1 ½ cup water
- 1 tbsp. flaxseed oil
- 1 tsp. vanilla extract
- 1 tsp. baking powder

Total number of ingredients: 7

METHOD:

1. Soak glucomannan powder in ½ cup water for a couple of minutes.
2. Combine all dry ingredients and set aside.
3. Mix vanilla extract and flaxseed oil with soaked glucomannan.
4. Put a non-stick pan on the stove over medium heat.
5. Slowly stir a cup of water into the dry flour mixture, and combine thoroughly.
6. Add the glucomannan into flour and protein mixture. Stir well.
7. Add heap of batter to the pan and spread out into a ¼ inch thick pancake.
8. Bake for 5 minutes on each side and repeat this for all pancakes.
9. Can be stored in fridge for 3 days or frozen for up to 2 months.

27. Breakfast Protein Bars

Serves: 16
Prep Time:
~35 min

Nutrition
information
(per serving)

Calories: 61 kcal
Carbs: 2.6g
Fat: 4.3g
Protein: 3.8g
Fiber: 1.3g
Sugar: 0.8g

INGREDIENTS:

- 1 cup cashew cheese spread
- 2 tbsp. softened cocoa butter
- 4 tbsp. coconut flour
- ½ cup full fat coconut milk
- 2 scoops vegan protein powder
- ¼ teaspoon stevia
- 1 tsp. vanilla extract

Total number of ingredients: 7

METHOD:

1. Preheat oven to 375°F.
2. Whisk together cocoa butter, cashew cheese spread, stevia, and coconut milk until mixed well.
3. Stir the coconut flour and protein powder through until completely combined.
4. Pour into a baking sheet lined with parchment paper, and bake for 30 minutes until the batter has set.
5. Let it cool, and slice into 16 bars.
6. Can be stored chilled for a week or frozen up to 2 months.

LOW-CARB
VEGAN LUNCHES

A nutritious lunch can give you the much-needed energy boost during the day. Recipes below are rich in fats and protein but have lower carbohydrate profiles.

You'll find soups, beans, and mushrooms that will energize you throughout the day. Most of these lunches are extremely low in net carbs and will maintain your body in a state of ketosis.

Enjoy these easy to prepare, yet great low carb lunch ideas that are perfect for any keto-vegan that knows how to utilize the kitchen. Some of the dishes can be prepared with an instant pot.

1. Mushroom Soup (Instant Pot)

INGREDIENTS:

- 1 onion (small, diced)
- 1 cup white button mushrooms (chopped)
- 1 cup portobello mushrooms (stems removed, chopped)
- 2 cloves garlic (minced)
- ¼ cup white wine
- 2 ½ cups mushroom stock
- 2 tsp. salt and pepper
- 1 tsp. fresh thyme

Cashew Cream:
- ½ cup raw cashews (soaked)
- ½ cup mushroom stock

Total number of ingredients: 11

METHOD:

1. Add the onions and mushrooms to the instant pot, stirring every now and then, and set on "Sauté" mode for about 10 minutes (until the mushrooms have shrunk in size).
2. Add the garlic and sauté for 2 more minutes.
3. Add the wine and stir in until it evaporates and the smell of wine isn't as strong.
4. Add the salt, pepper, thyme, and mushroom stock, and stir. Cancel the sauté mode.
5. Put the lid on and put it on manual, setting the time to 5 minutes.
6. Add cashews and water into a blender, and blend until smooth. Release the pressure from the pot, remove the lid, and transfer to the blender and blend until smooth.

Simple and stress free, this creamy soup is easy to make and sure to fill you up.

Serves: 3
Prep Time:
~10 min

Nutrition
information
(per serving)

Calories: 185 kcal
Carbs: 16.2g
Fat: 9.3g
Protein: 6.5g
Fiber: 2.2g
Sugar: 5.2g

2. Peanut Spinach Lentils (Instant Pot)

Serves: 2
Prep Time:
~5 min

Nutrition
information
(per serving)

Calories: 559 kcal
Carbs: 26.4g
Fat: 43.5g
Protein: 15.5g
Fiber: 18.3g
Sugar: 4.8g

INGREDIENTS:

- 2 tbsp. olive oil
- 1 tsp. cumin
- ¼ tsp. turmeric
- 2 green chilies (halved)
- 2 tbsp. garlic (chopped)
- 8 leaves curry (optional)
- 2 tomatoes (diced)
- 1 cup lentils (of choice)
- 2 cups spinach (roughly chopped)
- 2 tsp. salt
- 4-5 cups water

Total number of ingredients: 11

METHOD:

1. Add the olive oil and cumin to an instant pot and sauté for 30 seconds.
2. Mix in turmeric, chilies, garlic, and curry leaves. Add the peanut cheese spread, tomatoes, lentils, salt, and water and stir once.
3. Close the pot's pressure valve to seal it, raising the pressure to high for 15 minutes, allowing natural pressure release when done.
4. Add 2 more cups of water to help cook the lentils more.
5. Blend the soup using an immersion blender, and add the chopped spinach, mixing well.
6. Sauté until the soup comes to a boil and turn off the pot by pressing "cancel."
7. Add additional spices to taste.

With only 5 minutes of prep time, this nutritious, heart-healthy, and cruelty-free meal is a great go-to when looking for quick ketogenic vegan meals to make.

3. Refried Beans (Instant Pot)

Serves: 8
Prep Time:
~5 min

Nutrition
information
(per serving)

Calories: 146 kcal
Carbs: 15.6g
Fat: 6.9g
Protein: 5.2g
Fiber: 3.8g
Sugar: 0.7g

INGREDIENTS:

- 1 cup pinto beans (dried, soaked overnight)
- 1 cup water
- 1 tsp. garlic powder
- 1 tsp. onion powder
- ½ tsp. salt
- ¼ cup olive oil

Total number of ingredients: 6

METHOD:

1. Add drained beans, water, garlic powder, and onion powder to the instant pot, setting the timer for 20 minutes.
2. After the time is up, use the natural release method until all the pressure is relieved, remove the lid, and let beans cool for about 10 minutes.
3. Transfer the beans and liquid left in the pot into a blender, and process until smooth.

Refried beans are a great, filling side dish to a burrito bowl with veggies and avocados.

4. Veggie Medley (Instant Pot)

INGREDIENTS:

- 1 eggplant (large, cubed)
- ¼ cup olive oil
- 1 pepper (medium, cut into strips)
- 2 zucchinis (medium, sliced)
- 1 onion (wedged)
- 1 potato (medium, cubed)
- 10 tomatoes (cherry, halved)
- 1 tbsp. capers (strained and rinsed)
- 1 tbsp. raisins
- ¼ cup olives (seeds removed)
- 1 bunch basil (chopped, half for cooking and half for garnish)
- Salt and pepper (to taste)

Total number of ingredients: 13

METHOD:

1. Put eggplant cubes in a strainer and sprinkle with salt, leaving for 30 minutes.
2. Preheat pot by setting to "sauté" until it says "hot."
3. Add olive oil; then add potatoes and eggplants, cooking for about 3 minutes.
4. Next, add the peppers and onions and cook for another 3 minutes, doing the same as you add the zucchini, raisins, olives, salt, and pepper, and half of the basil.
5. Lock on the lid, setting the timer to 6 minutes of pressure cooking.
6. Once the time is up, open using the quick pressure release.
7. Transfer to a serving dish, and garnish with the leftover basil.

Who says you can't get full off veggies? Eat this medley alone or with a dish of your choosing.

Serves: 4
Prep Time:
~40 min

Nutrition
information
(per serving)

Calories: 263 kcal
Carbs: 26.1g
Fat: 16.1g
Protein: 3.2g
Fiber: 8.7g
Sugar: 9.7g

5. Veggie Soup (Instant Pot)

Serves: 8
Prep Time:
~15 min

———

Nutrition
information
(per serving)

Calories: 95 kcal
Carbs: 13g
Fat: 3.9g
Protein: 1.9g
Fiber: 3.3g
Sugar: 5.7g

INGREDIENTS:

- 2 tbsp. olive oil
- 1 onion (medium, chopped)
- 3 tbsp. parsley (fresh, minced)
- 1 clove of garlic (minced)
- 3 (14.5 oz.) cans vegetable broth
- 4 cups tomatoes (chopped)
- 1 cup celery (chopped)
- 1 cup carrots (sliced)
- 1 zucchini (halved and sliced)
- 2 tsp. basil (dried, crushed)
- ½ tsp. salt
- ½ tsp. Italian seasoning
- 1 tsp. red pepper flakes (crushed)
- 5 cups kale leaves (chopped)

Total number of ingredients: 14

METHOD:

1. Heat pot on "sauté" mode until it says "hot"; then add the oil.
2. Add the onion, cooking for about 5 minutes until it is tender. Add the parsley and garlic, stirring constantly for 30 seconds; then add the vegetable broth.
3. Stir in the celery, tomato, zucchini, carrots, Italian seasoning, and red pepper to the pot and turn off the heat. Close the lid.
4. Turn the steam option to "sealing," selecting high pressure for 6 minutes. When done, turn the cooker off again, choosing the quick pressure release option; then select "sauté."
5. Add kale, stirring for 3 minutes or so until the soup comes to a boil. Turn the cooker off and serve.

6. Tabbouleh

Serves: 6
Prep Time:
~20 min

Nutrition
information
(per serving)

Calories: 238 kcal
Carbs: 11.6g
Fat: 17.9g
Protein: 3.9g
Fiber: 3.3g
Sugar: 4.8g

INGREDIENTS:

- 1 tsp. salt
- 1 cucumber (peeled and diced)
- 1 cup cherry tomatoes (chopped)
- 2 onions (chopped)
- 3 cups spinach (chopped)
- 1 cup parsley (chopped)
- ½ cup mint (fresh, chopped)
- ½ cup lemon's juice
- 1 clove garlic (minced)
- ½ cup olive oil
- ¼ tsp. pepper

Total number of ingredients: 11

METHOD:

1. Mix lemon juice, garlic, olive oil, salt, and pepper.
2. Mix the rest of the ingredients and pour the sauce on top.
3. Toss well, adding more or less of your preferences and enjoy.

7. Stir Fry Satay Veggies

INGREDIENTS:

- 2 tbsp. soy sauce
- 1 red bell pepper
- 1 cup peanut butter
- 5 broccoli florets
- 1 carrot
- ½ cucumber
- 2 tbsp. chili paste
- 2 tsp. sesame oil
- 2 tbsp. sesame seeds
- Stevia sweetener to taste (optional)

Total number of ingredients: 10

METHOD:

1. Cut the pepper, broccoli, and carrot into small pieces.
2. Heat peanut butter with a tablespoon of soy sauce in a skillet with some sesame oil on medium heat.
3. Take out the mixture after 2 minutes, but keep the pan on the heat.
4. Sauté the peppers, carrot, and broccoli for 1 minute in the covered pan.
5. Stir fry the cauliflower with some fresh sesame oil until tender.
6. Mix the chili paste, the other tablespoon of soy sauce, and vinegar in a bowl.
7. Add a little bit of water for the sauce to remain liquid.
8. Use the sweetener to sweeten the recipe to taste
9. Divide the cauliflower over two plates and add the peanut butter mixture, peppers, broccoli, carrot and raw cucumber.
10. Pour the chili mixture over the full plates.
11. Top the dish with sesame seeds.

The chili paste is spicy! Use less if you're not a big fan of spicy food. If you want to add more veggies to this dish, feel free to add cucumber, bell peppers, mushrooms, spinach, and bok choy.

Serves: 4
Prep Time:
~25 min

Nutrition
information
(per serving)

Calories: 379 kcal
Carbs: 16g
Fat: 27.6g
Protein: 14.5g
Fiber: 5.5g
Sugar: 4.8g

8. Noodles with Avocado Pesto

Serves: 2
Prep Time:
~15 min

Nutrition information (per serving)

Calories: 295 kcal
Carbs: 16.4g
Fat: 23.1g
Protein: 5.4g
Fiber: 7.9g
Sugar: 6.2g

INGREDIENTS:

- 3 zucchinis (cut into thin ribbons with a vegetable peeler)
- Salt and pepper (to taste)
- 1 tbsp. olive oil
- ½ avocado (pitted)
- 1 cup fresh basil
- ¼ cup walnuts
- 2 garlic cloves (chopped)
- ½ juice of lemon
- ¼ cup cashew cheese (optional)
- ½ cup of water (optional for consistency)

Total number of ingredients: 11

METHOD:

1. Place ribbon zucchini in a bowl. Toss with salt and let sit.
2. Add avocado, basil, walnuts, lemon, garlic, and cashew cheese to a blender. Add water if needed.
3. Put zucchinis in a lightly-greased skillet and sauté for 5 minutes or until soft.
4. Place the dressing on the zucchini and gently toss, serve, and enjoy.

9. Jackfruit and Peanut Butter Dipping Bowls

Serves: 10
Prep Time:
~5 min

Nutrition
information
(per serving)

Calories: 207 kcal
Carbs: 17.3g
Fat: 13g
Protein: 5.3g
Fiber: 4.6g
Sugar: 1g

INGREDIENTS:

- 1 20 oz. can young jackfruit in water (drained, chopped)
- 1 tbsp. chili powder
- 1 cup kale (frozen)
- 1 cup peanut butter
- 1 tbsp. olive oil
- 1 tsp. onion powder
- 1 tsp. garlic powder
- 1 avocado (to serve)

Total number of ingredients: 8

METHOD:

1. Dump everything except the guacamole into a pot and stir until everything is mixed and the cauliflower is tender.

10. Avocado Salad Bowl

Serves: 2
Prep Time:
~5 min

Nutrition
information
(per serving)

Calories: 572 kcal
Carbs: 17.5g
Fat: 53.2g
Protein: 6g
Fiber: 10.3g
Sugar: 2.3g

INGREDIENTS:

- 1 avocado (halved, pitted)
- ¼ cup carrots (shredded)
- 3 tbsp. tahini
- Salt and pepper (to taste)

Dressing:
- ¼ cup olive oil
- ¼ cup lemon juice
- Salt (to taste)
- 1 tbsp. poppy seeds
- 1 tsp. ginger

Total number of ingredients: 9

METHOD:

1. Mix dressing ingredients well.
2. Mix the carrots in dressing; then place in the pitted avocado halves.
3. Drizzle the tahini on top and enjoy.

With all the good fats you need, this healthy, simple lunch is sure to keep you satisfied until dinner.

11. Dijon Avocado Salad

Serves: 2
Prep Time:
~5 min

Nutrition
information
(per serving)

Calories: 182 kcal
Carbs: 10.1g
Fat: 14g
Protein: 2.5g
Fiber: 8.8g
Sugar: 1.8g

INGREDIENTS:

- 1 avocado (sliced)
- 4 cups lettuce (mixed)
- 2 cloves garlic (minced)
- 2 tsp. Dijon mustard
- Salt and pepper (to taste)
- Chives, fresh herbs, olive oil (depending on what you prefer)

Total number of ingredients: 9

METHOD:

1. Mix garlic, Dijon mustard, salt and pepper and any of the optional ingredients you prefer.
2. Pour the mix on top of the lettuce and toss well.
3. Place the sliced avocado slices on top, and add additional salt, pepper, and olive oil to taste.

12. Caesar Salad

Serves: 4
Prep Time:
~5 min

Nutrition
information
(per serving)

Calories: 160 kcal
Carbs: 9.6g
Fat: 11.3g
Protein: 5.2g
Fiber: 6.8g
Sugar: 2.3g

INGREDIENTS:

- 1 avocado (ripe)
- 3 tbsp. lemon juice
- 2 tbsp. water
- 3 garlic cloves (minced)
- 1 tbsp. caper brine
- 1 tbsp. capers
- 2 tsp. Dijon mustard
- ¼ cup hemp seeds
- Salt and pepper (to taste)
- 12 cups romaine leaves (chopped)

Total number of ingredients: 11

METHOD:

1. Add all ingredients except the romaine leaves and hemp seeds into a blender and blend until smooth. The consistency should be a bit thick like pudding; add more water if needed.
2. Pour dressing in a bowl and add the hemp seeds, stirring well.
3. Coat the dressing atop the romaine leaves and enjoy.

This salad can serve as a side dish or a light lunch depending on your choosing! The hemp seeds in the dressing supply a cheesy-feeling texture. Get creative, adding any extra toppings you prefer.

13. Curried Kale Salad

Serves: 4
Prep Time:
~15 min

Nutrition
information
(per serving)

Calories: 94kcal
Carbs: 8.6g
Fat: 6g
Protein: 1.5g
Fiber: 2.3g
Sugar: 1.5g

INGREDIENTS:

- 1 onion (sliced)
- 1 tbsp. coconut oil
- 1 tbsp. curry powder
- 1 lemon's juice
- 1 bunch kale (chopped, steamed for 10 seconds)
- ¼ cup cilantro (fresh, chopped)
- 2 tbsp. mint (fresh, chopped)
- 2 tsp. olive oil
- ¼ tsp. salt

Total number of ingredients: 9

METHOD:

1. Preheat the oven to 400°F.
2. In a bowl, add the olive oil, lemon juice, curry powder, and onion, and place on a baking tray. Roast for about 30 minutes and allow to cool.
3. Add kale, cilantro and mint in a separate bowl and set aside. Add the oven mix and combine well.
4. Add the lemon juice, olive oil, and salt on top. Toss well.

14. Carrot Soup (Instant Pot)

Serves: 6
Prep Time:
~20 min

Nutrition
information
(per serving)

Calories: 73 kcal
Carbs: 16.5g
Fat: 0.3g
Protein: 1.1g
Fiber: 4.4g
Sugar: 8.9g

INGREDIENTS:

- 2 lbs. carrots (peeled, sliced)
- 4 cups vegetable broth
- ½ onion (chopped)
- ½ cup apple cider vinegar
- Salt and pepper to taste
- White vinegar (to taste)

Total number of ingredients: 7

METHOD:

1. Soak about 2 peeled carrots in the white vinegar until finished preparing remaining items.
2. Sauté onions in a lightly oiled pan until browned.
3. Put the broth and the rest of the carrots into the instant pot, setting to manual. When done, set natural pressure release.
4. Transfer this to a blender until mixed well. Add apple cider vinegar, onions, and salt to taste.
5. Top with the soaked carrots and enjoy.

15. Roasted Red Pepper Soup (Instant Pot)

Serves: 4
Prep Time:
~10 min

Nutrition
information
(per serving)

Calories: 226 kcal
Carbs: 12.2g
Fat: 17.8g
Protein: 3.9g
Fiber: 4.1g
Sugar: 5.8g

INGREDIENTS:

- 2 tbsp. coconut oil
- ½ cup roasted red pepper (about 2 peppers, chopped)
- 1 shallot (chopped)
- Salt (to taste)
- 1 tsp. paprika
- 1 tsp. red pepper flakes
- 4 cups cauliflower (florets)
- 4 cups vegetable stock
- 1 tbsp. apple cider vinegar
- 1 cup canned coconut milk
- 1 tsp. thyme (fresh)

Total number of ingredients: 11

METHOD:

1. In a pressure pot, melt the coconut oil and sauté the shallots for about 3 minutes. Add the red peppers and seasonings, stirring well and cooking for 3 minutes.
2. Add the cauliflower, thyme, vegetable stock and vinegar, bringing it to a simmer; cover the pot and cook the mix for about 15 minutes on high pressure.
3. Once the timer is up, allow for quick pressure release, carefully blend the mix in a blender, and return the mix to pot. Carefully add the coconut milk and stir well.

16. Peas and Asparagus Medley (Instant Pot)

Serves: 4
Prep Time:
~5 min

Nutrition
information
(per serving)

Calories: 149 kcal
Carbs: 9.8g
Fat: 10.8g
Protein: 3.3g
Fiber: 4.8g
Sugar: 5.5g

INGREDIENTS:

- 1 cloves garlic (minced)
- 1 cup English peas
- 2 tbsp. peanut oil
- 2 cups asparagus (cut into 2-inch pieces)
- ½ cup vegetable broth
- 1 juice of lemon and zest
- 2-3 tbsp. pine nuts (toasted)

Total number of ingredients: 7

METHOD:

1. Add the garlic, peas, asparagus, and broth to the instant pot and lock on the lid, cooking on manual for 2 minutes. When the time is up, release the pressure quickly.
2. Add the lemon zest and juice, and stir well. Pour in a bowl, add the nuts, and serve.

17. Marinated Artichokes (Instant Pot)

Serves: 4
Prep Time:
~15 min

Nutrition
information
(per serving)

Calories: 187 kcal
Carbs: 13.8g
Fat: 13.5g
Protein: 2.7g
Fiber: 7.1g
Sugar: 1.9g

INGREDIENTS:

- 4 artichokes
- 2 tbsp. lemon juice
- 2 tsp. balsamic vinegar
- ¼ cup olive oil
- 1 tsp. oregano (dried)
- 2 cloves garlic (minced)
- Salt and pepper to taste

Total number of ingredients: 8

METHOD:

1. Rinse the artichokes under cold water, removing the stems, tops, rough pieces, and thorns.
2. Place 2 cups of water and the artichokes (bottom up) in the pot fitted with a steamer basket.
3. Choose the steam setting and cook for 8 minutes.
4. Mix lemon juice, oregano, salt, pepper, vinegar, garlic, and olive oil in a lidded jar. Shake well and set aside.
5. Carefully remove artichokes when the time is up, and cut them in half, removing the cone with purple prickly leaves.
6. Pour the sauce over the artichokes, allowing them to set overnight.
7. When ready to serve, sear the artichokes in a pan or on the grill for about 5 minutes.

18. Brussels Sprouts (Instant Pot)

Serves: 5
Prep Time:
~10 min

Nutrition
information
(per serving)

Calories: 57 kcal
Carbs: 11.3g
Fat: 0.3g
Protein: 2.2g
Fiber: 4.0g
Sugar: 4.7g

INGREDIENTS:

- 6 cups Brussels sprouts (chopped)
- Salt and pepper to taste
- 2 tbsp. water
- 2 tbsp. balsamic reduction

Total number of ingredients: 5

METHOD:

1. Add "sauté" option on the pot, pouring in the Brussels sprouts, some water, and the salt and pepper.
2. Cover and stir every few minutes for about 5 minutes, uncover, and continue to sauté the Brussels sprouts until they crisp.
3. Transfer to a dish, adding the balsamic reduction, and enjoy.

19. Grapefruit Avocado Salad

Serves: 4
Prep Time:
~15 min

———

Nutrition
information
(per serving)

Calories: 214 kcal
Carbs: 13.8g
Fat: 16g
Protein: 3.7g
Fiber: 8.5g
Sugar: 3.9g

INGREDIENTS:

- ½ large grapefruit
- 2 avocados
- ¼ cup onion
- 6 cups of stemless kale
- 2 tbsp. sunflower seeds
- Pinch of salt
- Pinch of pepper

Total number of ingredients: 7

METHOD:

1. Wash the stemless kale and chop it into small pieces.
2. Chop the onion.
3. Cut the peeled half of the grapefruit.
4. Cut the avocados.
5. Mix everything together until the grapefruit and avocado blend into a dressing.
6. Add the pepper and salt to taste.
7. Top with sunflower seeds.

Avocado is a ketogenic treasure and mixes well with fruits and veggies. If you're ready for more carbs, then you can add the other half of the grapefruit to the salad. Alternatively, replace the extra half of the grapefruit with a tablespoon of lime juice.

20. Pad Thai Noodles

Serves: 4
Prep Time:
~10 min

Nutrition
information
(per serving)

Calories: 236kcal
Carbs: 3.9g
Fat: 19.5g
Protein: 8.8g
Fiber: 2.5g
Sugar: 1.3g

INGREDIENTS:

- 1 pack shirataki noodles
- ½ cup peanut butter
- 1 finely chopped onion
- ¼ cup coconut milk
- ¼ cup dark soy sauce
- ¼ cup lime juice
- 2 cloves garlic
- ½ chopped red chili

Total number of ingredients: 8

METHOD:

1. Drain and rinse noodles with water.
2. Combine all other ingredients in blender and blend until smooth.
3. Transfer shirataki noodles into a pot with boiling water and cook for 2-3 minutes.
4. Drain the noodles and fry in a pan without grease or liquids over medium heat to remove as much water as possible.
5. Place stir-fried noodles in a bowl and serve with ½ of the blender made sauce on top.
6. The sauce can be stored for up to a week in the fridge or frozen for up to 2 months.

KETOGENIC VEGAN DINNERS

A fter breakfast and lunch, there's still time left in the day to perform and enjoy. Depending on your culture and traditions, you usually have dinner at the start of the evening.

Try not to eat your meals too late. Get the nutrients your body needs to function after dinner and for your recovery during the night.

You'll have no problem keeping your body in a state of ketosis with these delicious, low-carb dinners. Some of the dishes can be prepared with an instant pot.

1. Low Carb Peanut Dip (Instant Pot)

INGREDIENTS:

- 2 tbsp. peanut oil
- 1 cup peanut cheese spread
- 1 low carb crust
- 1 cup onion (chopped)
- 1 tbsp. garlic (minced)
- 1 cup fire roasted tomatoes
- 1 tbsp. chipotle pepper (chopped)
- ½ cup water
- 1 tbsp. chili powder
- 2 tsp. ground cumin
- 2 tsp. salt
- 1 tsp. dried oregano

Total number of ingredients: 12

METHOD:

1. Select the "sauté" option on the instant pot, waiting till it reads "hot" to add the onions and garlic with olive oil, stirring for about 30 minutes.
2. Blend the canned tomatoes and the peanut butter until it is relatively smooth.
3. Mix the cumin, salt, chili powder, and oregano; then mix with the onions and garlic for 30 seconds, allowing them to soak in the flavor.
4. Pour the blender mix into the pot along with the water. Close the pot and cook on instant pressure for 10 minutes, allowing natural pressure release for 10 minutes after that.
5. Mix well, and serve with a low carb crust for dipping!

Serves: 6
Prep Time:
~10 min

Nutrition information
(per serving)

Calories: 451 kcal
Carbs: 18.9g
Fat: 37.7g
Protein: 9.8g
Fiber: 4.9g
Sugar: 3.7g

2. Spice-Rubbed Cauliflower (Instant Pot)

Serves: 4
**Prep Time:
~10 min**

**Nutrition
information
(per serving)**

Calories: 86 kcal
Carbs: 12.3g
Fat: 2.7g
Protein: 3.3g
Fiber: 7.5g
Sugar: 5.6g

INGREDIENTS:

- 2 lbs. cauliflower
- 2 tbsp. olive oil
- 2 tsp. paprika
- 2 tsp. ground cumin
- Salt to taste
- 1 cup cilantro (fresh, chopped)
- 1 lemon (quartered)

Total number of ingredients: 7

METHOD:

1. Insert the steam rack in the instant pot, adding 1 ½ cups of water.
2. Remove the leaves of the cauliflower, cut the end from the base, and place on the steam rack.
3. Combine the oil, salt, paprika, and cumin in a bowl; then pour over the cauliflower to coat.
4. Lock the lid and cook under pressure for 4 minutes; use the quick release to let out the steam, and open the lid.
5. Take the cauliflower out and cut it into 1 inch sized "steaks."
6. Divide onto plates, sprinkle the cilantro on top, and place a quartered lemon on each plate.

3. Satay Veggie Bowl

Serves: 4
Prep Time:
~15 min

Nutrition
information
(per serving)

Calories: 444 kcal
Carbs: 16g
Fat: 53.1g
Protein: 15.9g
Fiber: 9.8g
Sugar: 4.7g

INGREDIENTS:

- handful of olives
- olive oil, garlic powder, pepper, and salt to taste
- 1 cup broccoli (florets)
- 1 (15oz) block tempeh (cubed)
- 1 cup spinach (frozen)
- 3 cups peanut butter or cashew cheese

Total number of ingredients: **6**

METHOD:

1. In a greased skillet over medium heat, add broccoli, frozen spinach and stir for about a minute.
2. Add the tempeh and continue stirring, while it cooks, for about 2 minutes.
3. Add peanutbutter and mix well, keep stirring while cooking.
4. Adding salt and garlic powder to taste, stir well and wait until the spinach has softened and the tempeh is cooked.
5. Transfer to a bowl, and add olive oil, pepper, and salt to taste. Garnish with olives.

4. Shiritaki Noodles and Veggies

Serves: 1
Prep Time:
~15 min

**Nutrition
information
(per serving)**

Calories: 279 kcal
Carbs: 13.5g
Fat: 28.2g
Protein: 3.0g
Fiber: 4.6g
Sugar: 5.2g

INGREDIENTS:

- 1 package shiritaki noodles (rinsed, drained)
- 2 tbsp. peanut oil
- ¼ cup marinara sauce
- ½ cup mixed veggies (of choice)

Total number of ingredients: 4

METHOD:

1. Boil the noodles until soft.
2. Once done, transfer to a skillet and add the marinara sauce, oil, and mixed veggies.
3. Keep mixing, letting the mixture heat until the veggies are warm and incorporated.

5. Shiritaki Alfredo

Serves: 1
Prep Time:
~10 min

Nutrition
information
(per serving)

Calories: 377 kcal
Carbs: 11.3g
Fat: 34.3g
Protein: 5.6g
Fiber: 5.5g
Sugar: 1.0g

INGREDIENTS:

- 1 package shiritaki noodles (rinsed, drained)
- 2 tbsp. olive oil
- ¼ cup vegan cream cheese
- 1 cup spinach (frozen)
- Salt, pepper, and garlic powder (to taste)
- Almond milk (to reach desired consistency)

Total number of ingredients: 8

METHOD:

1. Dump all ingredients in a pan with olive oil and slowly add almond milk for a creamy feel.
2. Once all ingredients are mixed and the milk thickens, turn off the heat and serve.

6. Taco-Spiced Stir-fry

INGREDIENTS:

- 1 package cauliflower rice
- 1 tbsp. peanut oil
- 1 tbsp. taco seasoning
- ½ tbsp. chili powder
- 2 tbsp. guacamole
- ¼ cup sliced olives

Total number of ingredients: 6

METHOD:

1. Mix all ingredients, except the guacamole and olives, in a pan on medium heat until the cauliflower rice has softened.
2. Take off the stove and it cool when rice has softened, before serving.

Serves: 1
Prep Time:
~15 min

Nutrition
information
(per serving)

Calories: 293 kcal
Carbs: 18.7g
Fat: 22.5g
Protein: 4.0g
Fiber: 10.5g
Sugar: 3.7g

7. Green-Glory Soup (Instant Pot)

Serves: 6
Prep Time:
~15 min

___

Nutrition
information
(per serving)

Calories: 284 kcal
Carbs: 9.1g
Fat: 26.3g
Protein: 2.9g
Fiber: 3.1g
Sugar: 5.3g

INGREDIENTS:

- 1 head cauliflower (florets)
- 1 onion (diced)
- 2 cloves garlic (minced)
- 1 cup spinach (fresh or frozen)
- 1 bay leaf (crumbled)
- 1 cup coconut milk
- 4 cups vegetable stock
- Salt and pepper to taste
- Herbs for garnish (optional)
- ½ cup coconut oil

Total number of ingredients: 11

METHOD:

1. In a pressure pot on "sauté" mode, sauté onions and garlic until onions are browned. Once cooked, add the cauliflower and bay leaf and cook for about 5 minutes, stirring occasionally.
2. Add the spinach and continue cooking and stirring for 5 minutes.
3. Pour in the vegetable stock and set the timer for 10 minutes on high pressure to let the mix come to a boil; then allow quick pressure release and add the coconut milk.
4. Season with garnishes of choice as well as salt and pepper. Turn off the pot and mix the soup until it becomes thick and creamy with a hand blender.

8. Mediterranean-Style Pasta

Serves: 4
Prep Time:
~10 min

Nutrition
information
(per serving)

Calories: 117 kcal
Carbs: 7.9g
Fat: 8.7g
Protein: 1.8g
Fiber: 2.6g
Sugar: 4.2g

INGREDIENTS:

- 2 zucchinis (large, spiral-sliced)
- 1 cup spinach
- 2 tbsp. olive oil
- 5 cloves garlic (minced)
- Salt and pepper (to taste)
- ¼ cup tomatoes (sun dried for added flavor)
- 2 tbsp. capers
- 2 tbsp. parsley (chopped)
- 10 Kalamata olives (halved)

Total number of ingredients: 10

METHOD:

1. In a lightly oiled pan, add the spinach, zucchini, salt, pepper, and garlic, sautéing until the zucchini is tender; drain the excess liquid.
2. Add tomatoes, capers, olives, and parsley, mixing for about 3 minutes.
3. Remove from heat and toss well before serving, adding more or less of any item for preference.

9. Kale-Stuffed Mushroom Caps

Serves: 2
Prep Time:
~15 min

Nutrition
information
(per serving)

Calories: 81 kcal
Carbs: 7.3g
Fat: 4.8g
Protein: 3g
Fiber: 2.2g
Sugar: 1.1g

INGREDIENTS:

- 4 cups kale (fresh, chopped)
- 2 tbsp. olive oil
- 3 tsp. garlic (minced)
- 1 tsp. garlic powder
- ½ tsp. salt
- 4 portobello mushroom caps (large)

Total number of ingredients: 6

METHOD:

1. Sauté the garlic and olive oil in a pan. Before it burns, add the kale, stirring well for about 7 minutes. Then add the garlic powder and salt, stirring well for 3 more minutes. Turn off the heat.
2. Mix the other half of the olive oil and garlic, then rub on the mushroom caps.
3. Place caps on the grill on medium heat, allowing them to cook for about 10 minutes—5 minutes per side—until tender.
4. Remove from the grill and divide your kale mixture on top of each cap; serve and enjoy.

Check out this recipe for a delicious, unique treat to spice up any dinner or gathering.

10. Boiled Seasoned Veggies (Instant Pot)

Serves: 1
Prep Time:
~15 min

Nutrition
information
(per serving)

Calories: 816 kcal
Carbs: 66.1g
Fat: 55.8g
Protein: 12.5g
Fiber: 26.9g
Sugar: 32.2g

INGREDIENTS:

- 1 eggplant (cubed, medium)
- 2 zucchinis (halved and sliced)
- 8 oz. mushrooms (of choice, quartered)
- 6 cloves garlic (minced)
- 3 sprigs fresh rosemary (chopped)
- ¼ cup olive oil
- 2 tbsp. balsamic vinegar
- 2 tbsp. dried onion flakes
- ½ cup water
- Salt and pepper to taste

Total number of ingredients: 11

METHOD:

1. Preheat oven to 400°F.
2. In a bowl, mix all ingredients, lightly tossing and making sure all the vegetables are coated in spices and olive oil.
3. Throw mixture in a pressure pot with ½ cup of water and cook on high pressure for about 20 minutes, allowing for natural pressure release once time is up.
4. Open, and add more or less of the spices you prefer.

If you're a veggie lover, you are sure to love this dish. Vegetables are heart-healthy, filling, and kind alternatives to other non-vegan or ketogenic meals!

12. Cauliflower Soup (Instant Pot)

INGREDIENTS:

- 3 cups vegetable stock
- 2 tsp. thyme powder
- ½ tsp. matcha green tea powder
- 1 head cauliflower (about 2.5 cups, florets)
- 1 tbsp. olive oil
- 5 garlic cloves (minced)
- Salt and pepper to taste

Total number of ingredients: 8

METHOD:

1. In an instant pressure pot, add the vegetable stock, thyme, and matcha powder on medium heat. Bring to a boil.
2. Add the cauliflower and set timer for 10 minutes on high pressure, allowing for quick pressure release when finished.
3. In a saucepan, add garlic and olive oil until tender, and you can smell it; then add it to the pot along with salt and cook for 1 to 2 minutes.
4. Turn off the heat and. Blend the soup until smooth and creamy with a blender.

Serves: 6
Prep Time:
~10 min

Nutrition
information
(per serving)

Calories: 43 kcal
Carbs: 4.3g
Fat: 2.2g
Protein: 1.4g
Fiber: 1.3g
Sugar: 2.2g

13. Tahini Covered Eggplant

Serves: 1
Prep Time:
~20 min

Nutrition
information
(per serving)

Calories: 474 kcal
Carbs: 41.9g
Fat: 31.2g
Protein: 6.3g
Fiber: 21.9g
Sugar: 17.9g

INGREDIENTS:

- 1 eggplant (sliced)
- 1 garlic clove (minced)
- 1 tbsp. olive oil
- Salt and pepper (to taste)
- ½ cup chopped parsley

Sauce:
- 1 tsp. olive oil
- 1 onion (chopped)
- ½ garlic clove (chopped)
- Handful of parsley (chopped)
- ⅓ cup almond milk
- 1 tsp. tahini
- Salt (to taste)

Total number of ingredients: 12

METHOD:

1. Preheat oven to 350°F.
2. Mix all ingredients in the bowl with the eggplant.
3. Place on baking tray, and bake for 30 minutes.

Sauce:
1. Blend all ingredients. Add more or less to taste.

14. Oven-Baked Avocado Fries

Serves: 1
Prep Time:
~30 min

___

**Nutrition
information
(per serving)**

Calories: 474 kcal
Carbs: 30.7g
Fat: 56.8g
Protein: 8.2g
Fiber: 13.5g
Sugar: 1.3g

INGREDIENTS:

- 2 ripe avocados
- ½ cup almond milk
- ½ cup almond flour
- Salt and pepper to taste

Total number of ingredients: 5

METHOD:

1. Preheat oven to 425°F, and line a baking sheet with parchment paper.
2. Peel and pit the avocado. Slice into halves and again into "fries."
3. Dip the avocado fries in almond milk. Flour and season them with salt and pepper in that order.
4. Place avocado fries on the baking sheet with enough space between them.
5. Bake for **10** minutes on each side. Be careful not to burn (it goes quick!).
6. Serve with your favorite vegan cheese or dip.

15. Creamy Mushroom Soup

Serves: 8
Prep Time:
~5 min

Nutrition
information
(per serving)

Calories: 119 kcal
Carbs: 4.8g
Fat: 10.3g
Protein: 1.9g
Fiber: 1.9g
Sugar: 2.8g

INGREDIENTS:

- 2 cups cauliflower (florets)
- 1 ½ cup coconut milk (original)
- 1 tsp. onion powder
- ½ tsp. olive oil
- Salt and pepper (to taste)
- 1½ cups white mushrooms (diced)
- ½ onion (diced)

Total number of ingredients: 8

METHOD:

1. Place cauliflower, coconut milk, onion powder, pepper, and salt into a covered saucepan bringing to a boil on medium heat. Simmer for about 7 minutes, stirring well. Transfer to a blender and blend well.
2. Add the oil, onion, and mushrooms to a saucepan, heating until onions brown (around 8 minutes).
3. Add the cauliflower mix to the pan with onions and mushrooms. Bring to a boil, cover, and let the soup simmer for 10 minutes.

Want a filling, warm dinner to end a hectic or relaxing day? This easy recipe is sure to make you feel satiated and energized.

16. Satay Shirataki Noodles

Serves: 2
Prep Time:
~15 min

Nutrition information (per serving)

Calories: 119 kcal
Carbs: 15.5g
Fat: 43.2g
Protein: 20g
Fiber: 6.5g
Sugar: 3g

INGREDIENTS:

- 1 package (8 ounces) shirataki noodles
- 1 cup mixed greens
- Peanuts, toasted sesame seeds, parsley, spring onions, and cilantro (garnish to taste)

Sauce:

- 1 cup peanut butter
- 1 tbsp. low sodium soy sauce
- 1 tsp. rice vinegar
- ¼ tsp. garlic powder
- ½ tsp black pepper
- ¼ tsp. ground ginger

Total number of ingredients: 13

METHOD:

1. Blend all sauce ingredients and let them sit for 15 minutes.
2. Keep the sauce cool until ready to use
3. Rinse and drain the shirataki noodles well, and dry them on a cloth or paper towel.
4. In a dry, nonstick pan, heat the noodles on medium-low for a few minutes to dry them out.
5. Chop up the chosen vegetables, and add them to the noodles in the pan. Sauté for a couple more minutes to heat through.
6. Add peanut sauce to the pan and mix well.
7. Garnish with peanuts, toasted sesame seeds, and parsley, spring onions, or cilantro.

17. Cauliflower Kale Salad

Serves: 8
Prep Time:
~15 min

_____

Nutrition
information
(per serving)

Calories: 133 kcal
Carbs: 6.6g
Fat: 10.9g
Protein: 2.9g
Fiber: 2.7g
Sugar: 1.5g

INGREDIENTS:

- 2 cups white cauliflower (de-stemmed, sliced thin)
- ½ cup red pepper (chopped)
- ½ cup yellow pepper (chopped)
- 4 cups kale (fresh, de-stemmed)
- ½ cup pecans (toasted, chopped)
- 3 tbsp. olive oil
- ¼ cup lemon juice
- Salt and pepper

Total number of ingredients: 9

METHOD:

1. Dump the cauliflower, pepper, and onions into a bowl, and top with pecans.
2. Whisk the olive oil and lemon juice together along with the salt and pepper.
3. Place the sauce on top of the mixed vegetables, and toss well.

18. Mac n' Cheeze

INGREDIENTS:

- ¼ cup nutritional yeast
- ½ cup hemp seeds
- ¼ cup bell pepper (chopped, of choice)
- ½ tsp. salt
- ¼ tsp. garlic powder
- ¼ tsp. onion powder
- 2 packages shirataki macaroni

Total number of ingredients: 7

METHOD:

1. Preheat oven to 350°F.
2. Place all the sauce ingredients in a blender, and mix for about 2 minutes until smooth.
3. Rinse and drain the macaroni; then combine with the sauce mixture in a baking dish and cook for 45 minutes.

Serves: 2
Prep Time:
~15 min

Nutrition information (per serving)

Calories: 266 kcal
Carbs: 11.5g
Fat: 15.4g
Protein: 20.2g
Fiber: 8.9g
Sugar: 1g

19. Pumpkin "Cheddar" Risotto (Instant Pot)

Serves: 4
Prep Time:
~15 min

Nutrition
information
(per serving)

Calories: 119 kcal
Carbs: 8.2g
Fat: 7.2g
Protein: 6.2g
Fiber: 4.7g
Sugar: 2.7g

INGREDIENTS:

- 1 tsp. paprika
- 2 tbsp. olive oil
- 3 cups riced cauliflower
- ½ cup pureed pumpkin
- ¼ cup nutritional yeast
- ¼ cup vegetable broth
- Salt and pepper (to taste)

Total number of ingredients: 8

METHOD:

1. Add cauliflower, paprika, salt, pepper, and olive oil to an instant pot on "sauté," and stir.
2. Slowly add the veggie broth and put the lid on, cooking on high pressure for about 15 minutes, stirring occasionally.
3. Stir in the pumpkin puree and nutritional yeast, and close the lid for 5 minutes, allowing for quick pressure release when the time is up.
4. Taste the mixture once the cauliflower has softened, and add more or less of your preferences.

20. Baked Mushrooms

Serves: 4
Prep Time:
~10 min

___

Nutrition
information
(per serving)

Calories: 99 kcal
Carbs: 7.4g
Fat: 6.9g
Protein: 2.2g
Fiber: 2.5g
Sugar: 3.2g

INGREDIENTS

- 1 lb. portobello mushrooms (sliced)
- 2 tbsp. olive oil
- 1 large can tomatoes
- 2 cups vegan cheese (of choice, optional)
- 2 tbsp. garlic (minced)
- 2 tbsp. basil (fresh)
- 1 tbsp. parsley (fresh)
- 1 tsp. oregano (dried)
- Salt and pepper to taste

Total number of ingredients: 10

METHOD:

1. Preheat the oven to 400°F.
2. Mix sliced mushrooms with garlic and olive oil, and place on a baking tray. Cook for about 5 minutes.
3. Mix tomatoes and herbs in a bowl.
4. Place mushrooms in a baking tray, add herb sauce mix on top, and add vegan cheese (if desired).
5. Place back in oven for 20 minutes until cooked.

One of the simplest and satisfying meals. With only 1 major ingredient, yet multiple spices, this dish is sure to leave you making it a go-to dinner indulgence. Vegan cheeses excluded in macro count.

21. Squash Spaghetti with Mushroom Sauce

Serves: 8
Prep Time:
~15 min

Nutrition
information
(per serving)

Calories: 135 kcal
Carbs: 12.2g
Fat: 8g
Protein: 3.5g
Fiber: 2.3g
Sugar: 3.4g

INGREDIENTS:

- 1 large spaghetti squash (baked)
- 2 cups mushrooms (sliced, of choice)
- 1 onion (chopped)
- ½ cup raw cashew butter
- 2 tbsp. Dijon mustard
- 1 tbsp. sage (chopped, fresh)
- 1 tsp. thyme (chopped, fresh)
- Salt and pepper to taste
- 2 cups water
- 1 cup spinach

Total number of ingredients: 11

METHOD:

1. In a saucepan, add olive oil and mushrooms. Cook on medium heat until the mushrooms have browned; add the onion and cook until translucent.
2. In a bowl, add the Dijon mustard, sage, thyme, salt, pepper, and raw cashew butter. Mix until completely combined. Add the water, about ¼ cup at a time, mixing while doing so.
3. Pour this creamy mix on top of the mushrooms and onions, and lower the heat, mixing while doing so.
4. Add the spinach, then turn off the heat, allowing the spinach to wilt and the sauce to get creamy and thick.
5. Once the spaghetti squash is ready, divide into designated servings, and pour the sauce on it.

While this meal reaches the maximum, supported consumption of carbs in one meal, it is extremely filling! With this meal, be sure to eat light beforehand.

22. Buddha Bowl

Serves: 1
Prep Time:
~10 min

———

**Nutrition
information
(per serving)**

Calories: 192 kcal
Carbs: 27.1g
Fat: 18.4g
Protein: 9.1g
Fiber: 12.4g
Sugar: 6.4g

INGREDIENTS:

- 1 cup Brussels sprouts (chopped if preferred)
- 1 tbsp. peanut oil
- ½ cup carrots (thinly sliced)
- 1 cup frozen spinach
- 2-4 tbsp. hummus
- Salt and pepper to taste
- 1 tsp. garlic powder

Total number of ingredients: 8

METHOD:

1. In a greased skillet, sauté the Brussels sprouts, carrots, and spinach with the salt, pepper, olive oil, and garlic powder until softened.
2. Transfer to a bowl, and spoon the hummus on top of it with additional olive oil and salt.

23. Broccoli and Garlic (Instant Pot)

INGREDIENTS:

- 2 heads broccoli (florets)
- ½ cup water
- 6 garlic cloves (minced)
- 1 tbsp. peanut oil
- Salt to taste

Total number of ingredients: 5

METHOD:

1. Placing the broccoli onto the steamer rack, add ½ cup of tap water and cook at low pressure, selecting the option of "0 minutes." Select quick release when finished. Allow broccoli to cool.
2. Turn on "sauté" mode and wait until it says "hot" to add the garlic; then add the peanut oil and the minced garlic, stirring for 30 seconds.
3. Put the broccoli florets in for about 30 seconds, stirring and adding salt to taste.

If you're feeling a lighter, greener dinner, you can opt to just eating this veggie galore! If not, feel free to pair with another dish from the recipes provided!

Serves: 4
Prep Time:
~5 min

Nutrition
information
(per serving)

Calories: 61 kcal
Carbs: 5.4g
Fat: 3.3g
Protein: 2.2g
Fiber: 2.2g
Sugar: 1.1g

24. Low-Carb Hemp Curry

Serves: 10
Prep Time:
~50 min

———

Nutrition
information
(per serving)

Calories: 299 kcal
Carbs: 12.3g
Fat: 25.9g
Protein: 7.2g
Fiber: 5.4g
Sugar: 5.5g

INGREDIENTS:

- 4 tbsp. coconut or hemp oil
- 2 cans full-fat coconut milk
- 1 cup tomato puree
- 1 block (10 oz.) cubed hemp-fu
- 6 cups cauliflower rice
- 4 tbsp. masala curry spice
- ½ cup chopped onion
- 3 cloves chopped garlic
- 1-inch root chopped ginger root
- 1 tsp. salt

Total number of ingredients: 10

METHOD:

1. Heat oil in pan over high heat and fry onion and garlic for 3 minutes.
2. Turn heat to medium and add ginger, stirring thoroughly.
3. Add curry spices, tomato puree, and coconut milk and stir over medium heat until everything is combined.
4. Add in hemp-fu cubes, cover pan, and simmer for 15 minutes.
5. Add cauliflower rice, stir, and cook. Check every five minutes until rice is soft.
6. Cool down and serve; can be frozen or stored in fridge for a couple of days.

25. Ramen Noodles

Serves: 4
Prep Time:
~60 min

Nutrition
information
(per serving)

Calories: 136 kcal
Carbs: 6.9g
Fat: 10.4g
Protein: 7.0g
Fiber: 2.1g
Sugar: 2.1g

INGREDIENTS:

- 2 tbsp. peanut oil
- 4 tbsp. dark soy sauce
- 4 cups vegetable broth
- 1 tsp. pepper flakes
- 2 cloves minced garlic
- 1 tsp. minced ginger
- 2 packs shirataki noodles
- ½ block hemp-fu
- ¼ cup baby spinach
- ¼ cup sprouts (optional)
- ¼ cup shitake bits (optional)
- Seaweed (optional)
- Sesame seeds (optional)

Total number of ingredients: 13

METHOD:

1. Sautee shitake bits over medium heat in small sauce pan for a few minutes.
2. Take off heat and set aside.
3. Bake hemp-fu over scramble in a stir-fry pan with 1 tablespoon peanut oil over medium heat.
4. Add another tablespoon of peanut oil to the pan and toss in garlic, ginger and sautéed shitake bits. Stir thoroughly until combined.
5. Add in broth, soy sauce, and pepper flakes to taste.
6. Drain and rinse shirataki noodles. Add noodles to broth.
7. Let it simmer for 5-10 minutes.
8. Fill a bowl with one quarter of the ramen noodle soup, and save the rest for later.

26. Stuffed Portobello Nutshrooms

Serves: 2
Prep Time:
~60 min

—

Nutrition
information
(per serving)

Calories: 163 kcal
Carbs: 19.6g
Fat: 6.7g
Protein: 6.2g
Fiber: 5.9g
Sugar: 10.3g

INGREDIENTS:

- 6 portobello mushrooms
- 1 tbsp. chopped almonds
- 1 tbsp. ground flaxseed
- 1 tbsp. hazelnut spread
- ½ tsp. salt
- ½ tsp. smoked paprika powder
- 1 clove minced garlic
- Black pepper to taste

Total number of ingredients: 8

METHOD:

1. Preheat oven to 350°F.
2. Remove stems from mushrooms and clean them. Save stems for later.
3. Chop up the stems in small pieces.
4. Combine almonds, hazelnut spread, ground flaxseed, salt, paprika powder, garlic, and black pepper to the container of a blender and blend shortly until thoroughly mixed.
5. Divide the filling from the blender container over mushroom caps with a spoon.
6. Bake the mushrooms for 30 minutes and cool before serving.

This recipe is great if you're craving a sandwich with a twist! Have a pressed spinach and Portobello mushroom sandwich with a small handful of vegan cashew-cheese to indulge.

27. Cheesy Roasted Peppers

Serves: 2
Prep Time:
~45 min

Nutrition
information
(per serving)

Calories: 189 kcal
Carbs: 28.1g
Fat: 6.3g
Protein: 7.2g
Fiber: 9.7g
Sugar: 13.4g

INGREDIENTS:

- 2 cups cashew cheese spread
- 4 bell peppers, red, yellow or orange
- ½ cup Mexican salsa
- ½ tsp. salt
- ½ tsp. smoked paprika powder
- 1 clove minced garlic
- Black pepper to taste

Total number of ingredients: 7

METHOD:

1. Preheat oven to 375°F.
2. Grease a deep baking pan or line with baking sheet.
3. Halve the peppers, and remove seeds, stem, and placenta.
4. Make sure that the halved peppers fit inside the deep baking pan so you can cover the top with tin foil but the peppers don't touch the tin foil.
5. Brush peppers with high heat oil like MCT oil, arachnid oil, or flaxseed oil.
6. Mix salsa with salt, pepper, garlic, and cashew cheese spread in a medium bowl.
7. Stuff the peppers with the cashew cream mixture from the bowl.
8. Place the halved peppers in baking plate, and cover the pan with tin foil.
9. Bake for 30 minutes.
10. Remove foil, increase the temperature to 400°F, and bake for 15 minutes.
11. Eat when fresh and warm, or you can freeze them or keep fresh for 2-3 days; heat for 15 minutes at 350°F before eating.

28. Creamy Cauliflower Spaghetti

INGREDIENTS:

- 1 pack shirataki noodles
- ½ cup small cauliflower florets
- 1 clove minced garlic
- ¼ cup baked cashew-herb cheese
- 1 tbsp. olive oil
- 1 tsp. nutritional yeast
- Italian herbs (basil, oregano, rosemary, thyme and sage) to taste
- Salt & black pepper to taste

Total number of ingredients: 8

METHOD:

1. Heat olive oil in medium pan, and add garlic and cauliflower florets.
2. Stir fry over medium heat for a minute.
3. Drain and rinse noodles before adding them to the pan with the herbs and baked cream cheese.
4. Keep stirring, and add in the nutritional yeast with a tablespoon of water if the sauce is too thick until desired consistency is reached.
5. Add salt and pepper to taste and keep stirring over medium-low heat until cauliflowers are soft.
6. Put the spaghetti in a bowl and eat warm.

Serves: 1
Prep Time:
~15 min

Nutrition
information
(per serving)

Calories: 222 kcal
Carbs: 10.7g
Fat: 17.5g
Protein: 7.5g
Fiber: 4.8g
Sugar: 2.2g

29. Mexican Lasagna

INGREDIENTS:

- 1 pack shirataki lasagna sheets
- 1 tsp salt
- 1 cup Mexican salsa
- ½ cup spicy cheese sauce
- ½ cup vegan mozzarella

Total number of ingredients: 5

METHOD:

1. Preheat oven to 350°F.
2. Put lasagna sheet in a deep baking tray lined with parchment paper.
3. Brush lasagna sheet with olive oil, and add a layer of vegan mozzarella.
4. Add another lasagna sheet, and top it with a layer of salsa.
5. Lay another sheet on top of the salsa, and cover with the spicy cheese sauce.
6. Use another lasagna sheet, and cover with a thin layer of salsa.
7. Add sheet of lasagna to create final layer with spicy cheese sauce.
8. Sprinkle leftover mozzarella on top.
9. Cover with tin foil and bake for 25 minutes in deep baking tray.
10. Remove cover, and bake for another 8 minutes.
11. Let it cool after removing from oven and eat warm. Store up to 2 days in fridge, or freeze for up to 2 months; warm in oven for 10 minutes at 320°F before eating.

Serves: 4
Prep Time:
~60 min

Nutrition
information
(per serving)

Calories: 96 kcal
Carbs: 3.4g
Fat: 7.7g
Protein: 3.3g
Fiber: 1.5g
Sugar: 0.8g

30. Creamy Italian Herb Soup

Serves: 5
Prep Time:
~90 min

Nutrition information (per serving)

Calories: 517 kcal
Carbs: 20.3g
Fat: 45.6g
Protein: 8.5g
Fiber: 8.5g
Sugar: 9.1g

INGREDIENTS:

- 2 cans full fat coconut milk
- ½ cup coconut cream
- ¼ cup fresh parsley
- 1 cup broccoli florets
- 1 cup veggie broth
- 1 tbsp. olive oil
- 1 tsp. nutritional yeast
- 1 finely chopped onion
- 2 cloves minced garlic
- 1 cup fresh Italian herbs (basil, oregano, rosemary, thyme, and sage)
- Salt & black pepper to taste

Total number of ingredients: **11**

METHOD:

1. Caramelize onion and garlic in a large cooking pan over medium heat.
2. Add Italian herbs, stir, adding coconut milk while stirring.
3. Add remaining ingredients with salt and pepper to taste and cook for 30 minutes.
4. You can blend it after cooking or eat it when it's the right temperature.
5. If you want to store and freeze, you have to blend it.
6. Either transfer it directly to a heat safe blender, or let it cool, then blend until smooth.

31. Zucchini Risotto

Serves: 5
Prep Time:
~90 min

Nutrition
information
(per serving)

Calories: 80 kcal
Carbs: 5.8g
Fat: 5.6g
Protein: 2.1g
Fiber: 2.3g
Sugar: 2.9g

INGREDIENTS:

- ½ cup sliced zucchini
- 2 tbsp. olive oil
- 1 clove minced garlic
- 1/2 finely chopped onion
- 1 red diced bell pepper
- 3 cups cauliflower rice
- ½ cup (chunky)

- cashew cheese spread
- 1 tsp. nutritional yeast
- ¼ cup almond milk
- ¼ cup fresh basil
- ¼ cup fresh parsley
- Salt & black pepper to taste

Total number of ingredients: 11

METHOD:

1. Caramelize onion and garlic in a large cooking pan with olive oil over medium heat.
2. Add in diced and deseeded bell pepper, and stir fry for a minute.
3. Add zucchini and cook until it softens.
4. Pour in almond milk and add cauliflower rice. Let it cook for 10-15 minutes with a lid on the pan.
5. Stir in cashew cheese, basil, parsley, and nutritional yeast.
6. Taste to see if more herbs are needed, and use salt and pepper if necessary.
7. Cook until rice is soft, and remove from heat when soft and ready to eat.
8. Garnish with leftover parsley. Can be stored in fridge for 2-3 days, and frozen for up to 2 months.

VEGAN
FAT BOMBS

1. Coconut Berry Bombs

Serves: 16 cubes
Prep Time:
~5 min

Nutrition
information
(per serving)

Calories: 217 kcal
Carbs: 4.0g
Fat: 21.9g
Protein: 1.1g
Fiber: 2.2g
Sugar: 1.5g

INGREDIENTS:

- 1 cup coconut butter
- 1 cup coconut oil
- ½ cup fresh or frozen fruit of your choice (raspberries, blackberries, blueberries, etc.)
- ½ tsp. sweetener of your choice (for example: 3 drops of stevia)
- ¼ tsp. vanilla powder
- 1 tbsp. lemon juice

Total number of ingredients: 6

METHOD :

1. Place coconut oil, coconut butter, and fruit (only if you chose frozen fruit) in a pot and heat on stove.
2. Mix thoroughly, then let cool.
3. Place mixture in a blender.
4. Add remaining ingredients to blender.
5. Blend until smooth.
6. Spread mix evenly on a pan lined with parchment paper.
7. Place in refrigerator for about an hour or until cold and firm.
8. Once cold, cut into about 16 squares and put back into refrigerator.

For starters, this is a great recipe as it contains 21.9g of plant-based fats and only 4g of carbs per cube—wow! Moreover, this recipe is extremely versatile to cater to a plethora of taste buds. Just follow the directions above, adding whatever fruit you prefer!

2. Oats and Fudge Squares

Serves: 16 cubes
Prep Time:
~20 min

—————

Nutrition
information
(per serving)

Calories: 300 kcal
Carbs: 5.0g
Fat: 28g
Protein: 8g
Fiber: 4g
Sugar: 1.5g

INGREDIENTS:

- 1 cup coconut oil, melted (or melted oil of your choice)
- ½ cup shredded coconut, unsweetened
- ⅓ cup coconut flour
- ½ tsp. vanilla extract
- 2 cups hemp hearts

For the Fudge Middle:
- 10 oz. 100% dark chocolate.
- ½ cup coconut milk.

Total number of ingredients: 7

METHOD:

1. Melt chocolate and coconut milk in a saucepan and stir until smooth.
2. Mix melted coconut oil, shredded coconut, coconut flour, vanilla extract, and hemp hearts in heated saucepan. Mix well, then remove from heat.
3. Press half of shredded coconut mixture onto a lightly greased pan, then alternate and add the chocolate filling, layering evenly.
4. Place the other half of shredded coconut mixture on top and press gently.
5. Refrigerate overnight, then cut into squares.

Vegans try to avoid grains and oats, so behold the oats 'n' fudge recipe! They taste just like real oats, but without the carbs, and with plenty of fat. The secret to this recipe is the hemp hearts with 13.5g of fat per 3 tbsp. and only 2g of carbs, so be sure to have some on hand!

3. Mini Choco-Coco Cups

Serves: 10 cups
Prep Time:
~35 min

Nutrition
information
(per serving)

Calories: 39 kcal
Carbs: 7.9g
Fat: 3.7g
Protein: 5.8g
Fiber: 5.5g
Sugar: 1.4g

INGREDIENTS:

Coconut-based bottom:
- ½ cup coconut butter
- ½ cup coconut oil
- ½ cup unsweetened coconut, shredded
- 1 tbsp. vanilla extract
- 12 drops of stevia

Chocolate-based top:
- Sugar-free, milk free, 100% dark chocolate (If you prefer to make homemade chocolate sauce, it will work for this recipe as well!).

Total number of ingredients: 6

METHOD:

1. Line a mini-muffin pan with mini cupcake liners
2. Place coconut butter and coconut oil in a heated pan, and melt at low heat, stirring constantly.
3. Add shredded coconut and vanilla.
4. Pour mixture into cupcake liners, and let sit in freezer for 30 minutes until firm.
5. Melt chocolate, and scoop it over hardened coconut candies.
6. Place candies in refrigerator, and keep refrigerated until candy is firm.

These lovely bites will remind you of mini Reese's Cups but with a twist! For those of you with a coconut sweet tooth, this combination paired with the chocolate on top is great for satisfying your cravings and giving you a quick energy boost.

4. Nut Mania Fat Bomb

Serves: 36
Prep Time:
~15 min

Nutrition
information
(per serving)

Calories: 217 kcal
Carbs: 3.4g
Fat: 21.7g
Protein: 0.4g
Fiber: 1.7g
Sugar: 0.6g

INGREDIENTS:

- ½ cup cocoa butter
- 1 cup almond butter
- 1 cup coconut butter
- 1 cup coconut oil
- ½ cup coconut milk
- ¼ cup olive oil
- 1 tbsp. vanilla extract
- ¼ cup chopped almonds
- ¼ tsp. salt
- ¼ cup shelled pistachios, roasted

Total number of ingredients: 10

METHOD:

1. Melt cocoa butter over low heat, stirring frequently.
2. Add all other ingredients (except the almonds) to an electric mixing bowl, and mix thoroughly.
3. Stir in melted cocoa butter and mix again.
4. Spread mixture on a parchment lined pan.
5. Place chopped almonds on top.
6. Refrigerate overnight.

What better way to get satiated and get an energy boost from a quick bite than from a yummy nut-based treat? This recipe is versatile as you can use whatever nuts you want. Pistachios and almonds work best. Grab a few on the go to keep you full throughout the day.

5. Coconut Balls

Serves: 18
Prep Time:
~5 min

Nutrition
information
(per serving)

Calories: 143 kcal
Carbs: 1.5g
Fat: 14.9g
Protein: 0.5g
Fiber: 0.8g
Sugar: 0.3g

INGREDIENTS:

- 1 cup coconut oil (softened, not melted)
- 1 tsp. vanilla extract
- 5 drops of stevia
- 1 tsp. salt
- 3 tbsp. 100% cocoa powder
- 2 tbsp. almond butter (or whatever nut butter you prefer)
- ½ cup unsweetened coconut, shredded

Total number of ingredients: 7

METHOD:

1. Mix all the ingredients together. Make sure there are no clumps or uneven areas.
2. Take small, ball-shaped tablespoons of dough and roll them in shredded coconut.
3. Place finished bites on a pan lined with parchment paper and refrigerate until solid.

Many of these recipes opt for using coconut-based ingredients as they are high in fat and low on the carbohydrate scale. For you coconut lovers, you're in luck. If not, no worries, as there's an array of different flavored fat bombs coming up!

6. Lemon Zest Fat Bombs

Serves: 16
Prep Time:
~10 min

Nutrition
information
(per serving)

Calories: 78 kcal
Carbs: 1.7g
Fat: 7.7g
Protein: 0.5g
Fiber: 1.1g
Sugar: 0.5g

INGREDIENTS:

- ½ cup coconut butter (also sold in stores as creamed coconut, NOT coconut milk)
- ¼ cup coconut oil, softened
- Lemon zest, finely grated from 1-2 lemons
- 3 drops of stevia
- 1 pinch of salt

Total number of ingredients: 5

METHOD:

1. Mix together all the ingredients, ensuring even mixing.
2. Fill each mini cupcake mold with 1 tablespoon of the mixture.
3. Place tray in fridge for about an hour or until firm.

Here's a spin on the coconut chocolate cups mentioned above for those of you into that lemony flavor. This is a guilt-free indulgence with 7.7g of fat and only 1.7g of carbs, not to mention less than 1g of sugar, yet you still taste the lemony, sweet combination!

7. Strawberry Coconut Fat Bombs

Serves: 15
Prep Time: ~10 min

Nutrition information (per serving)

Calories: 81 kcal
Carbs: 1.6g
Fat: 8.1g
Protein: 0.4g
Fiber: 1g
Sugar: 0.6g

INGREDIENTS:

- ⅓ cup coconut butter
- ⅓ cup coconut oil
- 2 drops stevia sweetener (or whatever natural sweetener you personally prefer)
- ½ tbsp. 100% cocoa powder
- ⅓ cup fresh strawberries
- 1 tbsp. shredded coconut, unsweetened

Total number of ingredients: 6

METHOD:

1. To a pot, add coconut butter, coconut oil, syrup, and cocoa powder.
2. Cook over low heat until melted, stirring constantly.
3. To a frying pan, add strawberries with a bit of water and crush them down, stirring constantly.
4. Place strawberries in a blender, along with one tablespoon of the coconut oil mixture, and blend.
5. Fill each mold of your choice with one tablespoon of the coconut oil mixture and one tablespoon of the strawberry mixture.
6. Sprinkle shredded coconut on top of each mold.
7. Place in refrigerator and refrigerate overnight.

The combination of strawberries and coconut is delicious; even if you're skeptical at first, everyone should give it a try! This recipe's ingredients are very adaptable as you can substitute so many ingredients to fix the nutritional values to your dietary needs. You can change the preference of fruit, sweetener, and even oils and butters used to nut-based ones if you prefer!

8. Walnut Chocolate Bars

Serves: 15
Prep Time:
~10 min

Nutrition
information
(per serving)

Calories: 691 kcal
Carbs: 14.4g
Fat: 64.7g
Protein: 12.8g
Fiber: 0.5g
Sugar: 3.3g

INGREDIENTS:

- ½ cup coconut oil (melted)
- 4 tbsp. cocoa powder
- 1 tbsp. sugar (or sweetener of your choice)
- 2 tbsp. tahini paste
- ¼ cup halved walnuts

Total number of ingredients: 5

METHOD:

1. Place all the ingredients except the walnuts in a pot on low heat.
2. Stir constantly until melted.
3. Let cool.
4. Pour mixture into molds (or ice trays), and place in refrigerator.
5. Once bars are almost firm, add a halved walnut on top of each bar and   continue to refrigerate.

While we are trying to decrease our sugars, it seems that sugar works best in this recipe. A tablespoon has 12g of sugar, but this is for 15 bars. If you have a go-to natural sweetener that you find better, by all means use it!

9. Maple Pecan Fat Bombs

INGREDIENTS:

- 2 cups pecan halves
- 1 cup almond flour
- ½ cup shredded coconut, unsweetened
- ½ cup coconut oil
- ¼ tsp. stevia sweetener or maple syrup

Total number of ingredients: 5

METHOD:

1. Preheat oven to 350 °F.
2. Place pecans on a parchment-lined tray and place in oven.
3. Toast pecans for 5 minutes.
4. Remove pecans from oven and place on a cutting board.
5. Using a rolling pin, crush the pecans.
6. Place dry ingredients in a bowl and mix evenly.
7. Add wet ingredients and mix evenly. A crumbly-type dough will form.
8. Place dough on a parchment-lined pan and bake for 25 minutes.
9. Remove from oven and let cool at room temperature.
10. Once cooled, place in refrigerator.

While this fat bomb does take a bit more time, it's an amazing grab 'n' go on the way out to work or in the evening before you sleep. Each bar contains fat levels of 28g with about 5g of carbs. And, like most recipes, if pecans are not your preference, you can substitute with another nut of your choice.

Serves: 12
Prep Time:
~15 min

Nutrition
information
(per serving)

Calories: 285 kcal
Carbs: 5.1g
Fat: 28g
Protein: 3.7g
Fiber: 2.8g
Sugar: 1.8g

10. Peanut Butter Pecan Bars

Serves: 4
Prep Time:
~15 min

Nutrition
information
(per serving)

Calories: 678 kcal
Carbs: 14.2g
Fat: 64.4g
Protein: 9.8g
Fiber: 2g
Sugar: 7.5g

INGREDIENTS:

- ½ cup peanut butter
- ½ cup coconut oil
- 1 tsp. vanilla extract
- 1 tbsp. vanilla syrup
- 1 cup pecans

Total number of ingredients: 5

METHOD:

1. Place coconut oil and peanut butter in a bowl and mix.
2. Warm mixture in a microwave for 30 seconds, then take out and mix some more.
3. Place mixture back in microwave for another 30 seconds. Repeat process until mixture is smooth.
4. Add extract, syrup, and pecans and stir until well blended.
5. Separate mix into four separate rectangular molds to give thin, rectangular bar shape.
6. Place bars in refrigerator and let cool until firm.

11. Dark Chocolate Almond Clusters

Serves: 10 clusters
Prep Time:
~15 min

**Nutrition
information
(per serving)**

Calories: 249 kcal
Carbs: 6.1g
Fat: 22.1g
Protein: 7.2g
Fiber: 4.3g
Sugar: 0.7g

INGREDIENTS:

- 1 cup almonds
- ⅓ tsp. stevia
- 10 oz. store bought dairy-free, sugar-free dark chocolate

Total number of ingredients: 3

METHOD:

1. Mix almonds with sweetener, and separate into 8 clusters (the sticky sweetener should allow almonds to stick together).
2. Melt chocolate in a pot on low heat and let cool.
3. Dip each almond cluster into chocolate sauce and place on a tray lined with parchment paper.
4. Place tray in freezer for 30 minutes, then refrigerate.

Having chocolate cravings? This recipe has you covered. Again, if you prefer homemade chocolate sauce, this recipe will work just as well. It also works just as well if you substitute the stevia with another natural sweetener you're more accustomed to!

12. Raspberry Almond Chocolate Brittle

Serves: 8
Prep Time:
~5 min

Nutrition
information
(per serving)

Calories: 148 kcal
Carbs: 6.5g
Fat: 12.5g
Protein: 2.7g
Fiber: 2.1g
Sugar: 2.4g

INGREDIENTS:

- ¼ cup almond butter
- ¼ cup coconut butter
- 1 tbsp. cocoa powder
- ¼ cup raw almonds, chopped
- ¼ cup walnuts, chopped
- ¼ cup frozen raspberries

Total number of ingredients: 6

METHOD:

1. Place coconut butter, cocoa powder, and almond butter in a bowl and mix.
2. Defrost raspberries for 30 seconds **in microwave**.
3. On a non-stick pan, pour butter mixture and top with chopped nuts and melted raspberries.
4. Place tray in freezer for an hour, or until frozen, then break into about 8 pieces.

The combination of fruits, nuts, and chocolate will make this your favorite go-to fat bomb, at least for a while! While it doesn't have as much fat as the other recipes, it can do the trick for those of you looking for some tasty, quick energy.

13. Chocolate Orange Nut Clusters

Serves: 25 clusters
Prep Time:
~5 min

———

Nutrition
information
(per serving)

Calories: 66 kcal
Carbs: 1.5g
Fat: 9.3g
Protein: 1.1g
Fiber: 0,9g
Sugar: 0.2g

INGREDIENTS:

- ½ cup pure dark cocoa powder
- ¼ cup coconut oil
- 1 ⅓ cups walnuts, chopped (or any nut of your preference)
- 1 tsp. cinnamon
- ½ tbsp. orange zest (finely grated)

Total number of ingredients: 5

METHOD:

1. Place dark chocolate along with a bit of water in a pot.
2. Stir on low heat.
3. Add coconut oil, orange zest, chopped walnuts, and cinnamon, and stir well.
4. Spoon about one tablespoon each of the mixture into mini candy parchment cups.
5. Refrigerate overnight.

14. Fudgy Peanut Butter Cubes

Serves: 12
Prep Time:
~5 min

────────

Nutrition
information
(per serving)

Calories: 313 kcal
Carbs: 5.5g
Fat: 30g
Protein: 5.1g
Fiber: 2.2g
Sugar: 2.4g

INGREDIENTS:

- 1 cup peanut butter
- 1 cup coconut oil
- ¼ cup almond milk (preferably vanilla flavored for taste)

Chocolate Sauce:
- ¼ cup cocoa powder
- 2 tbsp. coconut oil

Total number of ingredients: 5

METHOD:

1. Place coconut oil and peanut butter in a pot.
2. Melt on stove at low heat. Mix until smooth.
3. Place in a blender and add almond milk.
4. Blend until smooth.
5. Pour mixture into a non-stick loaf pan and refrigerate until firm (about 2 hours).
6. Combine ingredients for chocolate sauce.
7. Once peanut butter fudge is firm, drizzle chocolate sauce over fudge.

Are you busy? You can still keep your nutrition up to speed with this tasty and quick 5 ingredient recipe.

15. Vanilla Fat Bombs

INGREDIENTS:

- 1 cup macadamia nuts
- ½ cup coconut oil (or oil of your choice)
- 2 tsp. vanilla extract

Total number of ingredients: 3

METHOD:

1. Place all ingredients in a blender and blend until smooth.
2. Pour mixture into an ice tray and place in fridge until firm.

For those of you who love recipes with less ingredients and barely any effort involved, you'll be sure to love this one! Three ingredients, high fat, low carb levels, and satisfying!

Serves: 14
Prep Time:
~15 min

Nutrition
information
(per serving)

Calories: 137 kcal
Carbs: 1.4g
Fat: 14.1g
Protein: 0.7g
Fiber: 0.8g
Sugar: 0.5g

16. Ginger Fat Bombs

Serves: 10
Prep Time:
~5 min

**Nutrition
information
(per serving)**

Calories: 137 kcal
Carbs: 2.7g
Fat: 13.7g
Protein: 0.8g
Fiber: 1.6g
Sugar: 0.8g

INGREDIENTS:

- ⅓ cup coconut butter
- ⅓ cup coconut oil
- ¼ cup shredded coconut, unsweetened
- 1 tsp. ginger powder

Total number of ingredients: 4

METHOD:

1. In a bowl, mix all ingredients until smooth.
2. Pour mixture into molds (for example, ice cube trays).
3. Place in fridge to set.

Another recipe with fewer than five ingredients! Also, if you find the batter not sweet enough, add a teaspoon of natural sugar or your sweetener of choice.

17. Mint Chocolate Fudge

Serves: 16
Prep Time:
~15 min

Nutrition
information
(per serving)

Calories: 445 kcal
Carbs: 15.8g
Fat: 40.4g
Protein: 4.7g
Fiber: 1.2g
Sugar: 7.5g

INGREDIENTS:

- 1½ cups coconut oil, melted
- 1¼ cups almond butter (or nut butter of choice)
- ½ cup favorite natural sugar or sweetener (all work just fine)
- ½ cup dried parsley flakes (crazy, right?!)
- 2 tsp. vanilla extract
- 1 tsp. peppermint extract
- 1 pinch of salt
- 10 oz. melted dark chocolate (optional, again I use store bought)

Total number of ingredients: 8

METHOD:

1. Add all ingredients in a blender. Blend until smooth.
2. Pour into a nonstick pan and freeze until firm.
3. If adding chocolate, drizzle on top once the fudge is firm.
4. Keep refrigerated.

This recipe's secret ingredient? Dried parsley. It allows for the offset of flavoring and gives color without the use of artificial coloring.

18. Peach-cake Cheeseballs

Serves: 8
Prep Time:
~90 min

Nutrition
information
(per serving)

Calories: 182 kcal
Carbs: 8g
Fat: 10.8g
Protein: 13.1g
Fiber: 1.6g
Sugar: 4.3g

INGREDIENTS:

- ½ cup coconut cream
- 2 tbsp. hazelnut spread
- 3 scoops vegan protein powder
- ½ cup ground hemp seed
- ¼ cup freeze dried peach powder
- 1 tsp. nutritional yeast

Total number of ingredients: 6

METHOD:

1. Melt coconut cream on low heat, and make sure it doesn't come close to boiling or simmering. It just needs to be fully melted.
2. Add hazelnut spread and make sure that it's thoroughly combined with the coconut cream.
3. Take pan off the heat, and add peach powder, protein powder, and ground hempseed.
4. Stir thoroughly until dough forms.
5. Roll into 16 balls, and store in fridge for a week or up to 4 months in the freezer.

19. Blueberry Walnut Bites

Serves: 12
Prep Time:
~35 min

Nutrition
information
(per serving)

Calories: 226kcal
Carbs: 6.1g
Fat: 17.2g
Protein: 12.5g
Fiber: 2.4g
Sugar: 2.5g

INGREDIENTS:

- 1 cup peanut butter
- 2 tbsp. softened coconut butter
- 4 tbsp. almond flour
- ¼ cup chopped almonds
- ½ cup full fat coconut milk
- 2 scoops vegan protein powder
- 2 tbsp. freeze dried blueberry powder
- ¼ tsp. stevia

Total number of ingredients: 7

METHOD:

1. Preheat oven to 375°F and grease a muffin plate with coconut oil.
2. Whisk peanut butter, coconut butter, stevia, and coconut milk until thoroughly mixed.
3. Stir the almond flour, almond bits, blueberry powder, and protein powder until completely combined.
4. Pour into a baking sheet lined with parchment paper and bake for 30 minutes until the batter has set.
5. Let it cool, and slice into 12 bites.
6. Can be stored chilled for a week or frozen up to 2 months.

CLEANSING LOW-CARB & PLANT-BASED RECIPES

1. Spicy Tofu Scramble

Serves: 1
Prep Time:
~20 min

Nutrition information (per serving)

Calories: 472 kcal
Carbs: 34.4g
Fat: 33.3g
Protein: 8.8g
Fiber: 15.1g
Sugar: 8.5g

INGREDIENTS:

- 1 onion, diced
- ½ green pepper, diced
- ½ cup mushrooms, chopped
- 1 oz. package extra firm tofu, drained
- 1 tsp. curry powder
- 1 tomato, chopped
- 1 avocado, pitted and sliced
- 1 tsp. olive oil
- 1 cup fresh spinach
- 1 pinch pepper

Total number of ingredients: 10

METHOD:

1. Sauté green peppers and onions in a skillet with olive oil for about 5 minutes.
2. Add in mushrooms.
3. Add dried tofu along with other spices and spinach.
4. Cook for about 10 minutes.
5. Place on a plate and top with sliced tomato and avocado.

When following a LCHF vegan diet, tofu is a great staple to have by your side. You can season it any way you like, and its nutritional profile is perfect for your dietary needs.

2. Baked Green Beans

Serves: 3
Prep Time:
~25 min

Nutrition
information
(per serving)

Calories: 98 kcal
Carbs: 11.8g
Fat: 4.4g
Protein: 2.8g
Fiber: 7g
Sugar: 2.2g

INGREDIENTS:

- 1 lb. fresh green beans, ends snipped
- 3 tbsp. ground flax meal
- 1 tsp. salt
- 1 pinch black pepper
- 1 tsp. olive oil

Total number of ingredients: 5

METHOD:

1. Preheat oven to 350 °F.
2. Mix all ingredients in a bowl.
3. Place on a nonstick baking tray and bake for 20 to 25 minutes.

This is a life saver recipe, you guys. An entire pound of seasoned green beans is sure to fight off any hunger cravings you may be having!

3. Baked Eggplant with Spicy Dressing

Serves: 1
Prep Time:
~20 min

Nutrition information (per serving)

Calories: 474 kcal
Carbs: 41.9g
Fat: 31.2g
Protein: 6.3g
Fiber: 21.9g
Sugar: 17.9g

INGREDIENTS:

- 1 eggplant, sliced
- 1 clove garlic, minced
- 1 tbsp. MCT oil
- 1 pinch salt
- 1 pinch pepper
- ½ cup chopped cilantro

Sauce:
- 1 tsp. MCT oil
- 1 onion, chopped
- ⅓ cup coconut milk
- 1 tbsp. curry powder
- 1 chopped green chili (optional)
- 1 pinch salt

Total number of ingredients: 13

METHOD:

1. Preheat oven to 350 °F.
2. Mix all the ingredients from Part 1 into a bowl.
3. Place on a nonstick baking tray and bake for 30 minutes.
4. For the sauce, place all ingredients for the sauce in a blender.
5. Blend until smooth.

Eggplants can leave you completely satisfied for an entire meal. Talk about pure plant power!

4. Veggie Detox Soup

Serves: 6
Prep Time:
~30 min

Nutrition
information
(per serving)

Calories: 44 kcal
Carbs: 9.1g
Fat: 0.3g
Protein: 1.2g
Fiber: 2.5g
Sugar: 3.2g

INGREDIENTS:

- ½ cup lemon juice
- 6 cups water
- ½ onion, diced
- 2 cloves garlic, minced
- ½ cup celery, diced
- 3 carrots, diced
- ½ cup broccoli florets
- 1 cup tomatoes, chopped
- ¼ tsp. cinnamon
- Salt and pepper to taste
- 2 cups kale

Total number of ingredients: 12

METHOD:

1. Sauté onions and garlic.
2. Add sautéed onions and garlic to a pot filled with boiling water, and stir on medium heat.
3. Add remaining vegetables except kale. Stir occasionally for 5 minutes.
4. Add spices, and let simmer for 15 minutes.
5. Add kale and lemon, and let simmer until all vegetables are soft.

The fiber contained in all these fresh veggies allows the net count of carbs to be less than 10g for an entire meal's serving. This soup is nothing but the best plant-powered medicine for you!

5. Spinach Pepper Quiche

Serves: 6
Prep Time:
~15 min

Nutrition
information
(per serving)

Calories: 98 kcal
Carbs: 11.4g
Fat: 1.9g
Protein: 9g
Fiber: 1.5g
Sugar: 1.5g

INGREDIENTS:

- 1 lb. extra firm tofu
- 1 tsp. onion powder
- 1 tsp. garlic powder
- 1 pinch salt
- ¼ cup cornstarch
- ¼ cup nutritional yeast
- 1 tbsp. Dijon mustard
- 1 tsp. lemon juice
- 2 cups fresh spinach
- 1 bell pepper, chopped
- 2 tsp. red pepper flakes

Total number of ingredients: 11

METHOD:

1. Heat oven to 350 °F.
2. Lightly grease a shallow pie dish.
3. Place all ingredients, except spinach and pepper, in a blender. Blend until smooth.
4. Place mixture in a bowl.
5. Chop spinach.
6. Add chopped spinach and pepper to mixture from Step 4 and mix well.
7. Pour mixture into pie dish and bake for 45 minutes.

The fiber in the spinach comprises 2/3 of the carb content. This enables a low level of net carbs, around 11g per meal serving.

6. Tofu and Broccoli Filled Avocado

Serves: 2
Prep Time:
~30 min

Nutrition
information
(per serving:
half avocado)

Calories: 290 kcal
Carbs: 10.6g
Fat: 27g
Protein: 2.1g
Fiber: 9.1g
Sugar: 1.5g

INGREDIENTS:

- 1 tbsp. Dijon mustard
- ½ clove garlic, sliced
- 3 tbsp. olive oil
- 1 avocado, halved and pitted
- 1 pinch chili flakes
- 1 pinch salt and pepper
- 1 pinch cumin
- 2 tbsp. lemon juice
- ⅓ package extra firm tofu, drained
- 1 cup broccoli florets

Total number of ingredients: 10

METHOD:

1. Prepare sauce by mixing lemon, mustard, olive oil, garlic, and spices in a bowl.
2. In a separate bowl, pour mixture over broccoli and tofu cubes to marinate then place in fridge.
3. Grill avocado with olive oil, salt, and pepper, then place marinated tofu and broccoli on grill.
4. Once charred, remove from grill.
5. Chop grilled tofu and broccoli, then spoon into avocado.

A great staple for LCHF vegans? Avocados. Extremely high in fat and fiber, equaling a low net carb count! More importantly? They're delicious!

7. Stuffed Portobello Mushrooms

Serves: 4
Prep Time:
~15 min

___

Nutrition
information
(per serving)

Calories: 120 kcal
Carbs: 11.5g
Fat: 7.1g
Protein: 2.6g
Fiber: 3g
Sugar: 5.8g

INGREDIENTS:

- 4 portobello mushrooms
- 2 tbsp. olive oil
- 1 onion, diced
- 1 zucchini, diced
- 1 roasted red pepper, diced
- 1 pinch each of the following spices: oregano, salt, black pepper, and pepper flakes
- 5 sundried tomatoes, diced
- 3 cloves garlic, sliced
- ¼ cup fresh spinach
- no-salt vegan cream cheese (see recipe)

Total number of ingredients: 12-13

METHOD:

1. Preheat oven to 350 °F.
2. Sauté all ingredients except mushrooms and vegan cheese, then spoon into mushrooms.
3. If using vegan cream cheese, spread on top of each mushroom.
4. Place mushrooms in oven and bake for 45 minutes.

This recipe is great because you have the freedom to stuff and spice the mushrooms with whatever veggies, whole foods, and/or spices you like!

8. Sesame Tofu with Eggplant

Serves: 4
Prep Time:
~20 min

Nutrition information (per serving)

Calories: 285 kcal
Carbs: 14.9g
Fat: 20.1g
Protein: 12g
Fiber: 6.1g
Sugar: 4.4g

INGREDIENTS:

- 1 lb. extra firm tofu, drained
- 1 cup cilantro, chopped
- 3 tbsp. rice vinegar
- 2 cloves garlic, chopped
- 1 eggplant, julienned
- Salt and pepper to taste
- ¼ cup sesame seeds
- ¼ cup of soy sauce, low sodium
- 1 tbsp. red pepper flakes, crushed
- 4 tbsp. sesame oil

Total number of ingredients: 10

METHOD:

1. Place 2 tablespoons of sesame oil and the cilantro, red pepper flakes, rice vinegar, and garlic in a bowl and mix.
2. Cook eggplant in a lightly greased skillet until soft then add seasoned mix from step 1.
3. In another skillet, add 2 tablespoons sesame oil, sesame seeds, and tofu, and sauté until crisp.
4. Pour in the soy sauce, and let tofu pieces soak in the soy sauce in order to appear caramelized.
5. Place tofu pieces on top of eggplant noodles and voila.

9. Pasta Pesto

Serves: 2
Prep Time:
~15 min

———

Nutrition
information
(per serving)

Calories: 234 kcal
Carbs: 17.3g
Fat: 16.2g
Protein: 5.8g
Fiber: 7.3g
Sugar: 6.3g

INGREDIENTS:

- 1 pack Shiritaki Pasta
- Salt and pepper to taste
- 1 tbsp. olive oil
- ½ avocado
- 1 cup fresh basil
- 2 cloves garlic, chopped
- ½ lemon
- ¼ cup cashew cheese spread
- ½ cup of water (only if needed to even out consistency)

Total number of ingredients: 10

METHOD:

1. Drain and rinse pasta with water.
2. Transfer shirataki pasta into a pot with boiling water and cook for 2-3 minutes.
3. Add avocado, basil, lemon, garlic, and cashew cheese spread to a bowl. Mix well, and add water if needed.
4. Pour dressing over pasta and toss gently.

This pasta is the perfect go-to to cleanse your system and make you a powerhouse for the rest of the day. Have this meal on a day when you have a high-level fat bomb to even out your nutrition levels!

10. Mushroom Tofu Lettuce Wraps

Serves: 2
Prep Time:
~25 min

Nutrition
information
(per serving)

Calories: 133 kcal
Carbs: 10.4g
Fat: 7.7g
Protein: 5.6g
Fiber: 6.1g
Sugar: 3.4g

INGREDIENTS:

- 1 oz. extra firm tofu
- ½ avocado, pitted and peeled
- ¾ lb. fresh mushrooms, chopped
- Lemon juice, to taste
- Salt and pepper
- 3 cloves garlic, minced
- Soy sauce (optional)
- 2 lettuce leaves

Total number of ingredients: 8

METHOD:

1. To a lightly greased skillet, add garlic and mushrooms.
2. Cook for 5 minutes, then add tofu.
3. Mix thoroughly and add soy sauce (if desired) and spices.
4. Keep cooking until tofu is cooked through.
5. Place on a bed of lettuce and add lemon juice.
6. Garnish with avocado slices.

By having a dish that uses tofu instead of meat for your proteins and dietary needs, as well as lettuce instead of bread, you can ensure optimum health.

11. Cumin Cashew Cream

Serves: 1 cup
Prep Time:
~4 min

Nutrition
information
(per serving)

Calories: 510 kcal
Carbs: 33g
Fat: 37.5g
Protein: 25.5g
Fiber: 7.5g
Sugar: 9g

INGREDIENTS:

- 3 tbsp. nutritional yeast
- ¾ cup raw cashews
- ¼ tsp. garlic powder
- 1 tsp. whole black peppercorns to taste
- 1 tsp. cumin to taste
- ¾ tsp. salt

Total number of ingredients: 4

METHOD:

1. Mix all the ingredients with a food processor or blender until desired consistency is reached, smooth or chunky.

LOW-CARB & PLANT-BASED SMOOTHIES

1. Shamrock Smoothie

Serves: 2
**Prep Time:
~5 min**

**Nutrition
information
(per serving)**

Calories: 39 kcal
Carbs: 5.1g
Fat: 1.8g
Protein: 0.6g
Fiber: 3g
Sugar: 3.1g

INGREDIENTS:

- 2 cups water
- ½ cup lettuce
- ¼ cup pineapple, chopped
- ½ cup cucumber, peeled and sliced
- ¼ cup kiwi, peeled and chopped
- ¼ cup avocado, peeled and pitted
- 3 tbsp. stevia

Total number of ingredients: 7

METHOD:

1. Blend all ingredients together in a blender. Add more or less of what you prefer.

2. The Ultimate Green Smoothie

Serves: 2
Prep Time:
~5 min

Nutrition
information
(per serving)

Calories: 104 kcal
Carbs: 8g
Fat: 7.1g
Protein: 2g
Fiber: 4.9g
Sugar: 1.9g

INGREDIENTS:

- 2 cups spinach
- ½ avocado, pitted and peeled
- ½ cucumber
- ½ cup parsley
- 1 cup water
- Ice cubes (optional)

Total number of ingredients: 6

METHOD:

1. Blend all ingredients together in a blender. Add more or less of what you prefer.

3. Nutty Green Smoothie

INGREDIENTS:

- ¼ cup coconut milk
- ½ avocado, pitted and peeled
- ½ cup water
- ½ cup fresh mint
- 2 tbsp. pistachios
- 1 tbsp. vanilla extract
- 2 drops stevia
- ¼ cup spinach

Total number of ingredients: 8

METHOD:

1. Blend all ingredients together in a blender. Add more or less of what you prefer.

A popular favorite! ... and look at the nutritional value of it! A 17g fat content!

Serves: 2
Prep Time:
~5 min

Nutrition
information
(per serving)

Calories: 212 kcal
Carbs: 9.1g
Fat: 16.6g
Protein: 2.9g
Fiber: 4.4g
Sugar: 2.7g

4. Coconut Berry Smoothie

Serves: 3
Prep Time:
~5 min

Nutrition
information
(per serving)

Calories: 166 kcal
Carbs: 14.7g
Fat: 10.5g
Protein: 3.6g
Fiber: 2.5g
Sugar: 7.5g

INGREDIENTS:

- ¾ cup frozen blueberries (or your choice of berries)
- ¾ cup almond milk
- 2 tbsp. ground chia seeds
- 2 tbsp. coconut oil
- 3 drops stevia

Total number of ingredients: 5

METHOD:

1. Blend all ingredients in a blender in a blender. Add more or less of what you prefer.

5. Fruity Chocolaty Avocado Smoothie

Serves: 2
Prep Time:
~5 min

Nutrition
information
(per serving)

Calories: 138 kcal
Carbs: 20.5g
Fat: 4.4g
Protein: 3.0g
Fiber: 3.35g
Sugar: 13g

INGREDIENTS:

- ½ cup cashew flavored almond milk
- ¼ avocado, pitted and peeled
- ⅓ cup frozen raspberries
- 1 tbsp. cocoa powder

Total number of ingredients: 4

METHOD:

1. Blend all ingredients together in a blender. Add more or less of what you prefer.

6. Chocolate Lover's Smoothie

Serves: 1
Prep Time:
~5 min

Nutrition
information
(per serving)

Calories: 232 kcal
Carbs: 9.2g
Fat: 19g
Protein: 3.8g
Fiber: 0.6g
Sugar: 2.9g

INGREDIENTS:

- 1 tsp. vanilla extract
- 1 tsp. almond butter
- ¼ cup coconut milk
- ¼ cup water
- ¼ cup cocoa powder
- A few dark chocolate chip chunks (optional)

Total number of ingredients: 6

METHOD:

1. Blend all ingredients together in a blender. Add more or less of what you prefer.

7. Strawberry Chocolate Milkshake

Serves: 2
Prep Time:
~5 min

Nutrition
information
(per serving)

Calories: 313 kcal
Carbs: 11.5g
Fat: 28.1g
Protein: 3.6g
Fiber: 1g
Sugar: 6g

INGREDIENTS:

- 1 cup coconut milk
- ½ cup fresh strawberries
- 3 drops stevia
- ¼ cup cocoa powder
- Ice cubes (optional, for thicker consistency)

Total number of ingredients: 5

METHOD:

1. Blend all ingredients together in a blender. Add more or less of what you prefer.

The coconut milk acts as a great nutritional substitute for regular milk by having a great fat to carb ratio per cup. Also, you can't go wrong with the simplicity of a 5-ingredient smoothie!

8. Raspberry Avocado Smoothie

Serves: 2
Prep Time:
~5 min

Nutrition information (per serving)

Calories: 212 kcal
Carbs: 9.1g
Fat: 16.6g
Protein: 2.9g
Fiber: 4.4g
Sugar: 2.7g

INGREDIENTS:

- ¼ cup coconut milk
- ½ avocado, pitted and peeled
- ½ cup water
- ½ cup fresh mint
- 2 tbsp. pistachios
- 1 tbsp. vanilla extract
- 2 drops of stevia
- ¼ cup spinach

Total number of ingredients: 8

METHOD:

1. Blend all ingredients together in a blender. Add more or less of what you prefer.

9. Pumpkin Acai Bowl

Serves: 1
Prep Time:
~10 min

Nutrition
information
(per serving)

Calories: 1300 kcal
Carbs: 24.3g
Fat: 96.5g
Protein: 32.3g
Fiber: 8.1g
Sugar: 2.5g

INGREDIENTS:

- ¼ cup pumpkin puree (optional)
- 1 cup almonds
- 1 pinch cinnamon
- 2 tbsp. pistachios
- ¼ cup blackberries (or berry of your choice)
- 1 tbsp. cocoa powder
- ½ avocado, pitted and peeled
- 1 cup water

Total number of ingredients: 8

METHOD:

1. Blend together water, cocoa powder, avocado, pumpkin puree, some of the berries, and the cinnamon in a blender until smooth.
2. Pour mixture into a serving bowl and top with leftover berries, and nuts.

10. PB&G Smoothie

Serves: 1
Prep Time:
~5 min

Nutrition
information
(per serving)

Calories: 189 kcal
Carbs: 5.4g
Fat: 8.3g
Protein: 4.5g
Fiber: 3.6g
Sugar: 9.6g

INGREDIENTS:

- 1 cup spinach
- 1 tbsp. peanut butter
- 2 drops stevia
- Water (depending on the desired consistency)
- 1 tbsp. cocoa powder

Total number of ingredients: 5

METHOD:

1. Blend all ingredients together in a blender. Add more or less of what you prefer.

The peanut butter and green smoothie is a favorite. Do you want a plant-based, green smoothie with a thick, creamy and sweet taste? This is the way to go.

11. Green Power

Serves: 1
Prep Time:
~5 min

**Nutrition
information**

Calories: 526 kcal
Carbs: 17.7g
Fat: 44.2g
Protein: 14.6g
Fiber: 7.2g
Sugar: 7.0g

INGREDIENTS:

- 1 cup of spinach
- ½ cup full-fat coconut milk
- 4 leaves kale
- 1 tsp. guarana powder
- 1 tsp. cocoa powder
- 1 celery stick, chopped
- 2 tbsp. peanut butter

Total number of ingredients: 8

METHOD:

1. Place the coconut milk, spinach, kale, guarana powder, cocoa powder, celery, and peanut butter into a blender.
2. Cover, and blend until smooth.
3. Pour into a glass and serve.

12. Coconut Avocado Smoothie

INGREDIENTS:

- 1 Hass avocado, diced
- ½ cup coconut milk
- ¼ cup coconut cream
- 1 pinch stevia to taste
- 8 ice cubes

Total number of ingredients: 5

METHOD:

1. Combine avocado, stevia, coconut milk, coconut cream, and ice cubes in a blender; blend until smooth.
2. Pour into glasses and serve.

Serves: 1
Prep Time:
~5 min

Nutrition
information

Calories: 724 kcal
Carbs: 25.9g
Fat: 68.5g
Protein: 9.3g
Fiber: 8.3g
Sugar: 4g

13. Razzy Green Morning Smoothie

Serves: 2
Prep Time:
~5 min

Nutrition
information

Calories: 429 kcal
Carbs: 26.9g
Fat: 32.7g
Protein: 6.8g
Fiber: 12.3g
Sugar: 13.6g

INGREDIENTS:

- 16 whole almonds
- 1 tablespoon ground flaxseed
- 1 cup frozen blueberries
- 1 cup baby spinach
- 1 cup raspberries
- 2 cups full-fat coconut milk

Total number of ingredients: 6

METHOD:

1. Place the almonds, spinach, and flaxseed into a blender; pulse until roughly ground.
2. Add the frozen blueberries, raspberries, and coconut milk, and puree until smooth.
3. Pour into glasses and serve.

14. Flu Shot

INGREDIENTS:

- 2 celery stalks, leafless
- ½ large carrots, sliced
- 1 clove raw garlic
- 1 large handful of spinach
- 1 lemon, peeled and parted
- ½ cup full-fat coconut milk
- ½ cup unsweetened coconut water
- ¼ cup fresh ginger root, sliced
- 1 pinch of cayenne pepper or hot sauce

Total number of ingredients: 11

METHOD:

1. Add all ingredients to blender.
2. Blend until smooth.
3. Give it a good stir, and pour into glass.

Serves: 1
Prep Time:
~5 min

Nutrition
information

Calories: 374 kcal
Carbs: 26.2g
Fat: 27.5g
Protein: 5.4g
Fiber: 9.1g
Sugar: 12.2g

LOW-CARB
VEGAN SALADS

1. Tofu Broccoli Salad

Serves: 2
Prep Time:
~15 min

───────────

Nutrition
information
(per serving)

Calories: 395 kcal
Carbs: 19.4g
Fat: 31.3g
Protein: 9.1g
Fiber: 3.9g
Sugar: 2.5g

INGREDIENTS:

Sauce:
- ¼ cup tahini
- 2 cloves garlic, minced
- Juice of 1 lemon
- 1 tbsp. sesame oil
- 2 tbsp. rice wine vinegar

Salad:
- 1 head broccoli, cut in florets
- 1 tbsp. walnuts, halved
- 1 oz. extra firm tofu
- 2 cups packaged mixed greens (or make your own)
- 1 tbsp. olive oil

Total number of ingredients: **10**

METHOD:

1. Blend all the sauce ingredients together in a blender. Add more or less of what you prefer.
2. Sauté tofu in a greased pan, add spices, and stir occasionally until done.
3. Add broccoli to pan and sauté in olive oil until tender.
4. Place tofu in a bowl and add the mixed greens, dressing, and nuts.
5. Enjoy!

2. Chickpeas and Greens Salad

INGREDIENTS:

- ½ cup kale
- ¾ cup broccoli florets
- 1 cup chickpeas, cooked
- 4 tbsp. hummus (store bought or homemade)
- 2 tbsp. sesame seeds
- 3 tbsp. pumpkin seeds

Total number of ingredients: 6

METHOD:

1. Steam the kale and broccoli. Once done, place in a bowl.
2. Add chickpeas, sesame seeds, and pumpkin seeds. Mix well.
3. Portion onto 4 plates.
4. Top each plate with a tablespoon of hummus.

Serves: 4
Prep Time:
~15 min

Nutrition
information
(per serving)

Calories: 166 kcal
Carbs: 20g
Fat: 6.8g
Protein: 6.1g
Fiber: 5.3g
Sugar: 0.4g

3. Avocado Kale Salad

Serves: 4
Prep Time:
~15 min

Nutrition
information
(per serving)

Calories: 290 kcal
Carbs: 17.1g
Fat: 22.5g
Protein: 4.9g
Fiber: 9.5g
Sugar: 3.4g

INGREDIENTS:

Salad:
- 1 ½ avocados, chopped
- ½ onion, sliced
- ½ cucumber, sliced
- 1 cup kale, chopped
- 1 red chili (optional), sliced

Dressing:
- 2 tbsp. lemon juice
- 1 avocado
- 1 tsp. cayenne pepper
- 1 pinch of salt
- 1 pinch of pepper
- ¼ cup chopped almonds (or nuts of your choice for topping)

Total number of ingredients: 11

METHOD:

1. Place all the ingredients for the salad in a bowl and toss.
2. Blend all the dressing ingredients together except the almonds.
3. Pour dressing over salad and toss.
4. Add chopped almonds on top.

4. Tabbouleh Dressing

Serves: 6
Prep Time:
~30 min

**Nutrition
information
(per serving)**

Calories: 183 kcal
Carbs: 5.4g
Fat: 17.7g
Protein: 0.6g
Fiber: 1.1g
Sugar: 2.5g

INGREDIENTS:

- ½ cup lemon juice
- ½ cup olive oil
- 1 onion, chopped
- 10 sprigs parsley, chopped
- 2 cups tomatoes, chopped
- salt and pepper to taste

Total number of ingredients: 7

METHOD:

1. In a bowl, mix parsley, tomatoes, and onions.
2. Gradually top with lemon juice, olive oil, salt, and pepper, and mix.
3. Keep mixing, tasting, and adding until preferred taste is achieved.

Mediterranean cuisine can be a bit tricky when it comes to a keto-vegan diet; however, their salads never disappoint. Tabbouleh is usually a side salad complimenting whatever else you may be eating.

5. Nut Broccoli Salad

Serves: 6
Prep Time:
~15 min

Nutrition
information
(per serving)

Calories: 349 kcal
Carbs: 17.5g
Fat: 26.4g
Protein: 10.3g
Fiber: 6.2g
Sugar: 6.2g

INGREDIENTS:

Salad:
- 5 cups broccoli
- 2 cups shredded carrots
- ½ cup walnuts
- ½ cup roasted peanuts
- ¼ cup onion, chopped

Sauce:
- ½ cup peanut butter
- Sriracha (optional)
- Salt and pepper to taste
- 2 tbsp. coconut oil
- Juice of ½ a lemon
- 2 tbsp. soy sauce
- 1 tsp. rice vinegar

Total number of ingredients: 12

METHOD:

1. 1. Mix all the salad ingredients in a bowl.
2. 2. In a separate bowl, mix together the dressing ingredients until smooth.
3. 3. Pour dressing over salad, and mix until evenly coated.
4. 4. Refrigerate to let all the flavors soak in, then serve!

6. Fattoush

Serves: 6
Prep Time:
~20 min

Nutrition
information
(per serving)

Calories: 194 kcal
Carbs: 15.5g
Fat: 13.3g
Protein: 2.7g
Fiber: 3.9g
Sugar: 4.8g

INGREDIENTS:

Salad:
- 1 pita bread (will be used for the bread crisps in the fattoush; you can use more or less depending on dietary preference)
- Salt and pepper to taste
- 1 head lettuce, chopped
- 1 cucumber, chopped
- 3 tomatoes, chopped
- 3 onions, chopped
- ½ tsp. sumac
- 4 radishes, sliced
- 1 cup parsley, chopped
- 1 tsp. olive oil

Lemon-Vinaigrette Sauce:
- Juice of 1 lemon
- ⅓ cup olive oil
- 1 tsp. sumac
- Salt and pepper to taste
- ½ tsp. ground cinnamon

Total number of ingredients: 15

METHOD:

1. Toast pita bread until crisp, break, and place in oiled skillet until browned.
2. Add salt, pepper, and sumac.
3. In a mixing bowl, mix the tomatoes, onions, cucumber, radish, lettuce, and parsley.
4. For the dressing, mix all the dressing ingredients in a small bowl.
5. Mix dressing with salad and toss, then add the pita chips and toss a bit more.

7. Mixed Greens with Raspberry Vinaigrette

Serves: 1
Prep Time:
~5 min

Nutrition information (per serving)

Calories: 937 kcal
Carbs: 17.7g
Fat: 95.4g
Protein: 8.1g
Fiber: 4.9g
Sugar: 9.1g

INGREDIENTS:

Salad:
- ½ cup mixed greens
- 3 tbsp. pine nuts, roasted
- 2 tbsp. homemade cumin cashew cream
- Salt and ground pepper to taste

Vinaigrette:
- ⅓ cup white wine vinegar
- ⅓ cup fresh raspberries
- ⅓ cup olive oil

Total number of ingredients: 8

METHOD:

1. Mix all salad ingredients together.
2. Blend dressing ingredients in a blender, then pour through a fine strainer into a cup to remove thick clumps.
3. Top salad with vinaigrette and enjoy!

8. Crumbled Broccoli Tofu Salad

Serves: 1
Prep Time:
~5 min

Nutrition
information
(per serving)

Calories: 232 kcal
Carbs: 22.3g
Fat: 10.1g
Protein: 12.6g
Fiber: 4.8g
Sugar: 8g

INGREDIENTS:

- ½ cup tofu (4oz)
- ½ head broccoli florets
- 1 onion, chopped
- 1 clove garlic, chopped
- 2 tsp. soy sauce
- 1 tsp. sesame seed oil
- 2 tsp. sesame seeds
- Salt and pepper to taste

Total number of ingredients: 9

METHOD:

1. Steam broccoli and tofu in a pot.
2. Once done, rinse under cold water, and put broccoli in a separate bowl.
3. Dry the tofu as much as possible by patting with a towel, then crumble and add in the bowl with the broccoli (keep them separated in the bowl, split in two sides).
4. Add the garlic, onions and ½ the soy sauce over the tofu only, and let soak for 5 minutes.
5. Add the rest of the soy sauce, sesame seeds, and oil over both items.
6. Toss gently, and add pepper and salt if desired.

9. Baby Kale Topped with Raspberry and Pecans

Serves: 4
Prep Time:
~15 min

_____

Nutrition information (per serving)

Calories: 294 kcal
Carbs: 8.2g
Fat: 27.7g
Protein: 3.7g
Fiber: 3.3g
Sugar: 2.6g

INGREDIENTS:

Salad:
- 1 cup raw pecans
- 6 drops stevia
- ¾ cup baby kale
- handful of raspberries (about a ¼ cup)

Maple Vinaigrette:
- 2 tbsp. olive oil
- 2 tbsp. balsamic vinegar
- 1 drop stevia or tsp. maple syrup
- 1 clove garlic, minced
- Salt and pepper to taste
- 2 tsp. Dijon Mustard
- 2 tsp. lemon juice

Total number of ingredients: 12

METHOD:

1. Preheat oven to 350 °F.
2. In a bowl, mix the pecans and stevia then place on a baking sheet and bake for 10 minutes.
3. Mix the ingredients for the vinaigrette in a bowl.
4. Place the kale in a bowl, and add the pecans, raspberries, and vinaigrette.

10. Avocado Mexican Salad

Serves: 4
Prep Time:
~15 min

**Nutrition
information
(per serving)**

Calories: 115 kcal
Carbs: 7.6g
Fat: 8.7g
Protein: 1.5g
Fiber: 4.7g
Sugar: 2.8g

INGREDIENTS:

- ½ tbsp. olive oil
- 1 pinch of salt and 1 pinch of pepper to taste
- 1 tsp. red wine vinegar
- ¼ onion, chopped
- 1 tbsp. fresh cilantro, chopped
- 1 ripe avocado
- ¼ head lettuce, chopped
- ½ jalapeno, chopped
- 12 cherry tomatoes, quartered

Total number of ingredients: 10

METHOD:

1. Combine oil, vinegar, tomatoes, salt and pepper in a bowl, and let sit for an hour.
2. Add jalapeño, onion, and cilantro, and toss.
3. Place chopped lettuce and sliced avocados on a plate, and spoon the mixture from Step 2 on top.

DESSERTS
& SNACKS

1. 2-Minute Microwave Cinnamon Pecan Bread

Serves: 4
Prep Time:
~5 min

Nutrition information
(per serving: 1 mini loaf)

Calories: 125 kcal
Carbs: 3.2g
Fat: 11.3g
Protein: 3g
Fiber: 2.3g
Sugar: 1.1g

INGREDIENTS:

- ⅓ cup almond flour (or any nut flour of your preference)
- 1 flax egg
- ½ tsp. baking powder
- ¼ tsp. salt
- ¼ tsp. cinnamon (optional)
- ¼ cup chopped pecans

Total number of ingredients: 6

METHOD:

1. In a bowl, add the almond flour, baking powder, cinnamon, and salt. Mix thoroughly.
2. Add the flax egg and pecans, and stir until evenly mixed.
3. Lightly oil (using olive oil) a cup big enough to fit the batter.
4. Pour the mixture into the cup and microwave for about 2 minutes or until firm.
5. Slice the mini loaf into about 4 or 5 pieces.
6. Toast the slices if you want.

2. Banana Nut Bread

Serves: 10
Prep Time:
~10 min

___

Nutrition
information
(per serving)

Calories: 253 kcal
Carbs: 14.1g
Fat: 20.4g
Protein: 6.7g
Fiber: 4.1g
Sugar: 6.7g

INGREDIENTS:

- 3 bananas, chopped
- 3 flax eggs
- 2 cups almond flour or oatmeal
- ⅓ cup walnuts (or any other keto friendly nut you prefer)
- ¼ cup coconut oil or olive oil (depending on availability or preference)
- ½ tsp. baking powder

Total number of ingredients: 6

METHOD:

1. Preheat oven to 350 °F.
2. Minimally grease a loaf pan with whichever oil you chose.
3. Add all the ingredients into one bowl and mix well.
4. Pour the mix into loaf pan.
5. Cook for 1 hour at 350 °F or until done.

Craving that natural sweet, sugary taste that comes from bananas? This banana bread recipe comes with a twist as it has walnuts, which give an extra spin to the normal banana bread! Also, the walnuts contribute 5.9g protein per slice. Indulge your sweet tooth with a dessert that contains half the carbs and sugar of a normal sweet loaf!

3. Almond Maple Crumble Dessert Loaf

Serves: 8
Prep Time:
~15 min

Nutrition
information
(per serving)

Calories: 178 kcal
Carbs: 6g
Fat: 14.9g
Protein: 6.3g
Fiber: 2.8g
Sugar: 1.8g

INGREDIENTS:

- 1½ cups almond flour (or any other nut flour).
- 4 flax eggs.
- ¼ cup finely ground flaxseed.
- 1 tbsp. whole flaxseed (optional).
- 2 tbsp. crushed almonds (optional).
- ½ tsp. salt.
- ½ tsp. baking soda.
- ½ tsp. apple cider vinegar.
- 2 drops stevia.

Total number of ingredients: 9

METHOD:

1. Preheat the oven to 300 °F.
2. Lightly grease a loaf pan with olive oil.
3. Add all the ingredients in a bowl and mix well.
4. Pour the batter into greased loaf pan.
5. Bake for about 45 minutes or until a knife comes out of the center clean.
6. Remove from oven and let cool completely before slicing.

The small splash of sweetener and apple cider vinegar allows for the most perfect sweetened combination, sure to have you coming back for another slice, and that's okay because this dessert is supportive of your carb and sugar restrictions! By taking a slice to satisfy that sweet tooth, you barely add on to your daily carb count with only 6g per slice!

4. Dark Chocolate Raspberry Cups

Serves: 14
Prep Time:
~20 min

Nutrition
information
(per serving)

Calories: 222 kcal
Carbs: 3.4g
Fat: 21.6g
Protein: 3.7g
Fiber: 0.6g
Sugar: 0.3g

INGREDIENTS:

Chocolate:
- 1 cup dairy-free, sugar-free dark chocolate (store bought)
- ½ cup cocoa butter
- 2 tbsp. coconut oil
- 1 tsp. vanilla extract

Fruit Topping:
- 1 ½ cups raspberries (fresh or frozen)
- 25 almonds (roasted for about 5 minutes)

Total number of ingredients: 6

METHOD:

1. Place one almond in each raspberry.
2. Space each almond-raspberry on a tray and freeze for about an hour.
3. Place all the chocolate ingredients into a pot over low heat and stir constantly until everything is mixed.
4. Pour the chocolate sauce into individual mini cupcake molds. At about midway mark, place 1-2 almond-raspberries, then cover with a bit more chocolate sauce.
5. Place in the fridge for about 30 minutes or until firm.

If you have not tried a raspberry and chocolate combination, you have not tasted the perfect fruity sweet! These are great as an evening snack or before heading out of the house. With 21.6g of fat, they are sure to satisfy your dietary needs as well.

5. Pumpkin Pie Bites

INGREDIENTS:

- ½ cup pumpkin puree
- 3 drops stevia
- ¼ cup coconut butter, softened
- ½ cup coconut oil, melted
- 2 tsp. cinnamon
- ½ cup pecans

Total number of ingredients: 6

METHOD:

1. Combine the pumpkin puree, coconut oil, and coconut butter in a bowl.
2. Stir in the sweetener and the cinnamon.
3. Mix together evenly and pour into mini molds or an ice cube tray.
4. Refrigerate until firm.

If you are a pumpkin lover, then you are sure to love this recipe! To keep it simple, ensure that you use a pre-made vegan, fresh pumpkin puree for best results! Or if you're up for the task, use a homemade version.

Serves: 15
Prep Time:
~20 min

Nutrition
information
(per serving)

Calories: 124 kcal
Carbs: 2.3g
Fat: 12.4g
Protein: 0.7g
Fiber: 2.0g
Sugar: 0.7g

6. Peanut Butter Brownies

Serves: 8
Prep Time:
~15 min

———

Nutrition
information
(per serving)

Calories: 142 kcal
Carbs: 6g
Fat: 8.8g
Protein: 10.2g
Fiber: 2.7g
Sugar: 1.9g

INGREDIENTS:

- 1½ cups water (room temperature)
- ½ cup peanut butter
- ¼ cup cocoa powder
- 6 drops stevia
- 2 tbsp. coconut flour
- 2 tsp. baking powder
- 2 scoops vegan protein powder of your choice (this recipe uses Vega chocolate-flavored protein powder)

Total number of ingredients: 7

METHOD:

1. Preheat oven to 350 °F.
2. In a bowl, mix the warm water, stevia, and peanut butter.
3. In a separate bowl, mix the cocoa powder, baking powder, Vega protein powder, and coconut flour.
4. Add the mixture from Step 2 to that of Step 3 and mix well.
5. Pour batter into a slightly greased pan and let bake for 40-45 minutes, or until a knife comes out of the center clean.

7. Chocolate Covered Strawberries

Serves: 16
Prep Time:
~20 min

Nutrition
information
(per serving: 4
Strawberries)

Calories: 119 kcal
Carbs: 5.4g
Fat: 9.7g
Protein: 3.1g
Fiber: 0.5g
Sugar: 2.4g

INGREDIENTS:

- **16 Strawberries**
- **¼ of 10 oz. milk-free and sugar-free dark chocolate bar**

Total number of ingredients: 2

METHOD:

1. Melt the chocolate in a pot until it turns into a liquid. Once liquid, keep stirring.
2. Remove from heat and allow to cool and thicken.
3. Dip strawberries in the cooled chocolate, then place them on a parchment-lined tray.
4. Place in the fridge for about an hour or until chocolate is perfectly set.

A simple, tasty treat sure to satisfy any chocolate fruity cravings while still being ketogenic and vegan due to the sugar-free, milk-free chocolate used.

8. Keto-Vegan Chocolate Mousse

Serves: 16
Prep Time:
~20 min

———

Nutrition
information
(per serving)

Calories: 470 kcal
Carbs: 12.8g
Fat: 41.3g
Protein: 5.1g
Fiber: 0.4g
Sugar: 4.6g

INGREDIENTS:

- 1 can coconut milk
- 5-10 drops stevia
- 3 tbsp. coconut oil
- ½ cup cocoa powder
- 2 flax eggs
- 1 tsp. vanilla

Total number of ingredients: 6

METHOD:

1. Pour ½ of the coconut milk into a pot, and add the stevia. Mix until everything is dissolved.
2. Add the rest of the ingredients in a blender and blend well.
3. Pour the coconut milk and stevia mixture into the blender, and blend again.
4. Pour the chocolate mousse into three separate jars and enjoy.

There are so many online adaptations of a delicious, fluffy chocolate mousse. Thanks to the stevia and flax eggs, this recipe satisfies your cravings while remaining keto-vegan.

9. White Chocolate Raspberry Chocolate Chip Squares

Serves: 16
Prep Time:
~20 min

Nutrition
information
(per serving)

Calories: 94 kcal
Carbs: 1.2g
Fat: 9.7g
Protein: 0.5g
Fiber: 0.4g
Sugar: 0.2g

INGREDIENTS:

- ¼ cup coconut oil
- ½ cup cocoa butter
- 1 tsp. vanilla extract
- 1 tsp. salt
- ½ cup fresh raspberries
- ¼ cup store bought dairy-free, sugar-free chocolate chips

Total number of ingredients: 6

METHOD:

1. Add a bit of water to a pan on medium heat.
2. Add cocoa butter and stir until it melts.
3. Add coconut oil, vanilla extract, and salt. Stir well.
4. Remove mixture from pan and place in blender.
5. Blend on high speed for 45 seconds.
6. Evenly place half of the raspberries and chocolate chips on a parchment lined tray.
7. Pour the mixture from Step 5 on top.
8. Add the remaining raspberries and chocolate chips on top.
9. Freeze for about 15 minutes, or until hardened, and break into serving sized pieces.

10. Almond Joy Squares

Serves: 15
Prep Time:
~20 min

Nutrition
information
(per serving)

Calories: 262 kcal
Carbs: 5.9g
Fat: 25.4g
Protein: 2.5g
Fiber: 1.0g
Sugar: 1g

INGREDIENTS:

Chocolate Base:
- ½ cup coconut oil
- ½ cup almond butter
- 1 tsp. stevia
- 6 tbsp. cocoa powder
- 2 tsp. vanilla powder

Coconut Top:
- 1 ⅓ cup shredded coconut, unsweetened
- 6 tbsp. coconut oil
- 1½ tsp. vanilla extract
- 15 almond halves

Total number of ingredients: 9

METHOD:

1. For the topping, melt coconut oil and almond butter on low heat, then add all the other chocolate base ingredients except the vanilla. Mix well.
2. Once the mixture has thickened, stir in the vanilla.
3. Pour the mixture on a nonstick tray and place in the freezer.
4. For the coconut top; melt the coconut oil in a pan and stir in the coconut shreds.
5. Add the remaining coconut top ingredients, and stir until it thickens.
6. Gently place the coconut mixture on top of the hardened chocolate.
7. Space the almonds on top of the coconut mixture, and place in fridge.

Missing that high sugar, artificial candy bar? Here's a healthy, low-carb, low-sugar, energy-packed alternative!

11. Coco-Nuts Cream Cookies

Serves: 10
Prep Time:
~50 min

Nutrition
information
(per serving)

Calories: 24 kcal
Carbs: 5.0g
Fat: 1.2g
Protein: 0.8g
Fiber: 2.8g
Sugar: 1.0g

INGREDIENTS:

- 6 tbsp. coconut or hempseed flour
- 8 tbsp. no-salt cream cheese spread
- ½ tsp. stevia

Filling:
- ¼ cup sugar free strawberry jam

Total number of ingredients: 4

METHOD:

1. Preheat oven at 350°F.
2. Whisk cashew cheese and stevia together in mixing bowl.
3. Stir in flour until completely mixed; knead if necessary.
4. Roll dough out to about 1/8 inch thick.
5. Cut out **10** bottom cookies and **10** top cookies with cookie cutter.
6. Bake on baking sheet with parchment paper for 10-12 minutes until edges turn golden.
7. Remove from oven and cool for **30** minutes.
8. Use teaspoon strawberry jam and spread on bottom cookies.
9. Top with other cookies, making a cookie sandwich.
10. Can be stored for a week or frozen up to two months.

12. Almond Cookies

Serves: 24
Prep Time:
~50 min

Nutrition
information
(per serving)

Calories: 77 kcal
Carbs: 1.7g
Fat: 6.2g
Protein: 1.3g
Fiber: 0.9g
Sugar: 0.6g

INGREDIENTS:

- 1 cup almond butter
- ¾ cup almond flour
- ½ tsp. stevia
- 1 tsp. baking soda
- 1 tsp. vanilla extract

Filling:
- 2/3 cup chopped almonds
- 2 tbsp. coconut flour
- ½ tsp. stevia
- 2 tbsp. water

Total number of ingredients: 9

METHOD:

1. Preheat oven at 350F.
2. Add almond butter, vanilla, and stevia together in mixing bowl and mix.
3. Stir in flour until completely mixed; knead if necessary.
4. Let dough rest for a few minutes.
5. Combine almonds, coconut flour, stevia, and water in a small mixing bowl and set aside.
6. Roll the cookie dough out between two sheets of parchment paper in a ¼ inch thick square.
7. Add a layer of filling to the dough by spreading it around, about a ½ inch away from the sides.
8. Roll the cookie dough slowly into a log on the parchment paper; use parchment paper if necessary.
9. Wrap it in the parchment paper and chill in in the freezer for 15 minutes until firm.
10. Remove from freezer and remove the parchment paper.
11. Cut into 24 ½ inch slices and place on cookie sheet or until there is no space left; make sure there is enough space between each cookie.
12. Make two batches if necessary.
13. Bake for 20-25 minutes until edges turn golden.
14. Remove from oven and cool for 30 minutes.
15. Bake the second batch after, and let cool.
16. Can be stored for a week or frozen up to two months.

13. Chai Latte

Serves: 8
Prep Time:
~60 min

Nutrition
information
(per serving)

Calories: 339 kcal
Carbs: 7.3g
Fat: 33.4g
Protein: 2.4g
Fiber: 2.9g
Sugar: 4.0g

INGREDIENTS:

- ¼ cup cocoa butter
- ¾ cup pre-made tea of your choice (lemon is recommended)
- 2 cups water
- 4 cups full fat coconut milk
- ½ tsp. stevia
- 1-inch cinnamon stick
- 6 cloves
- 6 green cardamom pods, cracked
- 6 black peppercorns
- 1 tsp. fresh minced ginger
- ¼ cup vegan half-and-half cream (optional)

Total number of ingredients: 11

METHOD:

1. Put the cocoa butter, water, coconut milk, stevia, cinnamon, cloves, cardamom, peppercorns, ginger in a pan and bring to a boil.
2. Once boiling, lower the flame and let simmer for 15-20 minutes or until cocoa butter is fully dissolved.
3. Let it cool, strain the mixture with a cheese cloth into a jar, and keep it covered.
4. Pour one cup of strained tea in a cup.
5. Heat it in the microwave if necessary, add half and half cream, and serve.

13. Peanut Butter Cocoa

INGREDIENTS:

- 2 cups full-fat almond milk
- 2 tbsp. peanut butter
- 2 tbsp. unsweetened cocoa powder
- ¼ tsp. stevia or sugar, to taste
- 1 tbsp. vegan nutella (optional)
- Coconut whipped cream (optional)

Total number of ingredients: 6

METHOD:

1. Combine all ingredients in blender; blend until smooth.
2. Serve cold or heat up in small saucepan over stove on low heat for 5 minutes.
3. Pour into glass, and serve with whipped cream if desired.

Serves: 2
Prep Time:
~5 min

Nutrition
information
(per serving)

Calories: 151 kcal
Carbs: 4.5g
Fat: 11.6g
Protein: 7.0g
Fiber: 2.7g
Sugar: 1.1g

14. Matcha Tea

Serves: 2
Prep Time:
~5 min

Nutrition
information
(per serving)

Calories: 306 kcal
Carbs: 8.3g
Fat: 28.7g
Protein: 3.1g
Fiber: 3.4g
Sugar: 4.5g

INGREDIENTS:

- 1 can full-fat coconut milk
- 1 ½ teaspoon green tea matcha powder
- 1 pinch stevia

Total number of ingredients: 6

METHOD:

1. Combine all ingredients in blender; blend until smooth.
2. Serve cold, or heat up in small saucepan over stove on low heat for 5 minutes.
3. Pour into glass, and serve with whipped cream if desired.

15. Raspberry Cheesecake

Serves: 16
Prep Time:
~5 min

Nutrition
information
(per serving)

Calories: 262 kcal
Carbs: 8.2g
Fat: 23g
Protein: 5.6g
Fiber: 1.7g
Sugar: 1.7g

INGREDIENTS:

Pie crust:
- 8 tbsp. hempseeds
- 8 tbsp. finely shredded coconut
- 1 tsp. vanilla extract.

Filling:
- 2 cups no-salt vegan cream cheese
- 2 cups soaked cashews
- 1 cup raspberries
- 4 tbsp. MCT oil
- 2 tbsp. lime juice
- ½ tsp. stevia

Total number of ingredients: 5

METHOD:

1. Soak cashews for 8 hours if not previously soaked.
2. Mix crust ingredients and add flattened layer in a deep baking dish or other container.
3. Combine filling ingredients in blender and process until smooth. Scrape down sides of blender when turned off until you have a smooth mixture.
4. Add an even layer of filling over the crust in the deep container, and let it chill in the freezer for 2 hours until firm.
5. Serve with a couple of fresh raspberries on top.
6. Can be stored in freezer for months.

16. Raspberry Lemon Ice Cream

Serves: 5
Prep Time:
~90 min

**Nutrition
information
(per serving)**

Calories: 198 kcal
Carbs: 8.3g
Fat: 17.5g
Protein: 1.8g
Fiber: 3.9g
Sugar: 4.0g

INGREDIENTS:

- 1 can full fat coconut milk
- 1 tsp. psyllium husk
- 1 cup water
- 1 cup raspberries
- 1 lemon with peel
- Pinch of stevia

Total number of ingredients: 6

METHOD:

1. Combine water and psyllium husk in small pan over medium heat, and stir thoroughly until psyllium husk is dissolved and gel forms.
2. Make about 1 tablespoon of lemon zest from the fresh lemon.
3. Combine coconut milk, stevia, raspberries, lemon zest, lemon juice from 1 lemon, and gel mixture from first step in blender and process until desired consistency.
4. Chill the mixture for 1 hour, and pour into ice cream maker.
5. With no ice cream maker, pour all but ½ cup blended mixture in ice cube tray and freeze.
6. Blend cubed frozen mixture with unfrozen mixture to create delicious ice-cream without an ice-cream maker.

17. Flaxseed Yogurt

Serves: 4
Prep Time:
~5 min

Nutrition
information
(per serving)

Calories: 230 kcal
Carbs: 9.2g
Fat: 16.9g
Protein: 10g
Fiber: 7.4g
Sugar: 0.7g

INGREDIENTS:

- ½ cup hemp seed
- ½ cup flax seed
- 1 cup almond milk
- 2 cups water
- ¼ cup lemon juice
- 2 tsp. psyllium husk
- ¼ teaspoon stevia

Total number of ingredients: 7

METHOD:

1. Make sure 1 cup water is piping hot by boiling it before adding it to a heat safe blender.
2. Combine 1 cup hot water and seeds in blender, and blend until smooth.
3. Add another cup of water, almond milk, and psyllium husk, and blend again for 30 seconds.
4. Add in lemon juice and stevia, and process for a few seconds.
5. Pour into container, and serve chilled.

18. Mini Hazelnut Doughnuts

Serves: 24
Prep Time:
~35 min

Nutrition
information
(per serving)

Calories: 116 kcal
Carbs: 2.8g
Fat: 9.8g
Protein: 4.8g
Fiber: 2.4g
Sugar: 1.1g

INGREDIENTS:

- 4 tbsp. ground hemp seed
- 2 cups almond flour
- ½ cup water
- ½ cup vegan nutella
- ¼ tsp. stevia
- 2 tbsp. flaxseed oil
- 1 tsp. vanilla extract
- 1 tsp. baking powder

Total number of ingredients: 8

METHOD:

1. Preheat oven to 350°F and grease muffin plate or doughnut pan with MCT oil.
2. Combine the hempseed with water, stir, and set aside.
3. Add stevia, flaxseed oil, and vanilla extract to hempseed mixture.
4. Mix baking powder with flour and set aside.
5. Combine vegan nutella with wet hempseed mixture, and stir thoroughly.
6. Mix the flour through the wet mixture, and make sure it's combined well.
7. Put scoops of batter into wells of the doughnut pan or muffin plate.
8. Bake for 30 minutes.
9. Let cool completely before removing from pan or baking plate.

LOW CARB VEGAN MEAL-PREPPING

There is so much we have learnt about ketogenic vegan diet. We have already seen some of the sources of the macros needed by the body, facts about fatty acids and how to balance some the macro-nutrients when dealing with a ketogenic vegan diet. Furthermore, we had a discussion on the importance of this kind of diet. In this section, we focus on how to do prep your meals to ensure that you stick to the rules of keto-vegan diet. Meal-prepping will help you to avoid the trap of unhealthy or fast food options. Knowledge is only one side of the coin, the other is execution.

All of us are under pressure to manage our time since most of us lead extremely busy lives. We are busy. There is no way around it, but we still need to eat and adhere to the strict rules of ketogenic vegan diet. That is exactly why the solution is meal-prepping. When it comes to eating healthy foods, preparation is always the best key to success. Spending your time on cooking and preparing meals is directly linked to having better dietary habits. Meal prepping or meal prep is now becoming a popular craze all throughout the world. It has been going mainstream and more people are now trying their hand on this kind of food preparation system. When engaged on special diets such as Weight Watchers or Ketogenic, you will enjoy the benefits of meal prepping because it can be quite difficult to prepare your dishes especially when you are following a strict diet.

Meal-prepping is exactly as the word is pronounced out; it simply means that an individual prepares a number of meals-- or even all of them --beforehand. Instead of eating ready-made meals which you would normally buy at a store you can now prepare your own. They will be better suited to your taste, contain no preservatives and will be a lot healthier. When you say meal-prepping, it simply means buying fresh produce, cleaning them, and slicing and preparing them soon as they reach your kitchen counter. The idea of meal-prepping is to carefully store ingredients into individual containers and place them for storage inside the fridge or frozen to maintain their freshness. It also makes things easier to prepare meals and create your full meals that would last you for a few days, a week or even months.

Not only will you be able to decide on the correct portions, but you will also be at liberty select the foods that are better for you. When hunger strikes and you do not have time to start cooking a decent meal, you will have already prepared meals to choose from instead of grabbing a pre-packaged meal or snack bought from a store which will only increase your calorie intake and may even harm your body.

IMPORTANCE
OF MEAL-PREPPING

Meal prep can be different from one person to another. Hence it is important that you will find a schedule that will work well for you. Let us look at the advantages of how meal prepping has become a life changer:

- Saves time. Meal-prepping enables you to eat healthy during the week without the hassle of preparing the meals for long hours. When you have an effective meal prep, you can easily prepare meals in a second plus it will lessen the time that you need to go to the supermarket just to buy your meal for the day.
- Saving money. Meal-prepping requires one to buy items like fresh herbs in bulk and use your freezer. This enables one to save more money.
- Allows for multitasking. Since you will have saved time by prepping your meals, you are able to do other tasks as you cook making it a good practice for those individuals who are on the go.
- Having healthy choices of food. Meal-prepping allows you to have your meals planned in a healthy way of your choice. Being busy makes one to go for the fast foods but with meal prep you will avoid fast foods and go for your healthy choices.
- Easy shopping. Meal-prepping helps you to stay organized and have a compiled list of the items you need to prepare your meals. Having a list is a great boost to prevent you from buying sugary products or processed foods that you do not need at all.
- No more stress. One of the greatest problems of busy people is making it home and preparing food. With meal prepping, you will be able to serve the food in a second making it less stressful.
- Learning portion control. When following a strict diet like the ketogenic vegan, portion control is very important. With meal prepping, you are able to determine what food you will consume and the number of calories in them.
- Adding variety to your meal. With meal-prepping, you will not eat the same food over and over again, but you will always have some variety in your meals.

- By creating healthy meals at home, consumption of harmful ingredients from processed food that cause unwanted weight gain are greatly reduced. These include: food additives (for instance, artificial colors and flavors,) preservatives, and overly refined starches. This is helpful when trying to quickly shed off unwanted weight.

If you want meal-prepping to help you lose weight, there are a few steps that you have to take. We have already talked about healthy meals. However, it is very simple to create unhealthy meals when you are meal-prepping as well. In order for you to ensure that your body is getting all of the nutrients that it needs, you need to make sure that you are creating healthy dishes, prepping healthy meals, and then actually eating them.

Breakfast is vital if you want to lose weight, however, it is a meal that so many of us skip or we just grab a cup of coffee as we run out of the door. Take the time to prep your breakfast.

It is vital that you pay attention to the calories that you are consuming. I know, I know, but I am eating healthy foods, why do I have to count calories? The fact is that eating too much of any food, even healthy foods will make you gain weight. Let's think about it for a moment. Imagine that you wake up in the morning and you drink a huge green smoothie that contains 800 calories. Then you eat a salad for lunch that contains another 800 calories. Before you factor in any snacks or dinner, you have already exhausted your daily calorie allowance in accordance with our ketogenic vegan diet in this book. You should determine how many calories you need in a day and break those calories down per meal. You will find guidelines about planning this in the chapter about balancing macro-nutrients in a ketogenic diet.

The next thing that you need to spend some time thinking about is your food struggles. Perhaps you are one of those people that have a hard time eating breakfast before you leave the house in the mornings. You will need to acknowledge this struggle and then be honest with yourself about what you will actually eat. You see, if you choose food that you are not going to eat in the morning you are no better off. If you are in a hurry in the morning, choose a low-carb protein bar or take a smoothie with you when you head to work.

If lunch is a struggle for you then you want to focus on prepping a healthy lunch option that you can grab on your way to work in the mornings. If that 3 pm lull seems to be when you are most tempted to eat junk, make sure that you pack a simple snack as well.

Dinners can be extremely difficult. Coming home after a long day at work, dealing with homework, chores, bills, emails, the phone ringing off of the hook, and in the midst of it, you are supposed to make dinner. It is no wonder so many people turn to easy, prepackaged foods, however, these foods are not going to provide your body with the nutrients that it needs. If preparing a healthy dinner is one of your food struggles, that is where you will want to focus when you first begin meal prepping.

Of course, food, in general, could be the struggle. It is very easy to get caught up in this life and feel like you don't have time to worry about or deal with food. This leads to meals that consist of nothing more than coffee or a can of soda. Eventually, you will become so hungry that you eat everything in sight and doing this over and over will lead to weight gain. If you struggle with getting enough food, you may want to prep 2 or 3 days' worth of meals and snacks at a time because you will need to prep all of your meals and snacks.

You want to create some snack, grab bags. Use a food container and place one portion of your food in it and grab one when you need a snack. This will not only ensure that you are not eating the entire container, but it is also going to ensure that you have a quick snack to grab and take with you when you are in a hurry.

BALANCING MACRO-NUTRIENTS IN A KETOGENIC DIET

The challenge of a ketogenic vegan diet lies in getting a sufficient amount of calories, mainly from proteins and fats. You may calculate your daily calories or weight loss using various tools available to you, for example: **happyhealthygreen.life/tools** As a rule of thumb, women are recommended to consume 2000 calories on a daily basis. For men, the amount is 2500.

A typical keto vegan diet, also known as a "long-chain triglyceride diet," usually includes a consumption ratio of 3 to 4 grams of fat for every 1 gram of carbohydrate and protein.

In order to ensure you are taking in accurate levels of each macro, you should make sure that you track your daily nutrient levels. The average percentage for each macro level for a ketogenic-vegan diet is 5% carbohydrates, 20% protein, and 75% fats.

Macro	Protein	Carbs	Fat	Total Calories
Ratio	20%	5%	75%	
Kcal & Grams	320 kcal/80 gr.	80 kcal/20 gr. net carbs	1200 kcal/ 133.3 gr.	1600
	360 kcal/ 90 gr.	90 kcal/22.5 gr net carbs	1350 kcal/ 150 gr.	1800
	400 kcal/ 100 gr.	100 kcal/25 gr net carbs	1500 kcal/ 166.7 gr.	2000
	500 kcal/ 125 gr.	125kcal/31.2 gr. net carbs	1875 kcal/ 208.3 gr.	2500
	600 kcal/ 150 gr.	150kcal/37.5 gr. net carbs	2250 kcal/ 250 gr.	3000

Let's look at our 1600 calorie keto-vegan meal plan. If you are supposed to eat 1600 calories per day and you are eating three meals plus two snacks, you need to be able to break your calories up so that you are getting enough throughout the day.

First, you will divide the number of calories that you eat each day by 4. This is 400 if you are eating a 1600 calorie a day diet. Therefore, your breakfast, lunch, and dinner should all be about 400 calories each. Then you will take the leftover 400 calories and divide that by 2 which is 200 and that is the number of calories your snacks can have in them.

Important things to keep in mind

1. Always check your labels

Carbs are calculated differently depending on where you live. The U.S., Canada and other countries have labels where total carbs include fiber. So in order to calculate net carbs, you must deduct fiber from the total amount of carbs.

On the other hand, countries like the U.K. and Australia don't include fiber in the total carb amount labeled.

If you want to track total carbs for a very low-carb diet, be sure that your diet supplements you with the necessary micronutrients. Extremely low-carb diets (20 grams of total carbs or less) can often be deficient in several micronutrients (magnesium, calcium, potassium, vitamin E, A, C, iron, thiamin, folate and zinc).

2. Artificial Sweeteners

Most artificial sweeteners are often marketed as "sugar-free" or "zero carbs". Unfortunately, this isn't always the case. Some sweeteners like Stevia, Erythritol and Monk Fruit extract contain very few carbs while others like Xylitol or Tagatose contain massive amounts.

So, if you use products that contain Erythritol, Xylitol or sweeteners containing fructo-oligosaccharides (FOS), always remember to account for the added carbs.

3. Products Labeled "Low-carb"

Avoid most products labeled "low-carb" and "sugar free", etc. Most of these products contain more carbs than the manufacturer claims and are often processed with unhealthy ingredients.

HOW TO COUNT CARBS?

Although most people on a low-carb diet count net carbs (total carbs minus fiber), the latest research hints at the importance of counting total carbs. In this scenario, consuming a very low-carb diet consisting of 20 grams or less of total carbs is the correct way to count carbs.

Although many believe that counting total carbs and ascribing to a very low-carb diet is the best way to lose weight, it is also important to understand how fiber works on blood sugar and, subsequently, overall metabolic health.

There are two types of fiber: soluble and insoluble. Most people think that dietary fiber does not affect blood sugar and that there are no calories given off at all, so they choose to use net carbs, total carbs minus fiber. However, this only applies to insoluble fiber, as this type of fiber cannot be absorbed by the body and doesn't affect blood sugar or ketosis.

Let's explain this in another way. Dietary fiber is indigestible and has two main components: insoluble fiber and soluble fiber. Once consumed, these fibers are fermented by the gut's microbiota into the short-chain fatty acid.

How does soluble fiber work?

The body absorbs calories from soluble fiber. The effect that it has on blood sugar is a bit more complicated. Ketosis can, in fact, be affected by soluble fiber because it is absorbed into the body and increases blood sugar, hence the discussion about using total carbs rather than net carbs.

When soluble fiber ferments in the large intestine, it starts producing gut hormones that help create a feeling of satiety. This appetite suppression is natural and contributes as the main reason that a low carb diet for weight loss can be very successful.

Recent studies have shown that soluble fiber plays a role in lowering blood sugar levels, although much more testing must be done to understand the effects of dietary fiber on metabolic health.

Total Carbs or Net Carbs?

High levels of ketones and low levels of glucose are not the main factors contributing to weight loss. Studies do not show that adding more ketones to the blood leads to greater and more rapid fat loss. In fact, the most important effect that a low-carb diet demonstrates, time and time again, is appetite suppression.

The body does not need to be in ketosis in order to lose weight. In fact, people who consume more than 50g of total carbs per day can continue to lose weight even though the body is not in any stage of ketosis.

There are differences of opinion whether to count total or net carbs regarding the "ideal" carb level. It has been suggested that ~ 50 grams of total carbs a day is enough to start nutritional ketosis. This is in between the range of 20-35 grams of net carbs depending on the fiber content. Most people on a ketogenic diet are successful in losing weight using this approach.

A different approach to a low carb diet recommends that you should have ~ 20 grams of total carbs a day. If you choose to track total carbs and follow a very low-carb diet, be sure to supplement your diet with necessary micronutrients, as extremely low-carb diets (20 grams of total carbs or less) are often deficient in several of these (magnesium, calcium, potassium, vitamin E, A, C, iron, thiamin, folate and zinc).

Above all, it is important to note that there is no wrong way to look at this. A ketogenic diet changes depending on what your goals are.

GETTING STARTED

Start simply and slowly. Remember that you are starting on a new venture so do not get overwhelmed and confuse yourself with too many details. Begin with some of your favorite, trusted recipes. Once you are comfortable, you can gradually incorporate new, healthier recipes and try out different ingredients and foods.

1. Choose a day

Take a hard look at your weekly program before you decide which day to choose for your meal-prepping. Do not try to squeeze it in on a weeknight after a long and hard day at the office. You will simply be too exhausted and will soon feel discouraged. Most people prefer Saturdays or Sundays when they are free from work and the family is home to lend a hand. You can even turn it into a fun, educational activity with the kids.

It might be easier to pick two different days of the week, for example Wednesdays and Sundays in order to lighten the load. These two days seem to be the preference amongst people more experienced in meal-prepping.

Initially though, do not try to prepare more than three meals in advance. As you gain more experience, you will be able to work faster and more efficiently and can increase the number of meals and snacks you can comfortably cope with.

2. Choose the meals

Your first choice is to decide whether you want to start with dinner, lunch or maybe breakfast. If you possess a big family, you might feel that in the evenings you have the least time and energy to cook big meals and therefore decide to start with one or more dinners. Lunch or breakfast might be a better option to start with if you live alone or are part of a couple. Remember, you are in control and should decide what is best for you.

Once you have come to a decision where to start, you are on to the next step: choosing your recipes. The most practical will be to use the exact same recipe for three different meals, but you may have a revolt on your hands if you dish up the exact same dinner three nights in a row. Defer the revolution by freezing one or two of them and dish them up over a longer period of time.

If you prepare a few meals a week, it is important to balance your meals. That means your next decision will be on balancing the macronutrients in each meal as you adhere to the keto ratio of 70% fats, 20% proteins and 5% carbohydrates. This is how different nutrients convert into calorie:

- *1g of Proteins = 4 Calories*
- *1g Carbs = 4 Calories*
- *1g Fats = 9 Calories*

For this purpose, you will need a kitchen scale. You can also use it to weigh your food portions.

3. Choose the correct containers

It is of the utmost importance that you use the correct containers for your food. Air tight containers are best to keep your food fresh and crispy both in the fridge and freezer. Using proper storage containers have many benefits and the success of your efforts rely on this.

The size of the containers you choose is quite important. Do you want to store individual portions or enough food for the whole family? How big are your portions? Ideally you want all of the containers to be the same size and shape to save space in your fridge or freezer and make them easier to stack but if this is not practical, buy different sizes for different foods. Do not empty the store on your first shopping trip, rather purchase a few and increase the number as you go along and find out exactly what your needs are.

Do not simply chuck the whole meal into one container. This will only spoil your hard work. Choose containers with dividers or different sections so that you can separate different foods. You do not want your meat and veggies to fuse into a stew. This will also prevent cross-contamination and improve the taste, look and freshness of your prepped meals.

Before you purchase any storage containers for food, always check the bottom to ensure that they are all BPA free. BPA stands for bispherol, an industrial chemical used to manufacture plastic containers. This chemical may seep into the food and be harmful to your health. BPA free containers may be used in the microwave and are absolutely safe.

Using clear containers can make life a lot easier. As your confidence grows and you prepare more meals in advance, it will help you to see what is stored inside them. Strictly follow the meal plan in this book or you may add sticker showing the date and name of the meal if you plan to freeze the prepped meals.

To summarize: Make sure that your storage containers are all BPA free, suitable for the microwave and dishwasher, freezer safe, are easy to stack and are reusable. The microwave is an essential equipment that you will always use to reheat the prepped food. If you follow these guidelines to the latter, you will save time and money and make your food prepping a lot easier.

How to prepare for the meal prepping day

1. First step - Take inventory

The first thing you ought to do when for your day of meal prepping is to take inventory of what you already have in your cabinets, freezer, and refrigerator.

Create a list of all of the items that you have. As you are going through the recipes that you plan on cooking check your list to determine if you already have any of the ingredients. Make sure that you put a check mark next to them if you are going to use them in a recipe so that you do not plan on using the same ingredient more than once. This is not only going to save you money and time, but it is also going to help you use up the foods that are taking up space in your kitchen.

2. Second step – Organize

While you are taking your inventory, you will want to organize. Clean out your cabinets, wipe them down and put all of the food back in them, making sure that they are organized. Do the same to your fridge, freezer and deep freeze.

It is very important that you clean out your refrigerator because, with all of the food that you are going to prep, you are going to want to make sure that you have enough space in your fridge. Make sure that when you put the prepped foods in the fridge, the foods that you are going to eat first are in the front.

3. Third step - Put on the calendar

So many times, people create meal plans, make wonderful grocery lists, buy all of the ingredients that they need, then by Tuesday, they have no idea what they are supposed to cook. In order to avoid this, put your meals on your calendar. You can buy a calendar for your kitchen so that you mark the meal plans in this book categorized in days on it.

This way, when it comes time to grab your prepped food out of the fridge, all you have to do is look at your calendar and you will know exactly what you need to grab. When you are adding the meals to your calendar, make sure that you check your schedule. There is no reason to prep lunch on Thursday if there is going to be a team lunch at work. There is no reason to prep dinner if you know you are going to be visiting family one evening for dinner. Making sure that you are not over prepping is going to make things a lot easier for you.

4. Fourth step 4 - Schedule it

There is no point in doing all of the preparation when it comes to meal prepping if you don't have the time to actually prep the meals. Make sure that you have time scheduled each week for your meal prepping, even if you have to split it up over a few evenings.

ESSENTIAL TOOLS WHEN MEAL-PREPPING

To ensure speedy weight loss, there are a few items you should invest in, such as:

1. Baking trays, cake racks, muffin tins, and other baking tools like: aluminum foil, muffin liners, parchment paper, saran wrap, silicon baking mats, etc. These make portioning out and pre-cooking dishes easier and faster. Baking snacks and meals are also far healthier than frying food and requires less effort than barbecuing or grilling food outdoors.

2. Food dehydrators are great for making fruit or vegetable snacks, but these can always dry slowly in a conventional oven.

3. Bento boxes, mason jars, and other food storage containers with air-tight lids for both liquids and solids. Use these to store portioned-out ingredients in the fridge until ready to use. To save money, choose vessels that have multiple purposes.

4. Mason jars can easily store freshly made fruit juices, shakes, and smoothies. With an airtight lid, these could be packed with one's daily lunch or taken to picnics or other outdoor events. These also make wonderful non-reactive containers for homemade ferments, pickles, and yogurt.

5. Invest also in several freezer- and microwavable-safe containers with tight-fitting lids. These will come in handy when making soups and stews or when precooking large batches of meals.

6. Blender (immersion or stovetop) and food processor. Use any appliance, machine, or tool that will make chopping easier because meal-prepping entails LOTS of chopping, mincing, and slicing. Using these will lessen physical stress when preparing dishes in large quantities.

7. Or, if preferring to do things the long way, consider chopping ingredients by hand as a form of physical exercise.

8. Other items to invest in are: food grater, quality sharp knives, mixing bowls, sturdy chopping/cutting board, and vegetable peeler. Optional tools that will make food prepping easier include: mandolin (vegetable chopper) spiralizer, rice shapers, and sandwich presses.

9. Colanders and strainers for rinsing and draining ingredients come particularly handy when draining noodles and rinsing out rice and veggies. Plastic colanders are great for rinsing out large volumes of fresh produce. Metal strainers come in handy when handling hot or fried food.

10. Labelling implements like dry erase markers, papers, sharpies, stickers, sticky notes, and transparent adhesive tape. Meticulously label containers or food packets when meal-prepping. Add details like: ingredients, portions, when or where these should be used, what recipe these should be included in, and date or time of when these should be served, etc.
Properly labelling containers or food packets will ensure that nothing in your fridge or pantry will ever go bad or unused. You don't have to bank on your memory when trying to create dishes in a hurry.

11. If preparing favorite drinks, dishes, or snacks, it might be a good idea to print out the recipes, laminate these, and attach to bottles and/or food containers, as needed. This helps lessen the need to redundantly write out labels.

12. Measuring cups and spoons and a kitchen counter scale are needed for measuring and portioning out ingredients and meals.
Optional: if steaming larger volumes of food, it would be better to invest in either an electric or stovetop steamer, preferably with several layers or tiers. Or, opt for bamboo steamers, which can be set over any large mouthed pot or wok. These can be used as serving dishes as well.

30-DAY LOW CARB MEAL-PLAN

This is our low carb meal plan, complete with shopping list for 30 days. The macro count for this meal plan is based on 1600 calories a day and easy to customize for higher caloric needs.

With 20 grams net carbs and a ratio of 5% carbs, 30% protein and 65% fats, we included a slightly higher protein balance for those with an active lifestyle to make sure that your body gets what it needs and stays in the best shape.

The meal plan consists of 5 days for each week including a shopping list for each week. That way it is easier to plan your shopping and prepping days.

Meal Plan Week 1

MEAL PLAN	MONDAY
Breakfast	*The Ultimate Green Smoothie* (1 serving) + 4 scoops low carb protein powder
	444 cal 4g carbs 17.1g fat 90g protein
	Salad - 1 cup raw arugula, ¼ cup sliced cucumber, 2 cherry tomatoes, 1 tablespoon flaxseed oil
	134 cal 0g carbs 13.7g fat 1g protein
A.M Snack	*Coconut Berry Bomb*
	1 serving
	217cal 1.8g carbs 21.9g fats 1.1g protein
Lunch	*Tofu and Broccoli Filled Avocado*
	1 serving
	290 cal 1.5g carbs 27g fat 2.1g protein
	Salad - 1cup bok choy, 1 tablespoon olive oil
	128 cal 0 carbs 13.6g fat 1g protein
P.M. Snack	*Raspberry Almond Chocolate Brittle*
	1 serving
	148 cal 4.4g carbs 12.5g fat 2.7g protein
Dinner	*Mac n' Cheeze*
	1 serving
	266 cal 2.6g carbs 15.4g fat 20.2g protein
Goal 1600 cal	1620 kcal
carbs	14.3 gr.
fats	121.2 gr.
protein	118.1 gr.

MEAL PLAN	TUESDAY
Breakfast	*Raspberry Avocado Smoothie* (1 serving) + 4 scoops low carb protein powder
	652 cal 8.7g carbs 26.6g fat 90.9g protein
	Salad - 1 cup shredded romaine lettuce, ¼ cup chopped zucchini, 1 tablespoon flaxseed oil
	132 cal 0g carbs 13.7g fat 1g protein
A.M Snack	*Nut Mania Fat Bomb*
	1 serving
	217 cal 1.7g carbs 21.7g fat 0.4g protein
Lunch	*Cauliflower Soup*
	1 serving
	43 cal 3.1g carbs 2.2g fat 1.4g protein
	Salad - 2 cups spinach
	133 cal 0 carbs 0g fat 1.7g protein
P.M. Snack	*Chocolate Orange Nut Clusters*
	4 servings
	264 cal 2.4g carbs 37.2g fat 4.4g protein
Dinner	*Pad Thai Noodles*
	1 servings
	236 cal 3.9g carbs 19.5g fat 8.8g protein
Goal 1600 cal	1606 kcal.
carbs	19.8 gr.
fats	120.9 gr.
protein	107.2 gr.

MEAL PLAN	WEDNESDAY
Breakfast	*Nutty Green Smoothie* (1 serving) + 4 scoops low carb protein powder
	652 cal 4g carbs 26.6g fat 90.7g protein
	Salad - 1 cup raw arugula, ¼ cup sliced cucumber, 2 cherry tomatoes, 1 tablespoon flaxseed oil
	134 cal 0g carbs 13.7g fat 1g protein
A.M Snack	*Lemon Zest Fat Bomb*
	2 servings
	156 cal 1.2g carbs 15.4g fat 1g protein
Lunch	*Tofu-Mushroom Lettuce Wraps*
	1 serving
	133 cal 4.3g carbs 7.7g fat 5.6g protein
	Salad - 1cup bok choy, 2 tablespoons olive oil
	128 cal 0 carbs 27.2g fat 1g protein
P.M. Snack	*Fudgy Peanut Butter Cubes*
	1 serving
	313 cal 3.3g carbs 30g fat 5.1g protein
Dinner	*Zucchini Risotto*
	1 serving
	161 cal 7.4g carbs 11.2g fat 5.1g protein
Goal 1600 cal	1635 kcal.
carbs	20.2 gr.
fats	124.1 gr.
protein	109.5 gr.

MEAL PLAN	THURSDAY
Breakfast	*The Ultimate Green Smoothie* (1 serving) + 4 scoops low carb protein powder
	444 cal 4g carbs 17.1g fat 90g protein
	Salad - 1 cup shredded romaine lettuce, ¼ cup chopped zucchini, 1 tablespoon flaxseed oil
	132 cal 0g carbs 13.7g fat 1g protein
A.M Snack	*Strawberry Coconut Fat Bomb*
	2 servings
	162 cal 1.2g carbs 16.2g fat 0.8g protein
Lunch	*Baked Green Beans*
	1 serving
	98 cal 4.8g carbs 4.4g fat 2.8g protein
	Salad - 2 cups spinach, 2 tablespoons olive oil
	252 cal 0 carbs 27.2g fat 1.7g protein
P.M. Snack	*Coconut Balls*
	2 servings
	286 cal 1.4g carbs 29.8g fat 1.0g protein
Dinner	*Tofu and Broccoli Filled Avocado*
	1 serving
	290 cal 1.5g carbs 27g fat 2.1g protein
Goal 1600 cal	1667 kcal.
carbs	12.9 gr.
fats	135.4 gr.
protein	99.4 gr.

MEAL PLAN	FRIDAY
Breakfast	*Raspberry Avocado Smoothie* (1 serving) + 4 scoops low carb protein powder
	652 cal 8.7g carbs 26.6g fat 90.9g protein
	Salad - 1 cup raw arugula, ¼ cup sliced cucumber, 2 cherry tomatoes, 1 tablespoon flaxseed oil
	134 cal 0g carbs 13.7g fat 1g protein
A.M Snack	*Maple Pecan Fat Bomb*
	1 serving
	285 cal 2.3g carbs 28g fat 3.7g protein
Lunch	*Creamy Mushroom Soup*
	1 serving
	119 cal 2.9g carbs 10.3g fat 1.9g protein
	Salad - 1cup bok choy, 1 tablespoons olive oil
	128 cal 0 carbs 13.6g fat 1g protein
P.M. Snack	*Ginger Fat Bombs*
	1 serving
	137 cal 1.1g carbs 13.7g fat 0.8g protein
Dinner	*Pad Thai Noodles*
	1 servings
	236 cal 3.9g carbs 19.5g fat 8.8g protein
Goal 1600 cal	**1636 kcal.**
carbs	18.9 gr.
fats	125.4 gr.
protein	108.1 gr.

Grocery List Week 1

- 1 container low carb vegan protein powder
- 3 packages of spinach
- 2 avocadoes
- 2 cucumbers
- 1 package parsley
- 3 (14 oz.) cans coconut milk
- 1 package pistachios
- 1 bottle of vanilla extract
- 1 bottle of stevia
- 1 package of fresh mint
- 3 bunches arugula
- 6 cherry tomatoes
- 1 bottle flaxseed oil
- 1 head romaine lettuce
- 1 package coconut butter
- 1 bottle coconut oil
- 1 small package blueberries
- 1 package vanilla powder
- 1 bottle lemon juice
- 1 package almond butter
- 1 package almond milk(500ml)
- 1 package of chopped almonds
- 1 package of salt
- 1 package of pistachios
- 1 lemon
- 1 package of pecans
- 1 bag of almond flour
- 1 package of shredded coconut
- 1 bottle Dijon mustard
- 1 bottle olive oil

- 1 package chili flakes
- 1 package pepper
- 1 package cumin
- 14 oz. non-GMO extra firm tofu
- 1 head broccoli florets
- 1 package vegetable stock
- 1 package thyme powder
- 1 package matcha green tea powder
- 1 head of garlic
- 908 grams mushrooms
- 1 head romaine lettuce
- 1 pound fresh green beans
- 1 package ground flax meal
- 1 package onion powder
- 1 head bok choy
- 1 package dark cocoa powder
- 1 package chopped walnuts
- 254 grams frozen raspberries
- 1 package cinnamon
- 1 orange
- 1 package peanut butter
- 1 package ginger powder
- 1 package nutritional yeast
- 250ml vanilla almond milk
- 2 bell peppers
- 1 package garlic powder
- 1 package hemp seeds
- 2 (908g packages) shirataki noodles
- 3 onions

- 1 bottle dark soy sauce
- 1 bottle lime juice
- 1 package red chili
- 3 red bell peppers
- 2 454g packages shirataki macaroni
- 1 head cauliflower
- 1 package raw cashews

Meal Plan Week 2

MEAL PLAN	MONDAY
Breakfast	*Chia Seed Pudding* (1 serving) + 4 scoops low carb protein powder
	771 cal 7.6g carbs 34.6g fat 94.6g protein
	Salad - 1 cup raw arugula, ¼ cup sliced cucumber, 2 cherry tomatoes, 1 tablespoon flaxseed oil
	134 cal 0g carbs 13.7g fat 1g protein
A.M Snack	*Ginger Fat Bombs*
	1 serving
	137 cal 1.1g carbs 13.7g fat 0.8g protein
Lunch	*Dijon Avocado Salad*
	1 serving
	182 cal 1.3g carbs 14g fat 2.5g protein
P.M. Snack	*Flaxseed Yogurt*
	1 serving
	230 cal 1.8g carbs 16.9g fat 10g protein
Dinner	*Mediterranean-Style Pasta*
	1 serving
	117 cal 5.3g carbs 8.7g fat 1.8g protein
	Salad - 1 cup shredded bok choy, 1 teaspoon vinegar, 1 tablespoon olive oil
	69.7 cal 0g carbs 13.6 g fat 1.0g protein
Goal 1600 cal	**1552 kcal.**
carbs	17.1 gr.
fats	115.2 gr.
protein	111.7 gr.

MEAL PLAN	TUESDAY
Breakfast	***Raspberry Avocado Smoothie*** (1 serving) + 4 scoops low carb protein powder
	652 cal 8.7g carbs 26.6g fat 90.9g protein
	Salad - 1 cup shredded romaine lettuce, ¼ cup chopped zucchini, 1 tablespoon flaxseed oil
	132 cal 0g carbs 13.7g fat 1g protein
A.M Snack	***Peach Cake Cheeseballs***
	1 serving
	182 cal 6.4g carbs 10.8g fat 13.1g protein
Lunch	***Caesar Salad***
	1 serving
	160 cal 2.8g carbs 11.3g fat 5.2g protein
P.M. Snack	***Chocolate Orange Nut Clusters***
	1 serving
	66 cal 0.6g carbs 9.3g fat 1.1g protein
Dinner	***Tofu and Broccoli Filled Avocado***
	1 serving
	290 cal 1.5g carbs 27g fat 2.1g protein
	Salad - 1 cup shredded bok choy, 1 tablespoon olive oil
	128 cal 0 carbs 13.6g fat 1g protein
Goal 1600 cal	**1548 kcal.**
carbs	20 gr.
fats	112.3 gr.
protein	114.4 gr.

MEAL PLAN	WEDNESDAY
Breakfast	*Nutty Green Smoothie* (1 serving) + 4 scoops low carb protein powder
	652 cal 4g carbs 26.6g fat 90.7g protein
	Salad - 1 cup raw arugula, ¼ cup sliced cucumber, 2 cherry tomatoes, 1 tablespoon flaxseed oil
	134 cal 0g carbs 13.7g fat 1g protein
A.M Snack	*Mini Hazelnut Doughnuts*
	2 servings
	232 cal 0.8g carbs 19.6g fat 9.6g protein
Lunch	*Curried Kale Salad*
	1 serving
	94 cal 6.3g carbs 6g fat 1.5g protein
P.M. Snack	*Peach Protein Bars*
	1 serving
	270 cal 3.9g carbs 19.3g fat 9.1g protein
Dinner	*Creamy Mushroom Soup*
	1 serving
	119 cal 2.9g carbs 10.3g fat 1.9g protein
	Salad - 2 cups spinach, 2 tablespoons olive oil
	133 cal 0g carbs 27.2 g fat 1.7g protein
Goal 1600 cal	**1637 kcal.**
carbs	17.9 gr.
fats	122.7 gr.
protein	115.5 gr.

MEAL	THURSDAY
Breakfast	*Matcha Pudding* (1 serving) + 4 scoops low carb protein powder
	684 cal 9.4g carbs 31.8g fat 91.1g protein
	Salad - 1 cup raw arugula, ¼ cup sliced cucumber, 2 cherry tomatoes, 1 tablespoon flaxseed oil
	134 cal 0g carbs 13.7g fat 1g protein
A.M Snack	*Fudgy Peanut Butter Cubes*
	1 serving
	313 cal 3.3g carbs 30g fat 5.1g protein
Lunch	*Dijon Avocado Salad*
	1 serving
	182 cal 1.3g carbs 14g fat 2.5g protein
P.M. Snack	*Chocolate Orange Nut Clusters*
	2 servings
	132 cal 1.2g carbs 18.6g fat 2.2g protein
Dinner	*Cheddar Cheese*
	1 serving
	47 cal 2.7g carbs 3g fat 1.3g protein
	Salad - 2 cups spinach, 1 tablespoon olive oil
	133 cal 0g carbs 13.7g fat 1.7g protein
Goal 1600 cal	1625 kcal.
carbs	17.9 gr.
fats	124.8 gr.
protein	104.9 gr.

MEAL	FRIDAY
Breakfast	*Chia Seed Pudding (*1 serving) + 4 scoops low carb protein powder
	771 cal 7.6g carbs 34.6g fat 94.6g protein
	Salad - 1 cup shredded romaine lettuce, ¼ cup chopped zucchini, 1 tablespoon flaxseed oil
	132 cal 0g carbs 13.7g fat 1g protein
A.M Snack	*Ginger Fat Bombs*
	1 serving
	137 cal 1.1g carbs 13.7g fat 0.8g protein
Lunch	*Caesar Salad*
	1 serving
	160 cal 2.8g carbs 11.3g fat 5.2g protein
P.M. Snack	*Fudgy Peanut Butter Cubes*
	1 serving
	313 cal 3.3g carbs 30g fat 5.1g protein
Dinner	*Sesame Seed Cheese*
	1 serving
	57 cal 1.2g carbs 4.9g fat 1.0g protein
	Salad - 2 cups shredded bok choy
	18 cal 0g carbs 0.3g fat 2.1g protein
Goal 1600 cal	1588 kcal.
carbs	16 gr.
fats	108.5 gr.
protein	109.8 gr.

Grocery list Week 2

- 1 container low carb vegan protein powder
- 1 package coconut butter
- 1 bottle olive oil
- 1 package shredded coconut
- 1 package ginger powder
- 1 package chia seeds
- 3 14oz cans coconut milk
- 1 package cocoa powder
- 1 bottle liquid stevia
- 1 package cinnamon
- 3 bunches arugula
- 1 bottle flaxseed oil
- 6 cherry tomatoes
- 4 -5 heads romaine lettuce
- 1 zucchini
- 1 cucumber
- 3 avocadoes
- 1 bunch fresh mint
- 1 bottle vanilla extract
- ½ cup spinach
- 1 package pistachios
- 1 package matcha powder
- 1 Small package strawberries
- 1 bottle coconut oil
- 1 package coconut cream
- 1 batch *hazelnut spread* (see recipe)
- 1 package hempseed
- 1 package dried peach powder
- 1 package nutritional yeast

- 1 bag almond flour
- 1 batch *vegan nutella* (see recipe)
- 1 package baking powder
- 1 pot peanut butter
- 500ml vanilla flavored almond milk
- 1 (454gram package) mixed lettuce
- 1 head garlic
- 1 bottle Dijon mustard
- 1 package salt
- 1 package pepper
- 1 bunch parsley
- 1 bottle lemon juice
- 1 container capers with brine
- 1 onion
- 1 package curry powder
- 1 lemon
- 1 bunch kale
- 1 bunch cilantro
- 1 package flaxseed
- 1 package psyllium husk
- 1 package stevia powder
- 1 package baking soda
- 1 package chopped pecans
- 1 bag coconut flour
- 1 package peanuts
- 1 package dehydrated peaches
- 1 package dark cocoa powder
- 1 package chopped walnuts
- 1 package cinnamon
- 1 orange

- 1 head bok choy
- 1 bottle vinegar
- 1 (454gram package) spinach
- 1 zucchini
- 1 bottle sun-dried tomatoes
- 1 bottle capers
- 3 Kalamata olives
- 1 package chili flakes
- 1 package cumin
- 1 (4oz. package) non-GMO extra firm tofu
- 1 head broccoli

- 1 head cauliflower
- 1 package onion powder
- 1 8oz. package white mushrooms
- 1 package agar-agar
- 1 package raw cashews
- 1 bottle sesame tahini
- 1 package paprika
- 1 package sea salt
- 1 package garlic powder
- 1 package cayenne
- 1 package dry mustard
- 1 package sesame seeds

Meal Plan Week 3

MEAL	MONDAY
Breakfast	*The Ultimate Green Smoothie* (1 serving) + 3 scoops low carb protein powder
	444 cal 4g carbs 17.1g fat 67.5g protein
	Salad - 1 cup raw arugula, ¼ cup sliced cucumber, 2 cherry tomatoes, 1 tablespoon flaxseed oil
	134 cal 0g carbs 13.7g fat 1g protein
A.M Snack	*Coconut Berry Bomb*
	1 serving
	217cal 1.8g carbs 21.9g fats 1.1g protein
Lunch	*Tofu-Mushroom Lettuce Wraps*
	1 serving
	133 cal 4.3g carbs 7.7g fat 5.6g protein
P.M. Snack	*Coconut Almond Loaf*
	1 serving
	250 cal 3.1g carbs 20.4g fat 6.5g protein
Dinner	*Shiritaki Alfredo*
	1 serving
	377 cal 5.8g carbs 34.3g fat 5.6g protein
	Salad - 2 cups shredded romaine lettuce, 1 tablespoon olive oil
	135 cal 0g carbs 13.6g fat 1.2g protein
Goal 1600 cal	**1583 kcal.**
carbs	19 gr.
fats	128.7 gr.
protein	87.7 gr.

MEAL	TUESDAY
Breakfast	*Raspberry Avocado Smoothie* (1 serving) + 3 scoops low carb protein powder
	652 cal 8.7g carbs 26.6g fat 75.4g protein
	Salad - 1 cup shredded romaine lettuce, ¼ cup chopped zucchini, 1 tablespoon flaxseed oil
	132 cal 0g carbs 13.7g fat 1g protein
A.M Snack	*Coconut Almond Loaf*
	1 serving
	250 cal 3.1g carbs 20.4g fat 6.5g protein
Lunch	*Pad Thai Noodles*
	1 servings
	236 cal 3.9g carbs 19.5g fat 8.8g protein
P.M. Snack	*Nut Mania Fat Bomb*
	1 serving
	217 cal 1.7g carbs 21.7g fat 0.4g protein
Dinner	*Guacamole*
	1 serving
	157 cal 2.0g carbs 8.0g fat 1.0g protein
	Salad - 2 cups swiss chard, 1 tablespoon olive oil
	133 cal 0g carbs 13.6g fat 1.3g protein
Goal 1600 cal	**1585 kcal.**
carbs	19.8 gr.
fats	123.5 gr.
protein	93.4 gr.

MEAL	WEDNESDAY
Breakfast	*Nutty Green Smoothie* (1 serving) + 4 scoops low carb protein powder
	652 cal 4g carbs 26.6g fat 90.7g protein
	Salad - 1 cup raw arugula, ¼ cup sliced cucumber, 2 cherry tomatoes, 1 tablespoon flaxseed oil
	134 cal 0g carbs 13.7g fat 1g protein
A.M Snack	*Lemon Zest Fat Bomb*
	2 servings
	156 cal 1.2g carbs 15.4g fat 1g protein
Lunch	*Mac n' Cheeze*
	1 serving
	266 cal 2.6g carbs 15.4g fat 20.2g protein
P.M. Snack	*Low Carb Corn Bread*
	1 serving
	138 cal 6.0g carbs 10.7g fat 3.5g protein
Dinner	*Creamy Mushroom Soup*
	1 serving
	119 cal 2.9g carbs 10.3g fat 1.9g protein
	Salad - 2 cups spinach, 2 tablespoons olive oil
	133 cal 0g carbs 27.2g fat 1.7g protein
Goal 1600 cal	**1620 kcal.**
carbs	16.7 gr.
fats	119.3 gr.
protein	120 gr.

MEAL	THURSDAY
Breakfast	*Chia Seed Pudding* (1 serving) + 4 scoops low carb protein powder
	771 cal 7.6g carbs 34.6g fat 94.6g protein
	Salad - 1 cup shredded romaine lettuce, ¼ cup chopped zucchini, 2 tablespoons flaxseed oil
	132 cal 0g carbs 27.4g fat 1g protein
A.M Snack	*Dried Fruit and Nut Granola*
	1 serving
	231 cal 3.7g carbs 19.8g fat 6.3g protein
Lunch	*Ramen Noodles*
	1 serving
	136 cal 4.8g carbs 10.4g fat 7.0g protein
P.M. Snack	*Strawberry Coconut Fat Bomb*
	2 servings
	162 cal 1.2g carbs 16.2g fat 0.8g protein
Dinner	*Cauliflower Soup*
	1 serving
	43 cal 3g carbs 2.2g fat 1.4g protein
	Salad - 2 cups swiss chard, 1 tablespoon olive oil
	133 cal 0g carbs 13.6g fat 1.3g protein
Goal 1600 cal	1648 kcal.
carbs	20.3 gr.
fats	124.2 gr.
protein	112.4 gr.

MEAL	FRIDAY
Breakfast	*Matcha Pudding* (1 serving) + 4 scoops low carb protein powder
	684 cal 9.4g carbs 31.8g fat 91.1g protein
	Salad - 1 cup raw arugula, ¼ cup sliced cucumber, 2 cherry tomatoes, 2 tablespoons flaxseed oil
	134 cal 0g carbs 27.4g fat 1g protein
A.M Snack	*Maple Pecan Fat Bomb*
	1 serving
	285 cal 2.3g carbs 28g fat 3.7g protein
Lunch	*Pumpkin "Cheddar" Risotto*
	1 serving
	119 cal 3.5g carbs 7.2g fat 6.2g protein
P.M. Snack	*Peanut Butter Cocoa*
	1 serving
	151 cal 1.8g carbs 11.6g fat 7g protein
Dinner	*Sesame Seed Cheese*
	1 serving
	57 cal 1.2g carbs 4.9g fat 1.0g protein
	Salad - 2 cups spinach, 1 tablespoon olive oil
	133 cal 0g carbs 13.7g fat 1.7g protein
Goal 1600 cal	**1641 kcal.**
carbs	18.2 gr.
fats	124.6 gr.
protein	111.7 gr.

Grocery List Week 3

- 1 container low carb vegan protein powder
- 3 bunches arugula
- 2 cucumbers
- 6 cherry tomatoes
- 1 bottle flaxseed oil
- 1 zucchini
- 2 (454g containers) spinach
- 4 avocadoes
- 1 bunch parsley
- 3 (14oz cans) coconut milk
- 1 bunch fresh mint
- 1 package pistachios
- 1 bottle vanilla extract
- 1 bottle liquid stevia
- 1 package chia seeds
- 1 package cocoa powder
- 1 package cinnamon
- 1 package matcha powder
- 1 small container strawberries
- 1 package coconut butter
- 1 bottle coconut oil
- 1 small package blueberries
- 1 package vanilla powder
- 1 bottle lemon juice
- 1 bag almond flour
- 1 bag coconut flour
- 1 package ground flaxseed
- 1 box salt
- 1 package baking powder
- 1 bottle apple cider vinegar

- 1 package chopped almonds
- 1 lemon
- 1 package chopped pecans
- 1 package sliced almonds
- 1 package roasted sunflower seeds
- 1 package roasted pumpkin seeds
- 1 package unsweetened dried cranberries
- 1 package cinnamon
- 1 package pecan halves
- 1 package unsweetened shredded coconut
- 1 small package (3.5oz) extra firm tofu
- 1 (454 gram package) of mushrooms
- 1 package pepper
- 2 heads garlic
- 1 head romaine lettuce
- 4454 gram packages shirataki noodles
- 1 jar peanut butter
- 2 onions
- 1 bottle dark soy
- 1 bottle lime juice
- 1 package red chili
- 1 package nutritional yeast
- 1 package hemp seeds
- 1 bell pepper
- 1 package garlic powder
- 1 package onion powder

- 1 package shirataki macaroni
- 1 bottle peanut oil
- 1 container vegetable broth
- 1 package pepper flakes
- 1 small ginger root
- 1 block hemp-fu
- 1 (254 gram) package baby spinach
- 1 package paprika
- 1 bottle olive oil
- 1 can pureed pumpkin
- 250ml vanilla flavored almond milk
- 1 (15oz. can) baby corn
- 1L plain almond milk

- 1 package stevia powder
- 1 bunch Swiss chard
- 1 batch *cashew cheese spread* (see recipe)
- 1 package frozen spinach
- 1 lime
- 1 red onion
- 1 bunch fresh cilantro
- 2 heads cauliflower
- 1 package matcha green tea powder
- 1 package agar-agar
- 1 package sesame seeds

Meal Plan Week 4

MEAL	MONDAY
Breakfast	*The Ultimate Green Smoothie* (1 serving) + 4 scoops low carb protein powder
	444 cal 4g carbs 17.1g fat 90g protein
	Salad - 1 cup raw arugula, ¼ cup sliced cucumber, 2 cherry tomatoes, 1 tablespoon flaxseed oil
	134 cal 0g carbs 13.7g fat 1g protein
A.M Snack	*Coconut Berry Bomb*
	1 serving
	217cal 1.8g carbs 21.9g fats 1.1g protein
Lunch	*Tofu and Broccoli Filled Avocado*
	1 serving
	290 cal 1.5g carbs 27g fat 2.1g protein
	Salad - 1 cup bok choy, shredded and 1 teaspoon balsamic vinegar
	13.7 cal 1.7g carbs 0.1g fat 1.1g protein
P.M. Snack	*Raspberry Lemon Icecream*
	1 serving
	198 cal 4.4g carbs 17.5g fat 1.8g protein
Dinner	*Mac n' Cheeze*
	1 serving
	266 cal 2.6g carbs 15.4g fat 20.2g protein
Goal 1600 cal	**1547 kcal.**
carbs	16 gr.
fats	112.7 gr.
protein	117.3 gr.

MEAL	TUESDAY
Breakfast	*Matcha Pudding* (1 serving) + 4 scoops low carb protein powder
	684 cal 9.4g carbs 31.8g fat 91.1g protein
	Salad - 1 cup raw arugula, ¼ cup sliced cucumber, 2 cherry tomatoes, 1 tablespoon flaxseed oil
	134 cal 0g carbs 13.7g fat 1g protein
A.M Snack	*Fudgy Peanut Butter Cubes*
	1 serving
	313 cal 3.3g carbs 30g fat 5.1g protein
Lunch	*Dijon Avocado Salad*
	1 serving
	182 cal 1.3g carbs 14g fat 2.5g protein
P.M. Snack	*Almond Cookies*
	1 serving
	77 cal 2.1g carbs 6.2g fat 2.4g protein
Dinner	*Cheddar Cheese*
	1 serving
	47 cal 2.7g carbs 3g fat 1.3g protein
	Salad - 2 cups spinach, 2 tablespoons olive oil
	133 cal 0g carbs 27.2g fat 1.7g protein
Goal 1600 cal	**1628 kcal.**
carbs	18.8 gr.
fats	125.9 gr.
protein	105.1 gr.

MEAL	WEDNESDAY
Breakfast	*Chia Seed Pudding* (1 serving) + 4 scoops low carb protein powder
	771 cal 7.6g carbs 34.6g fat 94.6g protein
	Salad - 1 cup shredded romaine lettuce, ¼ cup chopped zucchini, 2 tablespoons flaxseed oil
	132 cal 0g carbs 27.4g fat 1g protein
A.M Snack	*Coconut-Almond Loaf*
	1 serving
	250 cal 2.1g carbs 20.4g fat 6.5g protein
Lunch	*Ramen Noodles*
	1 serving
	136 cal 4.8g carbs 10.4g fat 7.0g protein
P.M. Snack	*Strawberry Coconut Fat Bomb*
	2 servings
	162 cal 1.2g carbs 16.2g fat 0.8g protein
Dinner	*Cauliflower Soup*
	1 serving
	43 cal 3g carbs 2.2g fat 1.4g protein
	Salad -2 cups swiss chard, 1 tablespoon olive oil
	133 cal 0g carbs 13.6g fat 1.3g protein
Goal 1600 cal	**1648 kcal.**
carbs	18.7 gr.
fats	124.8 gr.
protein	112.6 gr.

MEAL	THURSDAY
Breakfast	*Raspberry Avocado Smoothie* (1 serving) + 4 scoops low carb protein powder
	652 cal 8.7g carbs 26.6g fat 90.9g protein
	Salad - 1 cup shredded romaine lettuce, ¼ cup chopped zucchini, 1 tablespoons flaxseed oil
	132 cal 0g carbs 13.7g fat 1g protein
A.M Snack	*Protein Pancakes*
	2 servings
	226 cal 3.0g carbs 15.2g fat 15.6g protein
Lunch	*Pad Thai Noodles*
	1 servings
	236 cal 3.9g carbs 19.5g fat 8.8g protein
P.M. Snack	*Nut Mania Fat Bomb*
	1 serving
	217 cal 1.7g carbs 21.7g fat 0.4g protein
Dinner	*Guacamole*
	1 serving
	157 cal 2.0g carbs 8.0g fat 1.0g protein
	Salad - 2 cups swiss chard, 1 tablespoon olive oil
	133 cal 0g carbs 13.6g fat 1.3g protein
Goal 1600 cal	**1617 kcal.**
carbs	19.3 gr.
fats	118.3 gr.
protein	119 gr.

MEAL	FRIDAY
Breakfast	*Nutty Green Smoothie* (1 serving) + 4 scoops low carb protein powder
	652 cal 4g carbs 26.6g fat 90.7g protein
	Salad - 1 cup raw arugula, ¼ cup sliced cucumber, 2 cherry tomatoes, 2 tablespoon flaxseed oil
	134 cal 0g carbs 27.4g fat 1g protein
A.M Snack	*Coconut Berry Bomb*
	1 serving
	217cal 1.8g carbs 21.9g fats 1.1g protein
Lunch	*Curried Kale Salad*
	1 serving
	94 cal 6.3g carbs 6g fat 1.5g protein
P.M. Snack	*Raspberry Lemon Icecream*
	1 serving
	198 cal 4.4g carbs 17.5g fat 1.8g protein
Dinner	*Creamy Mushroom Soup*
	1 serving
	119 cal 2.9g carbs 10.3g fat 1.9g protein
	Salad - 2 cups spinach, 1 tablespoon olive oil
	133 cal 0g carbs 13.7g fat 1.7g protein
Goal 1600 cal	**1587 kcal.**
carbs	19.4 gr.
fats	123.4 gr.
protein	99.7 gr.

Grocery List Week 4

- 1 container low carb vegan protein powder
- 1 bunch arugula
- 1 head romaine lettuce
- 2 cucumbers
- 6 cherry tomatoes
- 1 zucchini
- 1 bottle flaxseed oil
- 454 gram package spinach
- 4 avocadoes
- 1 bunch parsley
- 1 package matcha powder
- 3 (14oz. cans) coconut milk
- 1 package chia seeds
- 1 small package of strawberries
- 1 bottle liquid stevia
- 1 package cocoa powder
- 1 package cinnamon
- 1 bunch fresh mint
- 1 package pistachios
- 1 bottle vanilla extract
- 1 package coconut butter
- 1 bottle coconut oil
- 1 small container blueberries
- 1 package vanilla powder
- 1 bottle lemon juice
- 1 jar peanut butter
- 250ml vanilla flavored almond milk
- 1 bag almond flour
- 1 bag coconut flour
- 1 package ground flaxseed
- 1 box salt
- 1 package baking soda
- 1 bottle apple cider vinegar
- 1 package sliced almonds
- 1 package chopped almonds
- 1 package glucomannan powder
- 1 bottle flaxseed oil
- 1 package baking powder
- 1 package hempseed
- 1 batch *vegan nutella* (see recipe)
- 1 package stevia powder
- 1 bottle Dijon mustard
- 1 head garlic
- 1 bottle olive oil
- 1 package chili flakes
- 1 package pepper
- 1 package cumin
- 1 (3.5 ounce package) extra firm tofu
- 1 head broccoli
- 1 bunch bok choy
- 1 bottle balsamic vinegar
- 1 (454gram package) mixed lettuce
- 1 bunch fresh parsley
- 1 bottle peanut oil
- 1 bottle dark soy sauce
- 1 container vegetable broth
- 1 package pepper flakes
- 3 (454gram packages) shirataki noodles

- 1 small ginger root
- 1 block hemp-fu
- 254 grams baby spinach
- 2 onions
- 1 bottle lime juice
- 1 package red chili
- 1 package curry powder
- 2 lemons
- 1 bunch kale
- 1 bunch cilantro
- 1 package psyllium husk
- 1 small package raspberries
- 1 batch *cashew cheese spread* (see recipe)
- 1 package shredded coconut
- 1 package cocoa butter
- 1 package almond butter
- 1 package chopped almonds
- 1 package nutritional yeast
- 1 bell pepper

- 1 package garlic powder
- 1 package onion powder
- 1 (454 gram) package shirataki macaroni
- 1 package agar-agar
- 1 package raw cashews
- 1 package sesame tahini
- 1 package paprika
- 1 box sea salt
- 1 package cayenne
- 1 package dry mustard
- 1 package thyme
- 1 package matcha green tea powder
- 1 head cauliflower
- 1 lime
- 1 red onion
- 1 bunch Swiss chard
- 254 grams white mushrooms

Meal Plan Week 5

MEAL	MONDAY
Breakfast	*Raspberry Avocado Smoothie* (1 serving) + 2 scoops low carb protein powder
	652 cal 8.7g carbs 26.6g fat 45.5g protein
	Salad - 1 cup shredded romaine lettuce, ¼ cup chopped zucchini, 1 tablespoon flaxseed oil
	132 cal 0g carbs 13.7g fat 1g protein
A.M Snack	*Coconut Berry Bomb*
	1 serving
	217cal 1.8g carbs 21.9g fats 1.1g protein
Lunch	*Cauliflower Soup*
	1 serving
	43 cal 3.1g carbs 2.2g fat 1.4g protein
	Salad - 2 cups spinach, 1 tablespoon olive oil
	133 cal 0 carbs 13.6g fat 1.7g protein
P.M. Snack	*Chocolate Orange Nut Clusters*
	4 servings
	264 cal 2.4g carbs 37.2g fat 4.4g protein
Dinner	*Pad Thai Noodles*
	1 servings
	236 cal 3.9g carbs 19.5g fat 8.8g protein
Goal 1600 cal	1547 kcal.
carbs	19.9 gr.
fats	134.7 gr.
protein	63.9 gr.

MEAL	TUESDAY
Breakfast	***Chia Seed Pudding*** (1 serving) + 4 scoops low carb protein powder
	771 cal 7.6g carbs 34.6g fat 94.6g protein
	Salad - 1 cup raw arugula, ¼ cup sliced cucumber, 2 cherry tomatoes, 2 tablespoons flaxseed oil
	134 cal 0g carbs 27.4g fat 1g protein
A.M Snack	***Ginger Fat Bombs***
	1 serving
	137 cal 1.1g carbs 13.7g fat 0.8g protein
Lunch	***Dijon Avocado Salad***
	1 serving
	182 cal 1.3g carbs 14g fat 2.5g protein
P.M. Snack	***Nuts & Seeds Bagels***
	1 serving
	139 cal 4.6g carbs 13.8g fat 4.1g protein
Dinner	***Baked Green Beans***
	1 serving
	98 cal 4.8g carbs 4.4g fat 2.8g protein
	Salad - 1cup shredded bok choy, 1 ½ tablespoon olive oil
	188 cal 0g carbs 20.4g fat 1.0g protein
Goal 1600 cal	**1659 kcal.**
carbs	19.4 gr.
fats	128.3 gr.
protein	106.8 gr.

MEAL	WEDNESDAY
Breakfast	*Matcha Pudding* (1 serving) + 4 scoops low carb protein powder
	684 cal 9.4g carbs 31.8g fat 91.1g protein
	Salad - 1 cup raw arugula, ¼ cup sliced cucumber, 2 cherry tomatoes, 1 tablespoon flaxseed oil
	134 cal 0g carbs 13.7g fat 1g protein
A.M Snack	*Maple Pecan Fat Bomb*
	1 serving
	285 cal 2.3g carbs 28g fat 3.7g protein
Lunch	*Pumpkin "Cheddar" Risotto*
	1 serving
	119 cal 3.5g carbs 7.2g fat 6.2g protein
P.M. Snack	*Ginger Fat Bombs*
	1 serving
	137 cal 1.1g carbs 13.7g fat 0.8g protein
Dinner	*Sesame Seed Cheese*
	1 serving
	57 cal 1.2g carbs 4.9g fat 1.0g protein
	Salad - 2 cups spinach, 1 ½ tablespoon olive oil
	193 cal 0g carbs 20.5g fat 1.7g protein
Goal 1600 cal	**1570 kcal.**
carbs	17.5 gr.
fats	119.8 gr.
protein	105.5 gr.

MEAL	THURSDAY
Breakfast	*The Ultimate Green Smoothie* (1 serving) + 4 scoops low carb protein powder
	444 cal 4g carbs 17.1g fat 90g protein
	Salad - 1 cup shredded romaine lettuce, ¼ cup chopped zucchini, 1 tablespoon flaxseed oil
	132 cal 0g carbs 13.7g fat 1g protein
A.M Snack	*Strawberry Coconut Fat Bomb*
	2 servings
	162 cal 1.2g carbs 16.2g fat 0.8g protein
Lunch	*Stuffed Portobello Mushrooms*
	1 serving
	120 cal 8.5g carbs 7.1g fat 2.6g protein
	Salad - 2 cups spinach, 1 ½ tablespoons olive oil
	193 cal 0g carbs 20.5g fat 1.7g protein
P.M. Snack	*Coconut Balls*
	2 servings
	286 cal 1.4g carbs 29.8g fat 1.0g protein
Dinner	*Tofu and Broccoli Filled Avocado*
	1 serving
	290 cal 1.5g carbs 27g fat 2.1g protein
Goal 1600 cal	**1645 kcal.**
carbs	16.6 gr.
fats	131.4 gr.
protein	99.2 gr.

MEAL	FRIDAY
Breakfast	*Nutty Green Smoothie* (1 serving) + 4 scoops low carb protein powder
	652 cal 4g carbs 26.6g fat 90.7g protein
	Salad - 1 cup raw arugula, ¼ cup sliced cucumber, 2 cherry tomatoes, 2 tablespoons flaxseed oil
	134 cal 0g carbs 27.4g fat 1g protein
A.M Snack	*Coconut Berry Bomb*
	1 serving
	217cal 1.8g carbs 21.9g fats 1.1g protein
Lunch	*Curried Kale Salad*
	1 serving
	94 cal 6.3g carbs 6g fat 1.5g protein
P.M. Snack	*Seed and Nut Topped Loaf*
	1 serving
	172 cal 4.6g carbs 13.2g fat 6.1g protein
Dinner	*Creamy Mushroom Soup*
	1 serving
	119 cal 2.9g carbs 10.3g fat 1.9g protein
	Salad - 2 cups spinach, 1 ½ tablespoons olive oil
	193 cal 0g carbs 20.5g fat 1.7g protein
Goal 1600 cal	1627 kcal.
carbs	19.6 gr.
fats	125.9 gr.
protein	104 gr.

Grocery List Week 5

- 1 container carb vegan protein powder
- 1 head romaine lettuce
- 2 zucchinis
- 1 bottle flaxseed oil
- 1 bunch arugula
- 2 cucumbers
- 6 cherry tomatoes
- 5 (14oz cans) coconut milk
- 3 avocadoes
- 1 bunch fresh mint
- 1 package pistachios
- 1 package vanilla extract
- 1 bottle liquid stevia
- 1 package chia seeds
- 1 package dark cocoa powder
- 1 package cinnamon
- 1 package matcha powder
- 1 small package strawberries
- 3 (454gram packages) spinach
- 1 bunch parsley
- 1 package hempseed
- 1 bag almond flour
- 1 bottle flaxseed oil
- 1 package baking powder
- 1 package coconut butter
- 1 bottle coconut oil
- 1 package shredded coconut
- 1 package ginger powder
- 1 package pecan halves
- 1 package vegetable stock
- 1 package thyme powder
- 3 heads cauliflower
- 1 box pepper
- 1 package salt
- 1 bottle olive oil
- 1 (454 gram package) mixed lettuce
- 1 head garlic
- 1 bottle Dijon mustard
- 1 package paprika
- 1 small can pureed pumpkin
- 1 package nutritional yeast
- 254gram package portobello mushrooms
- 4 onions
- 1 roasted red pepper
- 1 package oregano
- 1 package pepper flakes
- 1 sundried tomato
- 1 package curry powder
- 1 lemon
- 1 bunch kale
- 1 bunch fresh cilantro
- 1 orange
- 1 package ground flaxseed
- 1 package mixed nuts
- 1 bottle tahini
- 1 package psyllium husk powder
- 1 package stevia powder
- 1 package baking soda
- 1 package chopped pecans

- 1 bag coconut flour
- 1 package almond butter
- 1 small package whole almonds
- 1 package sesame seeds
- 1 package pumpkin seeds
- 1 package whole flax seeds
- 250ml almond milk
- 1 bottle apple cider vinegar
- 1 head bok choy
- 2 (454 gram packages) shirataki noodles
- 1 jar peanut butter
- 1 bottle dark soy sauce
- 1 bottle lime juice
- 1 package red chili

- 1 pound fresh green beans
- 1 package ground flax meal
- 1 package agar-agar
- 1 package garlic powder
- 1 package cumin
- 1 (3.5 oz. package) non-GMO extra firm tofu
- 1 head broccoli
- 1 package onion powder
- 1 (454 gram package) white mushrooms
- 1 package blueberries
- 1 package vanilla powder
- 1 bottle lemon juice

Meal Plan Week 6

MEAL	MONDAY
Breakfast	*Nutty Green Smoothie* (1 serving) + 4 scoops low carb protein powder
	652 cal 4g carbs 26.6g fat 90.7g protein
	Salad - 1 cup raw arugula, ¼ cup sliced cucumber, 2 cherry tomatoes, 2 tablespoons flaxseed oil
	134 cal 0g carbs 27.4g fat 1g protein
A.M Snack	*Lemon Zest Fat Bomb*
	2 servings
	156 cal 1.2g carbs 15.4g fat 1g protein
Lunch	*Mushroom Tofu Lettuce Wraps*
	1 serving
	133 cal 4.3g carbs 7.7g fat 5.6g protein
	Salad - 1cup bok choy, 1 tablespoon olive oil
	128 cal 0 carbs 13.6g fat 1g protein
P.M. Snack	*Strawberry Coconut Fat Bombs*
	3 servings
	243 cal 1.8g carbs 24.3g fat 1.2g protein
Dinner	*Zucchini Risotto*
	1 serving
	161 cal 7.4g carbs 11.2g fat 5.1g protein
Goal 1600 cal	**1633 kcal.**
carbs	18.7 gr.
fats	126.2 gr.
protein	105.6 gr.

MEAL	TUESDAY
Breakfast	*Raspberry Avocado Smoothie* (1 serving) + 4 scoops low carb protein powder
	652 cal 8.7g carbs 26.6g fat 90.9g protein
	Salad - 1 cup shredded romaine lettuce, ¼ cup chopped zucchini, 1 tablespoon flaxseed oil
	132 cal 0g carbs 13.7g fat 1g protein
A.M Snack	*Coconut Berry Bomb*
	1 serving
	217cal 1.8g carbs 21.9g fats 1.1g protein
Lunch	*Caesar Salad*
	1 serving
	160 cal 2.8g carbs 11.3g fat 5.2g protein
P.M. Snack	*Almond Cookies*
	1 serving
	77 cal 2.1g carbs 6.2g fat 2.4g protein
Dinner	*Tofu and Broccoli Filled Avocado*
	1 serving
	290 cal 1.5g carbs 27g fat 2.1g protein
	Salad - 1cup shredded bok choy, 1 tablespoon olive oil
	128 cal 0 carbs 13.6g fat 1g protein
Goal 1600 cal	**1565 kcal.**
carbs	16.9 gr.
fats	120.3 gr.
protein	103.7 gr.

MEAL	WEDNESDAY
Breakfast	*Chia Seed Pudding* (1 serving) + 4 scoops low carb protein powder
	771 cal 7.6g carbs 34.6g fat 94.6g protein
	Salad - 1 cup shredded romaine lettuce, ¼ cup chopped zucchini, 1 tablespoon flaxseed oil
	132 cal 0g carbs 13.7g fat 1g protein
A.M Snack	*Nut Mania Fat Bomb*
	1 serving
	217 cal 1.7g carbs 21.7g fat 0.4g protein
Lunch	*Ramen Noodles*
	1 serving
	136 cal 4.8g carbs 10.4g fat 7.0g protein
P.M. Snack	*Strawberry Coconut Fat Bomb*
	2 servings
	162 cal 1.2g carbs 16.2g fat 0.8g protein
Dinner	*Cauliflower Soup*
	1 serving
	43 cal 3g carbs 2.2g fat 1.4g protein
	Salad - 2 cups swiss chard, 2 tablespoons olive oil
	133 cal 0g carbs 27.2g fat 1.3g protein
Goal 1600 cal	**1633 kcal.**
carbs	18.3 gr.
fats	126 gr.
protein	106.5 gr.

MEAL	THURSDAY
Breakfast	*The Ultimate Green Smoothie* (1 serving) + 4 scoops low carb protein powder
	444 cal 4g carbs 17.1g fat 90g protein
	Salad - 1 cup raw arugula, ¼ cup sliced cucumber, 2 cherry tomatoes, 1 tablespoon flaxseed oil
	134 cal 0g carbs 13.7g fat 1g protein
A.M Snack	*Coconut Berry Bomb*
	1 serving
	217cal 1.8g carbs 21.9g fats 1.1g protein
Lunch	*Tofu and Broccoli Filled Avocado*
	1 serving
	290 cal 1.5g carbs 27g fat 2.1g protein
	Salad - 1 cup bok choy, shredded and 1 teaspoon balsamic vinegar
	13.7 cal 1.7g carbs 0.1g fat 1.1g protein
P.M. Snack	*Raspberry Lemon Icecream*
	1 serving
	198 cal 4.4g carbs 17.5g fat 1.8g protein
Dinner	*Mac n' Cheeze*
	1 serving
	266 cal 2.6g carbs 15.4g fat 20.2g protein
Goal 1600 cal	1547 kcal.
carbs	16 gr.
fats	112.7 gr.
protein	117.3 gr.

MEAL	FRIDAY
Breakfast	*Matcha Pudding* (1 serving) + 4 scoops low carb protein powder
	684 cal 9.4g carbs 31.8g fat 91.1g protein
	Salad - 1 cup raw arugula, ¼ cup sliced cucumber, 2 cherry tomatoes, 2 tablespoons flaxseed oil
	134 cal 0g carbs 27.4g fat 1g protein
A.M Snack	*Lemon Zest Fat Bombs*
	3 servings
	234 cal 1.8g carbs 23.1g fat 1.5g protein
Lunch	*Pumpkin "Cheddar" Risotto*
	1 serving
	119 cal 3.5g carbs 7.2g fat 6.2g protein
P.M. Snack	*Almond Cookies*
	2 servings
	154 cal 4.2g carbs 12.4g fat 4.8g protein
Dinner	*Sesame Seed Cheese*
	1 serving
	57 cal 1.2g carbs 4.9g fat 1.0g protein
	Salad - 2 cups spinach, 1 1/2 tablespoons olive oil
	193 cal 0g carbs 20.5g fat 1.7g protein
Goal 1600 cal	**1655 kcal.**
carbs	20.1 gr.
fats	127.3 gr.
protein	107.3 gr.

Grocery List Week 6

- 1 container low carb vegan protein powder
- 2 bunches arugula
- 15 cherry tomatoes
- 2 cucumbers
- 1 bottle flaxseed oil
- 3 heads romaine lettuce
- 2 zucchinis
- 4 (14ounce cans) coconut milk
- 4 avocadoes
- 1 bunch fresh parsley
- 1 package pistachios
- 1 bottle vanilla extract
- 1 bottle liquid stevia
- 1 bunch spinach
- 1 bunch parsley
- 1 (454-gram package) spinach
- 1 package chia seeds
- 1 package cocoa powder
- 1 package cinnamon
- 1 package matcha powder
- 1 small package strawberries
- 1 package coconut butter
- 1 bottle coconut oil
- 3 lemons
- 1 box salt
- 1 small package blueberries
- 1 package vanilla powder
- 1 bottle lemon juice
- 1 package cocoa butter
- 1 package almond butter
- 1 bottle olive oil
- 2 packages chopped almonds
- 1 package shelled pistachios
- 1 bag almond flour
- 1 (3.5-ounce package) non-GMO extra-firm tofu
- 1 (454-gram package) mushrooms
- 1 head garlic
- 1 bottle capers with brine
- 1 bottle Dijon mustard
- 1 package hemp seeds
- 1 bottle peanut oil
- 1 bottle dark soy sauce
- 1L container vegetable broth
- 1 package pepper flakes
- 1 small ginger root
- 1 (454-gram package) shirataki noodles
- 1 package ground flaxseed
- 1 block hemp-fu
- 1 (454-gram package) baby spinach
- 1 package cumin
- 2 heads broccoli
- 1 package paprika
- 4 heads cauliflower
- 1 package nutritional yeast
- 1 package shredded coconut
- 1 package stevia powder
- 1 package coconut flour
- 1 package psyllium husk
- 1 small package raspberries

- 2 red bell peppers
- 250ml almond milk
- 1 bunch fresh basil
- 1 head bok choy
- 2 bunches Swiss chard
- 1 package thyme
- 1 package onion powder
- 1 (454-gram package) shirataki macaroni
- 1 package agar-agar
- 1 package sesame seeds
- 1 package raw cashews
- 1 package garlic powder

LOW-CARB VEGAN PANTRY STACKING

Dry storage staples

Butters, oils, seeds, nuts and flours

Good for snacking and essential in many of our low-carb vegan recipes. We can store nut butters and nut-based cheeses in the freezer to increase their shelf-life.

Nuts:

- Peanuts and cashews – you can stir-fry, use for vegan cheeses and eat them on their own or mix with curries or soups
- Walnuts
- Almonds
- Pecans
- Hazelnuts
- Pistachios
- Macadamia nuts
- Brazil Nuts

Seeds:

- Chia seeds
- Hemp seeds
- Sunflower seeds
- Pumpkin seeds
- Hemp seeds
- Sacha seeds
- Flax seeds

Nut butters:

- Cocoa butter
- Coconut butter
- SunButter
- Almond butter
- Walnut butter
- Cashew butter
- Pecan butter

Flours:

- Almond flour
- Coconut flour

Refrigerated staples

Plant-based milks – they include soy, cashew, almond, rice or coconut milk.

Pickles and preserved vegetables – they include

- Dill pickles
- Pepperoncini, capers and
- olives
- Pickled jalapeños
- Pickled red onions
- Sun-dried tomatoes

Sauces and condiments – they include:

- Cilantro or herb sauce
- Chili oil
- Soy sauce
- Tahini and harissa
- Tamari
- Marinara sauce
- Vinegar (apple cider, balsamic or rice)

Vegetables – all vegetables are great but if bought fresh only for short term storage, must consume within a week when stored in the fridge. Here is a few of them:

- Pumpkins and squash
- Carrots, celery and onions
- Kale and hearty greens
- Fresh herbs like basil, mint, coriander, cilantro, thyme, chives and parsley
- Eggplant

Spices & Herbs – if bought fresh only for short term storage, must consume within a week when stored in the fridge. they include:

- Nutritional yeast
- Curry powder
- Ground turmeric, cumin and
- coriander
- Chili powder
- Dried rosemary
- Dried thyme
- Bay leaves

SPICES LIST & HOW TO MAKE THEM

Most spices are great to give an original twist to your favorite recipes. The easiest way to do this is with nut based cheeses. Just change up the recommended spices with any spice recipe that you like and enjoy!

The spice recipes include the following ingredients, (dried to it make easy for long term storage):

- Cumin, coriander and lime
- Oregano, basil, marjoram or mint
- Rosemary
- Mustard powder
- Bay leaves
- Thyme
- Garlic
- Turmeric

- Dill
- Sage
- Parsley
- Oregano
- Cardamom powder
- Garam masala
- Curry powder
- Chili powder
- Vanilla extract

- Black pepper
- Cayenne pepper
- Paprika
- Ground cinnamon
- Ground Cloves
- Nutmeg
- Ground ginger

SPICE
RECIPES

Berbere

This is an African spice made from:

- ½ cup chili powder or cayenne pepper
- ¼ cup sweet paprika
- 1 tbsp. salt
- ½ tsp. ground coriander
- 1 tsp. ground ginger
- ½ tsp. ground cardamom
- ½ tsp. ground fenugreek
- ¼ tsp. ground nutmeg
- 1/8 tsp. ground allspice
- 1/8 tsp. ground cloves.

Dukkah

An Egyptian spice made from a mix of:

- 1 cup toasted nuts
- ⅓ cup sesame seeds
- 2/3 cup hazelnuts
- 3 tbsp. coriander
- 3 tbsp. cumin
- 1 tsp. ground pepper

Harissa

A mixture of:

- 1 smoked red pepper
- ½ tsp. cumin
- ½ tsp. coriander
- ½ tsp. paprika
- 3 cloves garlic
- ½ tsp. sea salt
- ½ tsp. caraway
- 1 red onion

Ras el Hanout

A blend of:

- ¾ tsp. cumin
- ½ tsp. ginger
- ½ tsp. sea salt
- ½ tsp. black pepper
- 1¼ tsp. cinnamon
- ½ tsp. coriander
- ½ tsp. cayenne
- ¾ tsp. allspice

Chinese Five Spice

A mix of:

- 1 tsp. ground cinnamon
- 1 tsp. ground cloves
- ¼ tsp. fennel seed
- 1 tsp. star anise
- ¼ tsp. Szechuan peppercorns.

Gomasio

A Japanese condiment that is a mix of:

- 2 cups toasted sesame seeds
- 1 tbsp. coarse salt

Togarashi

A mix of:

- 3 tbsp. chili pepper
- 3 tbsp. citrus peel
- 2 tbsp. sesame seeds
- 3 tbsp. Seaweed

Fines Herbes

A blend of fresh or dry herbs:

- 2 tbsp. chervil
- 2 tbsp. chives
- 4 tsps. tarragon
- 2 tbsp. parsley
- ½ tbsp. thyme
- 2 tbsp. chervil

Khmeli Suneli

A Georgian mix of:

- 2 tsps. fenugreek
- 1 tbsp. coriander
- 1 tbsp. savory
- ½ tsp. black peppercorns.

Quatre Epices (Four spices)

A mix of:

- 2 tbsp. ground black and/or white pepper
- 1 tbsp. cloves
- 1 tbsp. nutmeg
- 1 tbsp. ginger.

Curry Powder

A mix of:

- ¼ cup turmeric
- 2 tbsp. coriander
- 2 tbsp. cumin
- 2 tbsp. fenugreek
- ½ tsp. red pepper.

Garam Masala

A mix of:

- 2 tbsp. cinnamon
- 2 tbsp. cardamom
- 1 tbsp. cumin
- 2 tbsp. turmeric
- 1 tsp. mustard
- 1 tsp. fennel seed
- 2 red chilis

Panch Phoron

A mix of:

- 1 tbsp. fenugreek
- 1 tbsp. nigella
- 1 tbsp. cumin
- 1 tbsp. black mustard
- 1 tbsp. fennel seeds.

Adobo

An all-purpose seasoning composed of:

- 1 tbsp. garlic
- 2 tbsp. oregano
- 3 tbsp. black pepper
- ¼ cup paprika
- 1 tbsp. garlic
- 2 tbsp. cumin

Chili Powder

A blend of:

- ancho chili
- 2 tbsp. paprika
- 1¼ tsps. cumin
- 2 tsps. Mexican oregano.
- ¾ tsp. onion

Jerk Spice:

A spicy Jamaican composed of:

- 1 tsp. red and black pepper
- 1 tsp. allspice
- ¼ tsp. cinnamon
- 2 tsps. thyme
- 2 tsps. salt

Advieh

A mix of:

- 1 tsp. dried rose petals
- 1 tsp. cinnamon
- 1 tsp. cardamom
- 1 tsp. cloves
- 1 tsp. nutmeg
- ½ tsp. cumin

Baharat

A mixture of:

- 1 tsp. black pepper
- 2 tbsp. cumin
- ½ tsp. cinnamon
- ¼ tsp. cloves.
- ¼ tsp. cardamom
- 1 tsp. coriander

Za'atar

A mix of:

- 2 tbsp. thyme
- 1 tbsp. sesame seeds
- ¼ cup sumac
- 2 tbsp. oregano
- 2 tbsp. marjoram

Pickling Spice

A blend of:

- 2 tbsp. bay leaves
- 2 tbsp. mustard seeds
- 1 tsp. peppercorns
- 2 tsps. coriander
- 1 tbsp. allspice

Pumpkin Pie Spice

A mix of:

- 4 tbsp. cinnamon
- ½ tsp. nutmeg
- 2 tbsp. ginger
- 1 tsp. cloves.

CONCLUSION

I would like to thank you for purchasing this book and taking the time to read it.

I do hope that it has been helpful and that you found the information contained within the sections useful!

The Ketogenic Vegan diet is beneficial to your health and stamina. The combination of the two is the best thing you can do for your physical and mental well-being. Try it and you will be an ardent follower for life.

Keep in mind that you are not limited to the diet plan and recipes provided in this book! Keep on exploring until you create your very own culinary masterpiece!

Stay healthy and stay safe!

BONUS REMINDER

Welcome to the reader's circle of happyhealthygreen.life. You can subscribe to our newsletter using this link:

http://happyhealthygreen.life/vegan-newsletter

By subscribing to our newsletter, you will receive the latest vegan recipes, tips about health & nutrition and plant-based cooking articles that make your mouth water, right in your inbox.

We also offer you a unique opportunity to read future vegan cookbooks for absolutely free...

Get your hands on free vegan recipes and instant access to 'The Vegan Cookbook'. Subscribe to the vegan newsletter and grab your free copy here at:

http://happyhealthygreen.life/vegan-newsletter

Enter your email address to get instant access. Support veganism and say NO to animal cruelty!

We don't like spam and understand you don't like spam either. We'll email you no more than 2 times per week.

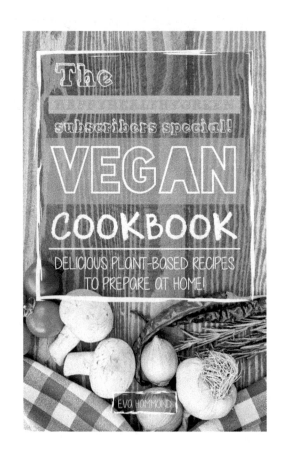

THANK YOU

Finally, if you enjoyed this book, then we would like to ask you for a small favor. Would you be kind enough to leave an honest review for this book? It'd be greatly appreciated by both the future reader and me!

You can send us your feedback at: **http://happyhealthygreen.life/about-us/evahammond/low-carb-vegan-bundle-review**

Did you discover any grammar mistakes, confusing explanations or wrongful information? Don't hesitate to send us an email! You can reach us at *info@happyhealthygreen.life*

We promise to get back at you as soon as time allows us. If this book requires a revision, we'll send you the updated eBook for free after the revised book is available.

SOURCES

http://ajcn.nutrition.org/content/85/1/238.full

http://sciencedrivennutrition.com/the-ketogenic-diet/

http://theconversation.com/what-are-ketogenic-diets-can-they-treat-epilepsy-and-brain-cancer-83401

http://www.healthline.com/nutrition/23-studies-on-low-carb-and-low-fat-diets#section9

http://www.medicalnewstoday.com/articles/319287.php

http://www.sandiegouniontribune.com/business/biotech/sd-me-ketogenic-health-20170905-story.html

https://draxe.com/keto-diet-food-list/

https://globenewswire.com/news-release/2017/08/29/1101488/0/en/Weight-Loss-Doctor-Nishant-Rao-Improves-Upon-the-Ketogenic-Diet-for-More-Consistent-Results.html

https://www.aocs.org/stay-informed/read-inform/featured-articles/prescribing-dietary-fat-therapeutic-uses-of-ketogenic-diets-february-2016

https://www.dietdoctor.com/low-carb/keto

https://ketodietapp.com/Blog/post/2014/11/30/Total-Carbs-or-Net-Carbs-What-Really-Counts

https://www.ncbi.nlm.nih.gov/pmc/articles/PMC2716748/

https://www.ncbi.nlm.nih.gov/pmc/articles/PMC2902940/

https://www.ncbi.nlm.nih.gov/pmc/articles/PMC3826507/

https://www.ncbi.nlm.nih.gov/pubmed/17447017

https://www.ncbi.nlm.nih.gov/pubmed/22673594

The Ketogenic Diet: A Complete Guide for the Dieter and Practitioner By Lyle McDonald *https://books.google.co.ke/books?id=JtCZBe-2XVIC&pg=PA101&lpg=PA101&dq=medical+findings+on+macronutrients+in+ketogenic+diet&source=bl&ots=dPINf4CRDB&sig=O6oxDuSjYOd81Pff11lJ-LUImME&hl=en&sa=X&redir_esc=y#v=onepage&q=medical%20findings%20on%20macronutrients%20in%20ketogenic%20diet&f=false*

www.mdpi.com/2072-6643/9/5/517/pdf

CPSIA information can be obtained
at www.ICGtesting.com
Printed in the USA
BVHW090322130819
555687BV00007B/542/P